EMBODIMENT AND AGENCY

EMBODIMENT AND AGENCY

Edited by

SUE CAMPBELL, LETITIA MEYNELL,
AND SUSAN SHERWIN

THE PENNSYLVANIA STATE UNIVERSITY PRESS
UNIVERSITY PARK, PENNSYLVANIA

LIBRARY OF CONGRESS CATALOGING-IN-PUBLICATION DATA

Embodiment and agency / edited by Sue Campbell,
Letitia Meynell, and Susan Sherwin.
    p.   cm.
Includes bibliographical references and index.
Summary: "A collection of essays in feminist philosophy.
Contributors theorize how we act through differently acculturated
bodies in a variety of interpersonal and political contexts. Addresses
recent feminist challenges to bring the body more fully and
positively into theory"—Provided by publisher.
ISBN 978-0-271-03522-2 (cloth : alk. paper)
1. Feminist theory.
2. Agent (Philosophy).
3. Mind and body.
I. Campbell, Sue, 1956–.
II. Meynell, Letitia.
III. Sherwin, Susan, 1947–.

HQ1190.E45 2009
306.4—dc22
2008053957

Copyright © 2009 The Pennsylvania State University
All rights reserved
Printed in the United States of America
Published by The Pennsylvania State University Press,
University Park, PA 16802-1003

The Pennsylvania State University Press is a member of the
Association of American University Presses.

It is the policy of The Pennsylvania State University Press to
use acid-free paper. This books is printed on Natures Natural,
containing 50% post-consumer waste, and meets the minimum
requirements of American National Standard for Information
Sciences—Permanence of Paper for Printed
Library Material, ANSI Z39.48–1992.

CONTENTS

Acknowledgments   vii

Introduction: Minding Bodies   1
Letitia Meynell

PART I: BECOMING EMBODIED SUBJECTS

1

Emotional Metamorphoses: The Role of Others   25
in Becoming a Subject
Kym Maclaren

2

Racial Grief and Melancholic Agency   46
Angela Failler

3

A Knowing That Resided in My Bones: Sensuous Embodiment
and Trans Social Movement   58
Alexis Shotwell

4

The Phrenological Impulse and the Morphology of
Character   76
Rebecca Kukla

5

Personal Identity, Narrative Integration, and Embodiment   100
Catriona Mackenzie

6

Bodily Limits to Autonomy: Emotion, Attitude, and
Self-Defense   126
Sylvia Burrow

PART II: EMBODIED RELATIONS, POLITICAL CONTEXTS

7
Relational Existence and Termination of Lives: When Embodiment Precludes Agency   145
Susan Sherwin

8
A Body No Longer of One's Own   164
Monique Lanoix

9
Premature (M)Othering: Levinasian Ethics and the Politics of Fetal Ultrasound Imaging   184
Jacqueline M. Davies

10
Inside the Frame of the Past: Memory, Diversity, and Solidarity   211
Sue Campbell

11
Collective Memory or Knowledge of the Past: "Covering Reality with Flowers"   234
Susan E. Babbitt

12
Agency and Empowerment: Embodied Realities in a Globalized World   250
Christine M. Koggel

List of Contributors   269

Index   273

ACKNOWLEDGMENTS

We would like to express our gratitude to the contributors to this volume for their commitment to the project and their good will in responding to suggestions. We gratefully acknowledge financial support from the Social Sciences and Humanities Research Council (SSHRC) and acknowledge the invaluable administrative and editorial support of Khadija Coxon and Jan Sutherland. Thanks also to Françoise Baylis, Carolyn Ells, Helen Fielding, Trish Glazebrook, Cressida Heyes, Lorraine Code, Carolyn McLeod, Amy Mullin, Christine Overall, and Alexis Shotwell. We are also very grateful to Sandy Thatcher, Kathryn Yahner, and the staff at the Pennsylvania State University Press, and to the anonymous reviewers of the volume.

INTRODUCTION

MINDING BODIES

Letitia Meynell

1. INTRODUCTION

Feminist theory is peculiarly well suited to exploring the concepts of agency and embodiment. For historical, conceptual, and political reasons both topics have enjoyed considerable feminist attention. It is thus surprising that the many intersections that exist between these concepts have tended to be neglected, by both feminist theorists and nonfeminists alike. Theorizing about agency has often ignored all but the most rudimentary aspects of embodiment, and theories about the body have tended to forget that, typically, the human body *is* an agent, inevitably transforming through its actions both the world and itself. It is this strange gap between theorizing embodiment and theories of agency that the authors in this volume are particularly concerned to bridge.

2. THE TRADITION

Although somewhat mysterious in a feminist context, it is relatively easy to understand why the division between agency and embodiment is ubiquitous in traditional European thought,[1] as it is firmly rooted in the distinction between

---

1. There have been endless conversations about the appropriate name for the culture and tradition that has variously been called the West, the North, the First World, and the One Third World. As Chandra Talpade Mohanty has convincingly argued, all names are fraught, covertly distorting certain historical facts and implicitly endorsing various current politics (2003, 226–28). Using "the West" to refer to this tradition seems particularly ludicrous given its geographical

Thanks to Sue Campbell and Susan Sherwin for their invaluable input into this chapter and to Andrew Fenton, Matthew Mitchell, and Perwais Hayat for their advice and support.

mind (or soul) and body. The demarcation between mind and body (and the metaphysical problems arising from it) has been a mainstay of European thought, and while this demarcation is often associated with Plato and Descartes (Spelman 1982; Leder 1990), it is also at the heart of the Abrahamic religious traditions. In these religions, persons are thought to survive bodily death and receive in the "afterlife" punishment or reward for their actions in their previous embodied lives.[2] In this tradition, the person *is* the soul/mind, not the crude material stuff of the body. Moreover, virtuous and rational persons concern themselves with the life of the immortal soul/mind, rather than mere bodily concerns. What Spelman has called "somatophobia" (fear and loathing of the body) is a recurring theme of the European tradition (Spelman 1982).

This disdain for the body has resulted in the effective disappearance of the body from traditional European discussions of agency. Agency is clearly distinguished from mere bodily activity and is intimately tied to the mind. Activity is, after all, common to all life—even plants will grow and turn toward the sun. Agency, crucially, implies rationality and free will. In the European tradition, the agent was identified as the mind; thus the life of the mind became the locus for discussions of epistemology and ethics. Justification and judgment, those features of knowledge that distinguish it from mere belief, were thought to be achieved by minds. Similarly, ethical judgments, just as much as any other kind, are the purview of minds; so, too, is the will, which provides the capacity to act and to choose to do good or evil. While few, if any, thinkers in the European tradition have doubted that both knowledge of the world and action require a body, it has typically been treated as a mere medium through which information passes and by which the will pursues its ends. When properly functioning, the body is entirely generic. Indeed, often the

---

inadequacies and its explicit exclusion of the indigenous traditions of the Western hemisphere. I have, problematically, chosen to refer to this tradition and its culture as "European" throughout this chapter. Unfortunately, this name inevitably disappears the many important influences on European culture from India, Persia, Africa, the Middle East, and China and implicitly reifies a Eurocentric account of the history of civilization that is white supremacist. However, this Eurocentrism is characteristic of this tradition, and I hope that my use of the term forefronts this uncomfortable fact, which the more familiar "Western" might not. My use of "European" is meant to include the dominant culture of North America and Australia post European colonization, as well as the communities of European descent in Africa. In brief, it refers to those cultures that draw their lineage from the Greco-Roman Christianized world.

2. It should be noted that this is a generalization, and some sects of these faiths understand the soul as embodied so that, rather than the soul continuing to live on after death, the whole body must be reformed at some point in time—that is, resurrected—to enjoy the "afterlife." Indeed, mind-body dualism came late to the Judaic tradition, although it predates the Christian and Islamic eras.

body has only been noticed in theories of agency as something that may fail to function as expected or as commanded by the mind. Such failures have been taken as further proof of the inferiority of the body and bodily concerns when compared to the lofty life of the mind.

Experiences that, from a pre-theoretical view, might suggest that the mind-body distinction should not be so sharply drawn have been carefully dissected within this tradition. Thus desires and needs (phenomena where the mind appears ethically and rationally directed by and toward the body) were classified into rational desires or duties on one hand and mere appetites and preferences on the other, thus repeating and maintaining the mind-body split and the moral and epistemic hierarchy valuing the life of the mind over that of the body. Similarly, memory and imagination—in life, embodied experiences rich with affect—have often been reduced to ideas of the mind, one a source of knowledge, the other a source of creativity. The emotions, or "passions," are also a case in point as they have typically been considered bodily states that required very strong control by the rational faculties.

There are notable exceptions, for instance, Hume's account of emotions and moral psychology (1739/1969), which reversed the relation of control, rendering reason the servant of the emotions. Indeed, a few philosophical and political theorists have gone even further, rejecting somatophobic dualism, in whole or in part. John Dewey's notion of experience (Dewey 1980; Kestenbaum 1977), Merleau-Ponty's phenomenology of perception (2002), Heidegger's accounts of facticity and "being-in-the-world," and more recently, Michel Foucault's critique of power and modernity (Foucault 1979; 1980; 1990) have all explored the importance of embodiment to an understanding of human agency. Unfortunately, their implications for theories of agency have often been marginalized in canonical representations of the European tradition (Spicker 1970).

While one might think such heady stuff is the purview only of philosophy, it is not uncommon for members of the general public to think of themselves in dualistic ways—as minds that happen to be in particular bodies. Hence it seems quite natural to read science fiction stories of transplanting brains and downloading minds or ghost stories in which people's lives of thoughts, desires, and feelings continue after their deaths. In these stories the body is treated as a mere vessel. Changing bodies seems to be like moving house—habits, challenges, and perspectives may alter, but the person inside remains one and the same. Even many common attitudes about emotions reflect the traditional philosophical views about the relation of mind to body. Thus crimes of passion may be treated more leniently precisely because the perpetrators are thought to have been overcome by their emotions and hence not responsible for their actions. Their embodied emotional state is supposed to have made it impossible for them to think and act rationally. An action, it seems, only belongs to a responsible agent when it is rationally chosen; emotions and other bodily responses can be disowned as aberrations. The implication is that subjects are only fully agents insofar as they can overcome their embodiment—mind and body are conceived as distinct and, indeed, in opposition.

Although the mind-body distinction and its many implications were prevalent throughout the history of European philosophy, the vision of "man" as rational agent took on new importance in the humanism of the Enlightenment. While this humanism displaced religion from the heart of the community (and, in some cases, from the hearts of individuals), mind-body dualism remained entrenched, and it continued to form the framing assumption for epistemology and ethics. Even now, within a mainstream philosophical community that attempts to keep religious assumptions out of metaphysics and that typically endorses some form of materialist monism (the position that there is no mind-body distinction because the mind *is* the brain) the implications of rejecting dualism have not yet reverberated through the discipline. While the theoretical tensions caused by the suppression of the body have prompted some contemporary philosophers of emotion and mind to challenge the tradition of somatophobic dualism (e.g., Damasio 1994; Clark 1998; Kelly 2003), the gulf between agency and embodiment, implied by mind-body dualism, remains in both ethics and epistemology.

In the Enlightenment, zeal for scientific reasoning, rationality, and freedom were naturalized but not embodied. Liberal political thought arose from the idea that rationality and free will are natural capacities of "all" humanity. These capacities are taken to be equally valuable among all people and worthy of protection. The rise of the autonomous, radically independent individual as the locus for liberal political thought brought with it not only democracy but capitalism and the belief that the free market was a kind of economic state of nature in which "man," both as an individual and as a species, could flourish. The myths of the "self-made man" and entirely self-interested, rational economic agents resulted in a view of human autonomy that ignored the influences of personal relationships, communities, social position, and embodiment. Moreover, it fostered a sense that the state had an obligation to defend negative freedoms from interference rather than enforce positive freedoms of access to resources or opportunities. As the agent was thought to be naturally and fundamentally free when outside the legal constraints of society, the role of the state was to protect these freedoms as much as possible under the constraints imposed by engaging in the shared project of nation building.

While attention to positive freedoms might have directed attention toward agents as situated, embodied, and in need of resources, mainstream European political thought has not encouraged this view of persons. Moreover, women's culturally mediated activities of child bearing, mothering, and caring for others (particularly their emotional and bodily needs) positioned them, symbolically, as antithetical to the ideal autonomous agent; hence, women and their traditional activities have been invisible in most political, ethical, and epistemological theories in the European tradition. In other words, insofar as bodily circumstances are relevant to agents' activities and capacities, traditional theory has treated those whose bodily demands interfere with acting independently and "rationally" (as was assumed to be the case for women, racialized minorities, people with disabilities, and others) as incapable of fully meeting the criteria for competent agency and, hence, legitimately denied some of the privileges of agents. Thus, the mind-body distinction has had a crucial role in dividing theories of successful agency from considerations of embodiment. This paradigmatically metaphysical topic has not only shaped ethics and epistemology but has informed politics, economics, and science and continues to play a dominant role in contemporary society.

3. FEMINIST RESPONSES TO THE TRADITION

Much of feminist theory can be understood as a reaction to and correction of dominant traditions of thought. Just as we can see the influence of the mind-body distinction in European epistemology, ethics, and political theory, so it has also provided the metaphysical framework against which feminist theory has evolved. An investigation of the history of what this distinction has meant for women and how it has been used to maintain their inferiority and support their oppression shows that "agency" and "embodiment" have always been interestingly intertwined. But it also helps to explain how the conversations on these topics evolved in isolation from each other and why discussions of agency and of embodiment have typically applied quite different strategies of resistance against traditional European thought.

As feminist historians have persuasively shown, the oppression of women in the European tradition has often been justified by the view that women's bodies overwhelm their rational capacity and thus undermine their agency

(Schiebinger 1989). This was born from the related, though logically distinct, views that women were both deficient in rational capacity and more at the mercy of the contingencies of their embodiment (Tuana 1993). For much of European history the differences of agentic capacities between the sexes could be understood as God-given, no more mysterious or in doubt than the difference between subject and sovereign. As the Apostle Paul tells us, "the husband is the head of the wife just as Christ is the head of the church, the body of which he is the Savior. Just as the church is subject to Christ, so also wives ought to be, in everything, to their husbands" (Ephesians 5.23–24, New Revised Standard Version).

However, with the scientific revolution and Enlightenment came the secularization of politics and theories of human nature. Along with theories about men's natural rights came both calls for the recognition of women's rights and a sense that tradition—religious or otherwise—was insufficient grounds upon which to deny them. As Londa Schiebinger explains, once natural rights of equality and freedom were taken to be the logical consequence of natural features of man, calls for women's rights "could be countered only by proof of natural inequalities" (Schiebinger 2000, 9). Thus scientific efforts to identify and explain the essential and profound natural differences between males and females flourished, searching for features of bodies that could be used to explain differences in agentic capacities and thus justify differences in education, opportunity and legal rights.

3.1. *Agency*

Feminists, eager to defend the legal rights and equal rational capacities of women, argued that any differences that science might find between men's and women's bodies were not relevant to their agentic capacities. Appearances to the contrary resulted from differing education and differences in labor between the sexes, but, as one early feminist put it, "the mind has no sex"[3] (Schiebinger 1989, 1). In the second wave of feminism, this basic idea came to be expressed by distinguishing biological sex from social gender. Roughly speaking, sex was taken to be the category of biological description while gender was a social concept. That women typically have uteruses that often have the capacity to bear children is a biological fact about the female sex; that women are underrepresented in the study of physics and those

---

3. Schiebinger attributes the phrase to François Poullain de la Barre ("L'esprit n'a point de sexe") from *De l'egalité des deux sexes, Discours, physique et moral, où l'on voit l'import de se défaire de prejugez* (1673).

professions related to physics is a social fact about women's gender. The sex-gender distinction and the turn to thinking of the differences between men and women's lives as the result of social constructions, rather than emerging from biological fact, reinforced the view that the details of embodiment did not matter as much as the body being sufficiently clearly marked to allow categorization into social identities.

The idea that women could be rational agents prompted serious consideration of agency in the context of women's lives and traditional roles. Feminists began to consider epistemology and ethics from the perspective of women's lives—their experiences, their interests, and their labor. In other words, they looked at the effects of gender in the acquisition of knowledge and activities of daily life. This theorizing produced new understandings of the self and agency that radically departed from traditional conceptions.

Against the traditional liberal view of the radically autonomous subject, feminists argued that the self is not radically autonomous, but is importantly relational. While some theorists have understood the self as emerging solely through the interactions of close interpersonal relationships, others have understood relationships to include "the full range of influential human relations, personal and public . . . [thus] emphasizing political dimensions of the multiple relationships that structure an individual's selfhood" (Sherwin 1998, 19). These thinkers have argued that the agent cannot escape her political context; the agent's position in social hierarchies influences what she can know, what she wants, and what moral rights and obligations she might have.

In critiquing the liberal subject, feminist theorists have thus recognized that respecting and fostering the agency of women and members of other subordinated groups requires concepts of agency that are more theoretically creative and less politically exclusive than the dominant European ideal. Many feminists have worked on reconceptualizing the indispensable notion of autonomy in ways that recognize the importance of relational support to the possibilities of autonomous agency (e.g., Meyers 1989; Sherwin 1998; Mackenzie and Stoljar 2000). Others have attended to the transformative possibilities for critical agency that come with seeing the self as importantly socially constituted. Theorists like Maria Lugones (1989) and Sandra Harding (1991) among others have argued, for example, that the complex ways individuals are situated in the social can give rise to important critical positions for the exercise of political and epistemic agency.

However, in directly engaging dominant philosophical conceptions of agency, conceptions that neglect or disparage the body, feminist theorists have often themselves lost sight of the ways in which self-understanding and action are inevitably achieved through the body. Although they have decisively shown that any adequate theories of agency must be able to make sense of women's lives without reinforcing oppressive norms, they have often failed to fully contest the very distinction upon which the exclusion of women from traditional theories rested—the mind-body distinction. Thus, feminist theories of agency and autonomy might be seen to implicitly reify the view that the life of the mind is distinct from and superior to the life of the body, simply through neglect.

3.2. Embodiment

Londa Schiebinger credits 1970s feminism with reinserting the body into history. Prior to this, the body was considered "too vulgar, trivial, or risqué to merit serious attention" (Schiebinger 2000, 1). Feminist theories of the body have been wide-ranging and multifaceted, some historical, others arising concomitantly with the shift in feminist theories of self and autonomy, some only indirectly engaging embodiment through theories of emotion, others engaging embodiment directly through philosophical phenomenology. Early accounts of the significance of embodiment in second wave feminism sometimes echoed familiar strains from the European tradition that associated men and masculinity with the mind, rationality, and agency, while linking women and femininity with the body, emotionality, and receptivity. These thinkers maintained that sex differences were essential differences—rooted in women's biology as natural mothers or in men and women's psychology through a psychoanalytic etiology (e.g., Keller 1987). Sexism, according to such views, was not rooted in the differences themselves, which were just a fact of nature, but in their inequitable valuation.

Many feminists, however, regarded this difference feminism as deeply misguided. One branch of feminist scholarship took the marking of gender on the body as evidence of the profound effects of social construction. This approach posits the body as a site of vulnerability and constraint upon which gender is carved. Theorists such as Sandra Bartky (1990), Susan Bordo (1993), Marilyn Frye (1983), and Iris Marion Young (2005) have made powerful contributions to our grasp of how oppressive systems operate through bodies socially marked and shaped as subordinate, creating "practiced and subjected" bodies (Bartky 1990, 71). The encoding of various meanings onto the body and the many ways that oppression is materialized through bodies was a focus that found ready support from feminist theorists in a number of areas. Feminist historians, for example, have documented the many ways in which the female body has been conceived as inferior to the male's and as central to defining feminine identity. Moreover, they have traced the history of the role of science in creating our current folk theories of sex, race, and sexuality (Schiebinger 1989; Fausto-Sterling 2000). More recently, the feminist health movement has shown that a failure to take the possibility of significant statistical differences between sexed bodies seriously can both be understood as a symptom of sexist oppression and result in practices that seriously harm women (Baylis, Downie, and Sherwin 1998). (A familiar example of this critique involved the realization in the 1990s that many of the diagnostic signs of and treatments for heart disease were inadequate for diagnosing and treating women.) Though the focus on marked and socialized bodies has been, at the same time, an expression of feminists' deep political commitment to acknowledging and fostering the agency of marginalized political subjects, it is fair to say that much feminist theory has engaged the issue of embodiment with an overwhelming focus on how oppressive practices constrain and damage agentic possibilities. Although this focus has been indispensable to an adequate analysis of oppression, it has done little to show how the body is the ground for agency more positively conceived.

There are, however, important resources in feminist theory for addressing these gaps. In particular, feminist theory is replete with a number of methodological strands that challenge the distorting legacy of mind/body dualism (though what follows is by no means an exhaustive list). First, the growth in feminist theory since the 1970s has been paralleled by a growth in theory of emotions (Rorty 1980; de Sousa 1987; Stocker 1999). Historically, emotions have been viewed as irrational, crucially embodied, part of our animal evolutionary past, and often peculiarly feminine. Yet their role in directing attention and motivating action has been an undeniable dimension of agency. Increasingly, emotion theorists, with substantial support from neuroscience (Damasio 1994), have argued that emotions have a crucial role in good judgment, and a rich literature has grown up exploring the ontology of emotions and their ethical, epistemic, and political significance. It is true that these theories focus on the cognitive and conceptual aspect of emotions; nevertheless this work has the capacity to challenge the tradition of mind-body dualism and provides a rich basis upon which to engage theories of both the body and agency. Many feminists now consider the emotions to be crucial components in ethics and epistemology (Calhoun 1984; Jaggar 1989; Scheman 1996; Campbell 1997). Indeed, the authors in this text simply assume the value of emotions to agency.

Secondly, poststructuralist, postmodern, and psychoanalytic modes of feminist theorizing have given rise to an array of devastating feminist critiques of the hierarchical dualisms that ground European thought. These dimensions of feminist theory have also yielded sophisticated post-Foucauldian conceptions of power that recognize in subjection possibilities for subversion and resistance, enacted through bodies. In Judith Butler's work (1990; 1993), the embodied enactment and reinforcement of oppressive social norms is ineliminably tied to the power to undermine these same norms through subversive performance. In a similar vein, Donna Haraway's (1991) cyborg embodies the potential of new partial perspectives, grounded in the breakdown of animal/human, organism/machine, and physical/nonphysical dichotomies. Freed from a unified organic essence and a mythology of lost innocence, the cyborg is a wily political agent whose fractured identity defies categorization and operates as a basis for resistance. Elizabeth Grosz's account of agency as the multiple forces that act in and through a subject also poses a powerful challenge to multiple dualisms—including the dualism of inside and outside—that have informed dominant European understandings of bodies and minds (1994; 1995).

Third, many feminist theorists and activists have explored positions that rest "on the margins" of mainstream (read white, middle-class, culturally Christian, heterosexual, able-bodied) feminism. These theorists have used their own embodied realities as a challenge to do theory in ways that forefront the very embodied agency of those whose bodies are most disparaged by our current oppressive social orders. Theorists such as Patricia Hill Collins (2000), Audre Lorde (1984; 1986), Felly Nkweto Simmonds (1999), Susan Wendell (1996), Patricia Williams (1991), and Jacquelyn Zita (1998) have called on feminists to see that the ability to ignore the body in theorizing positive agency rests on the ignorance and privilege of those bodies that have not been marked by modes of oppression other than gender. Postcolonial feminist theorists, such as Chandra Talpade Mohanty (2003), have carried this concern with embodied agency into close contextual studies of women's work and agency in the postcolonial contexts shaped by the interaction of global capitalism, with local ideologies of gender, class, caste, and ethnicity.

Finally, some feminists have drawn on phenomenology, particularly the work of Merleau-Ponty, to give an account of the lived body from the perspective of the subject (Bigwood 1991; Fielding 1996; Sullivan 1997; Weiss 1999; Stoller 2000; Young 2005). Interestingly, phenomenology is one of the few schools within the European tradition that has drawn together theories of embodiment and agency. For phenomenologists the lived body grounds the possibility of all experience. Against the tradition of treating the person as a mind in the vessel of the body, Merleau-Ponty took human being to be situated, embodied being-in-the-world. Although his work is not entirely ignored, it is definitely relegated to a certain philosophical niche and is typically overlooked by Anglo-American schools of thought.

Feminists have only begun to confront the depth of mind/body dualism in our theoretical traditions and have begun to rebuild philosophy from a more plausible basis, firmly grounded in real lives. This volume contributes to this project by re-envisioning knowledge, morality, and politics as grounded in living, marked, diverse, active bodies and addressing ongoing conversations from this robust physical and political basis. The authors in this volume also draw strongly on the rich, sophisticated discussions of autonomy that have grown out of close feminist inspection of the traditional liberal subject, bringing these discussions into close conversation with reflections on embodiment. They recognize that paying attention to embodiment, far from being a distraction, is an important and fecund ground for theorizing agency.

4. THE VOLUME

4.1. *Becoming Subjects: Agency Embodied*

As Lois McNay notes, theories of identity formation of subjects in oppressive circumstances have typically been negative, treating "subjectification as subjection" (2000, 2). While McNay traces this trend to Foucauldian social construction and Lacanian psychoanalysis, it is fair to say that this tendency goes right to the roots of feminist theory. In his early liberal feminist treatise, John Stuart Mill, for example, offers a vivid account of subjectification as subjection:

> in the case of women, a hot-house and stove cultivation has always been carried on of some of the capabilities of their nature, for the benefit and pleasure of their masters. Then, because certain products of the general vital force sprout luxuriantly and reach a great development in this heated atmosphere and under this active nurture and watering, while other shoots from the same root, which are left outside in the wintry air, with ice purposely heaped all round them, have a stunted growth,

and some are burnt off with fire and disappear; men, with that inability to recognize their own work which distinguishes the unanalytic mind, indolently believe that the tree grows of itself in the way they have made it grow, and that it should die if one half of it were not kept in a vapour bath and the other half in the snow. (Mill 1869/1997, 21)

Although Mill's account is perceptive, both identifying the delusion of those who police gender norms and suggesting that no body can entirely flourish under the extremes of gender socialization, Mill's gendered subject is nevertheless entirely passive. Whether subjected to or freed from oppressive forces, women become subjects passively, either through "hot-house and stove" social construction or through nature taking its course through the body's ontogeny. Freed from oppression, girls become women in the fertile soil of liberal society just as acorns become oak trees.

Subsequent feminist attention to the real ways in which girls become women has emphasized that emotionally rich relationships of care, which are complex and importantly mutual, are the means by which individual humans become subjects and agents. The reciprocity of these relationships expressly implies that the subject herself has a role in becoming subject, but as the authors in Part I reveal, the agency of becoming subject goes far beyond the mutuality of parent-child relationships. These authors explore how we become individually and collectively identified subjects through the agentic possibilities that arise from specific modes of embodiment in a variety of contexts.

Kym Maclaren sets the tone for this section and for the volume, providing a useful account of Merleau-Ponty's phenomenology through an engaging example of identity development in young children in "Emotional Metamorphoses: The Role of Others in Becoming a Subject." Maclaren introduces a number of themes that recur throughout the volume: the importance of others in constituting the self, the epistemic and ethical role of emotions, the project of autonomy, and the importance of grounding theory in real lives and moral psychology, rather than relying on abstract idealization. Maclaren offers a new conceptualization of the subject as agent, using phenomenology as a powerful tool for reconfiguring the subject as "being in the world" as she struggles to understand her experience and become herself. This struggle is particularly fraught in Maclaren's example of sibling rivalry, regression, and self-overcoming in the development of young children. Her account of psychological development serves as an explanation of the way in which particular relationships, physically enacted through bodies, provide new resources for understanding one's place in the world and developing a sense of self that belongs there.

Angela Failler and Alexis Shotwell develop these themes while also introducing another: the influence of oppressive political contexts on our attempts to create selves. While they raise a familiar feminist issue—the lived politics of marginalized identities—each argues that we must reconceive agency through reflecting on aspects of embodiment to understand the positive possibilities of self-creation. In "Racial Grief and Melancholic Agency," Failler takes up the challenges of self-becoming in a racialized context. Following Anne Anlin Cheng's extension of Freudian melancholy into social critique (2000), Failler offers a psychoanalysis of American racism, revealing the ongoing process of becoming a racialized subject through disavowals and incorporations of various lost others. This process is both profoundly political and personal, enacted in society and inscribed on the body. In contrast to the simplified analyses of so-called power feminists, Failler offers a nuanced account of the perils of victim identification; she explores melancholia as a legitimate expression of grief that can also be a site for agency. Like Maclaren, Failler attempts to theorize new dimensions of agency that show how embodied relations that are often regarded as conflicted and oppositional can be a resource for agentic capacities.

Similar struggles for self-definition, mediated between social construction and biological reality, are negotiated by Alexis Shotwell in "A Knowing That Resided in My Bones: Sensuous Embodiment and Trans Social Movement." Guided by trans narratives and other genderqueer biographies, Shotwell navigates the epistemology of embodiment through the concept of sensuous knowledge—a type of embodied understanding that calls for political action. Through this knowledge genderqueer subjects can propel positive projects of self and social transformation. Through transitioning, trans subjects come to be at home in their own bodies; thus, genderqueer transformations are seen to be deeply personal transformations that are also political. Being at home in one's body is shown to be entwined with being at home in one's community.

Shotwell's characterization of sexual transitioning as a site for agency finds a counterpoint in Rebecca Kukla's critical discussion of body modification and the discourse of the mismatch between the inner agent and her outer body that justifies it. In "The Phrenological Impulse and the Morphology of Character," Kukla suggests that we remain captivated by the idea that parts of the body can be taken as signs of character and that we can thus truly become ourselves by surgically altering our bodies. Kukla explores how the background assumptions of nineteenth-century phrenology and mind-body dualism—complicated by the possibility of a mismatch between them—still resonate in the twenty-first century. Contemporary plastic surgery acts as an external means of crafting one's own character and correcting deceptive "deformities" so as to either reveal the real self and its capacities or to become a new self. The character, limited by having the wrong appearance, is freed; the knife restores the natural order. Kukla's account foregrounds the complex politics behind these transformations.

Catriona Mackenzie revisits and integrates many of the themes raised in the first four papers, providing the reader with a careful theoretical analysis of the role of narrative in self-becoming and both the constraints of political oppression and embodied possibility in this activity. Her essay, "Personal Identity, Narrative Integration, and Embodiment," follows a growing feminist critique of traditional European accounts of personal identity, abandoning the attempt to explicate necessary and sufficient conditions for personal identity in favor of an analysis of narrative self-constitution. Drawing on Merleau-Ponty's phenomenology, Mackenzie shows that a narrative approach to self that ignores the importance of embodied subjectivity cannot explain the dialectic of continuity and change that characterize our attempts to become integrated subjects. Crucial to Mackenzie's account is the idea of the bodily perspective, comprising body schema—the non-conscious, non-intentional organization of experience and action that guides ordinary daily activity—and body image—the "perceptual awareness of one's body . . . mental representations of one's body, beliefs about it, and emotional attitudes toward it." This bodily perspective forms the lens through which the subject experiences and understands her life and thus is the basis of all possible action. The first-person self-narrative is also informed by the responses of others who perceive her body; thus, the subject is vulnerable to having her own bodily perspective challenged and changed by others. In this way Mackenzie offers insight into the ways in which oppressive norms can be internalized, without thereby stripping the subject of agency.

Sylvia Burrow completes Part I by offering a concrete suggestion for developing agency through embodied practice. In "Bodily Limits to Autonomy: Emotion, Attitude, and Self-Defense," Burrow argues that training in self-defense can contribute to autonomy, investigating the role of the body and bodily awareness in confronting sex oppression. Building on Diana Tietjens Meyers's account of autonomy as a set of competencies (1989; 2004), Burrow extends the analysis to involve bodily competencies arising from self-defense training. These are not limited to the physical skills by which one can defend oneself from personal violence, but also extend to self-confidence and associated attitudes that provide the emotional basis for developing autonomy. By offering a tangible method for overcoming the bodily encoded limits associated with sex oppression and feminine identity, Burrow directs our attention to the larger political themes that run through the second part of the volume.

4.2. Embodied Relations: Political Contexts

The papers in Part II engage central political issues—national policies on the distribution of scarce medical resources, political goals of religious movements, Aboriginal reclamations of postcolonial histories, international conflict, and globalized economics—exploring the wide variety of ways in which politics constrains and creates possibilities for meaningful action. Susan Sherwin and Monique Lanoix focus on state-sponsored or institutionally managed contexts of care where moral commitments arising from personal relationships, embodied practices, and bodily and agentic capacities confront the public policy and political institutions that inform and shape these relationships, constraining personal agency. Jacqueline Davies and Sue Campbell foreground the ways in which the deep values and commitments that inform our interpretive practices (themselves a product of historical contingencies that engage larger political movements) construct and constrain the ways in which agents can think of themselves and present themselves. Susan Babbitt and Christine Koggel bring the discussion into the international arena, demanding that global economics and international policies be held accountable to the lived realities of human agents, the pursuit of justice, and the hope of genuinely improving human lives. All of the essays in this part challenge the reader to reconceptualize agency and embodiment in ways adequate to political realities and personal relationships, exploring the limits of bodies and agency.

The first three papers of this section, by Susan Sherwin, Monique Lanoix, and Jacqueline Davies, address the relationships between bodies in particular medical contexts, where differences in embodiment between caregiver and care receiver may have serious consequences for the agentic possibilities of both. While these relationships are crucially ethical and personal, each of these three papers brings out ways in which the agency of the subjects is constrained by outside political forces.

In "Relational Existence and Termination of Lives: When Embodiment Precludes Agency," Susan Sherwin reveals the power of a relational analysis in challenging and changing the contemporary discourse around ethical relationships and policy decisions in key medical contexts. Specifically, Sherwin confronts public policy that addresses the obligations that particular others have to those at the boundaries of moral personhood in the contexts of abortion and end-of-life decisions for individuals in persistent vegetative states. Sherwin's contextual approach embeds personhood in the social environments that constitute and maintain persons, and questions the moral and political meanings of embodied states that preclude agency. The capacity to relate is importantly mutual, and Sherwin argues that forms of embodiment that exclude certain critical agentic capacities need to be recognized as morally significant differences. Public policy decisions that burden those in relations of care for humans at the borders of moral personhood with ethical and legal obligations must meet the demands of justice and conform with the goals and values implicitly held by the social collective responsible for the policy.

Monique Lanoix effectively extends and reframes Sherwin's analysis looking at the institutionalized and economic mediation of the care relationships that typify the end of life. In "A Body No Longer of One's Own," Lanoix investigates the politics of control and the limits of agency negotiated by those who cannot fulfill the activities of daily living without some assistance and by the people who care for them. Despite the obvious centrality of bodily needs, limitations, and labor in these relationships, Lanoix argues that current institutionalized practices of care actually ignore the body. She explains that the current economic structuring of care labor compromises the caregiver and alienates the care receiver from her own body under a misleading public discourse of consumer autonomy. Lanoix advocates a reconfiguring of care activities around relational models of autonomy that reconceptualize the relationship between caregiver and -receiver as mutual, and highlight the personal and intimate nature of the care labor itself.

Jacqueline Davies also addresses the ways in which third parties may inform ethical relationships and, in some cases, attempt to create ethical relationships where, arguably, none exist. In "Premature (M)Othering: Levinasian Ethics and the Politics of Fetal Ultrasound Imaging," Davies shows how pro-life groups endorse using fetal ultrasound as a means of forcing pregnant women, prematurely, into an ethical relationship with the "unborn child," displacing the pregnant woman's embodied experience of her pregnancy in favor of the supposedly objective authority of the visual image. The argument implicit in these tactics looks, at first glance, like an application of Levinas's ethics—the pregnant woman is confronted by the fetal face of the Other, who demands that she respond ethically to her or his needs and thus become mother. However, Davies argues that rather than mediating between a mother and child, the ultrasound operates as a surrogate moralist, brandishing the image of a fetal face and ventriloquizing its voice. The image presents the fetus as the face of the Other and thus creates a mother who must meet the ethical demand of the encounter—that is, a mother whose motherhood is defined by the impossibility of choosing abortion. The ethical relation that *might* exist between pregnant woman and fetus is hijacked by a third party that masquerades as providing information (and thus as an aid to autonomy) while in fact radically constraining pregnant women's bodily self-determination and moral integrity.

Sue Campbell continues to explore the power of others in interpreting experience and ethical relevance, turning toward the importance of others' embodied imaginative engagement with representations of the past. In "Inside the Frame of the Past: Memory, Diversity, and Solidarity," Campbell applies performance theory to the epistemology of memory as a method of illuminating the relational and reconstructive aspects of remembering. Although she begins her analysis by showing how memory performances and their reception often function to affirm personal relationships through creating an imaginary of shared values, Campbell extends her analysis to oppositional rememberings that challenge the audiences from which they seek uptake. Her central example is a First Nations work, *The Scrubbing Project*. Utilizing Maria Lugones's account of "world"-traveling (Lugones 1989), Campbell argues that even when audiences are ill at ease in others' memory "worlds," their engagement can contribute important resources to marginalized social memory, opening the possibility for relationships of solidarity. Campbell reveals the deep politics of collective memory, using performance theory to draw attention to the importance of communicative uptake in making memories meaningful.

The final two papers of the volume continue the theme of collective moral agency, each addressing the position of agents in the context of global politics and international injustice. In counterpoint to Campbell, Susan Babbitt challenges the focus on collective memory as the basis for imagining a just future. In "Collective Memory or Knowledge of the Past: 'Covering Reality with Flowers,'" Babbitt draws on insights from Palestinian author Mourid Barghouti (2003) and Marxist (particularly Cuban) political figures, exhorting us to look with "open eyes" and engage concretely with the contingent present, rather than seeking to understand the present through mythologies of the past. Arguing against an intellectualist conception of collective memory as increased knowledge about the past or increased attention to others' perspectives, she contends that acts are made meaningful for agents by virtue of being relevant for their current self-conceptions and future plans. Thus, people can only find an explanatory purpose in alternative accounts of the past when they already need and desire to move into the future differently. Babbitt's analysis is primarily directed toward our collective envisioning of a more just future and demands that this humanistic project not be hobbled by attachments to the past and identities rooted in collective histories. Rather, to achieve true freedom, we must actively avoid intellectual despotism, embrace the insecurity that follows from a lack of certainty, and start from an experiential understanding of our lived individual and social reality.

Christine Koggel completes the volume by offering a characterization of agency in a globalized context of postcolonial oppression that is sensitive to the multiple and varied challenges of the lives of the economically marginalized. Koggel argues in "Agency and Empowerment: Embodied Realities in a Globalized World" that the current focus on agency and empowerment in international development and discussions of social justice, though laudable, requires a relational conception of persons in order to be successful. This relational analysis reveals the power dynamics that are characteristic of the inequalities of contemporary liberal, capitalist society, and international economic bodies—dynamics frequently invisible to those in power. She argues that the real facts of daily living for the socially marginalized—especially the ways in which basic bodily needs are pursued and achieved, despite a context of displacement and denial—is only visible through a relational account. Koggel's essay concludes the volume by addressing some of the central ethical challenges facing contemporary society: the problems of social justice in the face of global capitalism. In framing the problem as one of how to enhance the agency of the oppressed without denying their current agency in the context of real bodily needs, limitations, and physically enacted relations of power, she moves us closer toward an "embodied ethics" (Weiss 1999, chap. 7). Through engaging the body, in its physical and political context, not merely as the tool of the agent, but the site of agency, the authors in this volume reveal the importance of integrating the concepts of agency and embodiment and understanding them as crucially in relation with one another.

REFERENCES

Barghouti, Mourid. 2003. *I Saw Ramallah*. Trans. Ahdaf Soueif. New York: Anchor Books.

Bartky, Sanda Lee. 1990. Foucault, Femininity, and the Modernization of Patriarchal Power. In *Femininity and Domination: Studies in the Phenomenology of Oppression*, 63–82. New York: Routledge.

Baylis, Françoise, Jocelyn Downie, and Susan Sherwin. 1998. Reframing Research Involving Humans. In *The Politics of Women's Health: Exploring Agency and Autonomy*, ed. Feminist Health Care Ethics Research Network, coord. Susan Sherwin, 234–60. Philadelphia: Temple University Press.

Bigwood, Carol. 1991. Renaturalizing the Body (With a Little Help from Merleau-Ponty). *Hypatia: A Journal of Feminist Philosophy* 6(3): 54–73.

Bordo, Susan. 1993. *Unbearable Weight: Feminism, Western Culture, and the Body.* Berkeley and Los Angeles: University of California Press.

Butler, Judith. 1990. *Gender Trouble: Feminism and the Subversion of Identity.* New York: Routledge.

———. 1993. *Bodies That Matter: On the Discursive Limits of "Sex."* New York: Routledge.

Calhoun, Cheshire. 1984. Cognitive Emotions? In *What Is an Emotion? Classic and Contemporary Readings*, ed. Cheshire Calhoun and Robert Solomon, 327–42. Oxford: Oxford University Press.

Campbell, Sue. 1997. *Interpreting the Personal: Expression and the Formation of Feelings.* Ithaca: Cornell University Press.

Cheng, Anne Anlin. 2000. *The Melancholy of Race: Psychoanalysis, Assimilation, and Hidden Grief.* Oxford: Oxford University Press.

Clark, Andy. 1998. Embodied, Situated, and Distributed Cognition. In *A Companion to Cognitive Science*, ed. William Bechtel and George Graham, 506–17. Oxford: Blackwell.

Collins, Patricia Hill. 2000. *Black Feminist Thought: Knowledge, Consciousness, and the Politics of Empowerment.* 2nd edition. New York: Routledge.

Damasio, Antonio. 1994. *Descartes' Error: Emotion, Reason, and the Human Brain.* New York: Avon Books.

De Sousa, Ronald. 1987. *The Rationality of Emotion.* Cambridge: MIT Press.

Dewey, John. 1980. *Art as Experience.* New York: Perigee Books.

Fausto-Sterling, Anne. 2000. *Sexing the Body: Gender Politics and the Construction of Sexuality.* New York: Basic Books.

Fielding, Helen. 1996. Grounding Agency in Depth: The Implications of Merleau-Ponty's Thought for the Politics of Feminism. *Human Studies* 19(2): 175–84.

Foucault, Michel. 1979. *Discipline and Punish: The Birth of the Prison.* Trans. Alan Sheridan. New York: Vintage Books.

———. 1980. Body/Power. In *Power/Knowledge: Selected Interviews and Other Writings, 1972–1977*, ed. Colin Gordon, trans. Colin Gordon, Leo Marchall, John Mepham, and Kate Sober. New York: Pantheon Books.

———. 1990. *The History of Sexuality: An Introduction.* Trans. Robert Hurley. New York: Vintage Books.

Frye, Marilyn. 1983. *The Politics of Reality.* Freedom, Calif.: Crossing Press.

Grosz, Elizabeth. 1994. *Volatile Bodies: Towards a Corporeal Feminism.* Bloomington: Indiana University Press.

———. 1995. *Space, Time, and Perversion: Essays on the Politics of Bodies.* New York: Routledge.

Haraway, Donna. 1991. A Cyborg Manifesto: Science, Technology, and Socialist-Feminism in the Late Twentieth Century. In *Simians, Cyborgs, and Women: The Reinvention of Nature*, 149–82. New York: Routledge.

Harding, Sandra. 1991. Who Knows? Identities and Feminist Epistemologies. In *(En)gendering Knowledge: Feminists in Academe*, ed. Joan E. Hartmann and Ellen Messer-Davidow, 100–120. Knoxville: University of Tennessee Press.
Hume, David. 1739/1969. *A Treatise of Human Nature*. London: Penguin.
Jaggar, Alison. 1989. Love and Knowledge: Emotion in Feminist Epistemology. In *Women, Knowledge, and Reality: Explorations in Feminist Philosophy*, ed. Marilyn Pearsall and Ann Garry, 166–90. Boston: Unwin Hyman.
Keller, Evelyn Fox. 1987. Feminism and Science. In *Sex and Scientific Inquiry*, ed. Sandra Harding and Jean F. O'Barr, 233–46. Chicago: University of Chicago Press.
Kelly, Sean. 2003. Merleau-Ponty on the Body. In *The Philosophy of the Body*, ed. Michael Proudfoot, 62–76. Oxford: Blackwell.
Kestenbaum, Victor. 1977. *The Phenomenological Sense of John Dewey: Habit and Meaning*. New York: Humanities Press.
Leder, Drew. 1990. *The Absent Body*. Chicago: University of Chicago Press.
Lorde, Audre. 1984. The Uses of the Erotic: The Erotic as Power. In *Sister Outsider*, 53–59. Trumansburg, N.Y.: Crossing Press.
———. 1986. *A Burst of Light*. New York: Firebrand Books. 1988.
Lugones, Maria. 1989. Playfulness, "World"-Traveling, and Loving Perception. In *Women, Knowledge, and Reality: Explorations in Feminist Philosophy*, ed. Marilyn Pearsall and Ann Garry, 419–34. Boston: Unwin Hyman.
Mackenzie, Catriona, and Natalie Stoljar, eds. 2000. *Relational Autonomy: Feminist Perspectives on Autonomy, Agency, and the Social Self*. New York: Oxford University Press.
McNay, Lois. 2000. *Gender and Agency: Reconfiguring the Subject in Feminist and Social Theory*. Cambridge: Polity Press.
Merleau-Ponty, Maurice. 2002. *The Phenomenology of Perception*. New York: Routledge.
Meyers, Diana Tietjens. 1989. *Self, Society, and Personal Choice*. New York: Columbia University Press.
———. 2004. *Being Yourself: Essays on Identity, Action, and Social Life*. Lanham, Md.: Rowman and Littlefield.
Mill, J. S. 1869/1997. *The Subjection of Women*. Mineola, N.Y.: Dover.
Mohanty, Chandra Talpade. 2003. *Feminism Without Borders: Decolonizing Theory, Practising Solidarity*. Durham: Duke University Press.
Rorty, Amelie Oksenberg, ed. 1980. *Explaining Emotions*. Berkeley and Los Angeles: University of California Press.
Scheman, Naomi. 1996. Feeling Our Way Towards Moral Objectivity. In *Mind and Morals: Essays on Cognitive Science and Ethics*, ed. Larry May, Marilyn Friedman, and Andy Clark, 221–36. Cambridge: MIT Press.
Schiebinger, Londa. 1989. *The Mind Has No Sex? Women and the Origins of Modern Science*. Cambridge: Harvard University Press.
———. 2000. Introduction to *Feminism and the Body*, ed. Londa Schiebinger, 1–24. Oxford: Oxford University Press.
Sherwin, Susan. 1998. A Relational Approach to Autonomy in Health Care. In *The Politics of Women's Health: Exploring Agency and Autonomy*, ed. Feminist Health Care Ethics Research Network, coord. Susan Sherwin, 19–47. Philadelphia: Temple University Press.

Simmonds, Felly Nkweto. 1999. My Body, Myself: How Does a Black Woman Do Sociology? In *Feminist Theory and the Body: A Reader*, ed. Janet Price and Margrit Shildrick, 50–63. New York: Routledge.
Spelman, Elizabeth V. 1982. Woman as Body: Ancient and Contemporary Views. *Feminist Studies* 8(1): 109–31.
Spicker, Stuart. 1970. *The Philosophy of the Body: Rejections of Cartesian Dualism*. Chicago: Quadrangle Books.
Stocker, Michael, with Elizabeth Hegeman. 1999. *Valuing Emotions*. New York: Cambridge University Press.
Stoller, Silvia. 2000. Reflections on Feminist Merleau-Ponty Skepticism. *Hypatia: A Journal of Feminist Philosophy* 15(1): 175–82.
Sullivan, Shannon. 1997. Domination and Dialogue in Merleau-Ponty's Phenomenology of Perception. *Hypatia: A Journal of Feminist Philosophy* 12(1): 1–19.
Tuana, Nancy. 1993. *The Less Noble Sex: Scientific, Religious, and Philosophical Conceptions of Woman's Nature*. Bloomington: Indiana University Press.
Weiss, Gail. 1999. *Body Images: Embodiment and Intercorporeality*. New York: Routledge.
Weiss, Gail, and Honi Fern Haber. 1999. *Perspectives on Embodiment: The Intersections of Nature and Culture*. New York: Routledge.
Wendell, Susan. 1996. *The Rejected Body*. New York: Routledge.
Williams, Patricia J. 1991. *The Alchemy of Race and Rights*. Cambridge: Harvard University Press.
Young, Iris Marion. 2005. *On Female Body Experience: Throwing Like a Girl and Other Essays*. New York: Oxford University Press.
Zita, Jacquelyn. 1998. *Body Talk: Philosophical Reflections on Sex/Gender*. New York: Columbia University Press.

PART ONE

BECOMING EMBODIED SUBJECTS

ONE

EMOTIONAL METAMORPHOSES:
THE ROLE OF OTHERS IN BECOMING A SUBJECT

Kym Maclaren

1. INTRODUCTION

In their most passionate forms, emotions can seem to be psychological or bodily forces that *interrupt* and put in abeyance our agency and autonomy. We sometimes cry or laugh *despite ourselves;* or in the heat of an emotional moment, we may be driven to acts that, in a "cooler, more rational" moment, when we "have control over ourselves" we would never contemplate doing. It is not surprising, then, that emotion has often been conceived, both within philosophy and without, as a force that opposes itself to reason and, correspondingly, to one's autonomy.

Nonetheless, this impression that emotion is irrational and at odds with autonomy is, I contend, based upon traditional and problematic conceptions of what it is to be a self or subject, the agent of one's actions. One such problematic conception, still very much operative these days (if not in our philosophical treatises, then often in our practical lives), is the moralistic conception of a subject as inherently rational, and as actualizing her own autonomy through answering to her own rationality. From this perspective, when someone becomes "emotional" and behaves in ways that, from an external perspective, appear inappropriate to the situation at hand, we tend to suppose that this person is "losing control of herself," giving up on a rational way of considering the situation, and indulging in her irrational emotional impulses. She has, we might say, *chosen* to indulge herself in her emotions, and thus *freely* relinquished her own *freedom*. She is therefore fundamentally at fault for her behavior.

This essay offers a criticism of this moralistic conception of agency and selfhood, and it does so through a consideration of emotion and the emotional metamorphoses that we can undergo—either toward increasingly compulsive, "mad" ways of being, or toward new epiphanies and a new sense of oneself and one's place in the world. Relying on an existential understanding of the "subject as agent" as an *achievement,* or what one becomes, rather than as a pre-given, always present entity, I argue that emotion is not opposed to reason, but is rather an essential element of our rational development toward autonomous ways of being. Proponents of the moralistic conception of the subject, on this account, are wrong to think that a person's emotional behavior is simply her own fault, as if she had *allowed* herself to fall away from a rationality to which she has access; they mistakenly presuppose a fully developed rational self, and simultaneously fails to recognize the essential role that *others* play in a person's emotional metamorphoses. As a result, the moralistic conception of the subject can, I suggest, be oppressive and destructive, actually helping to bring about "mad" and compulsive behavior, instead of inspiring a greater rationality, as its proponents suppose it does.

To make these claims, I draw on the phenomenological tradition of philosophy, and especially on the work of Martin Heidegger and Maurice Merleau-Ponty. The first section articulates a phenomenological account of emotion, which locates emotions not in some solipsistic consciousness, but in our embodied engagements with the world and with others. Implied in this phenomenological account of emotion is a conception of bodily intentionality, which is elucidated in the second section. The third section argues that we are implicated in and moved by *others'* bodily intentionalities, and that these implications in others can lead to emotional tensions in our immediate experience of the world. I then consider how these emotional tensions can draw us in two different directions of emotional metamorphoses: toward compulsive and "mad" behaviors, where there is a relative loss of self (section 4); or toward epiphanies and the birth of a new, more autonomous self (section 5). Both of these metamorphoses, I argue, are conditioned by our implication in others' bodily intentionalities. This exploration of the nature of emotion and our emotional metamorphoses will suggest an alternative conception of what it is to be (or become) a subject, and propose serious reasons for thinking that the moralistic conception of the subject is problematic.

2. EMOTION AS BEING IN THE WORLD

The phenomenological notion of human reality as *being in the world* arises from a criticism of modern philosophy, and especially a criticism of the Cartesian conception of the subject. According to the Cartesian conception, the subject is related to its objects primarily through *knowing* and *judging*. That is to say, this subject is metaphysically distinct from its objects and accesses them in their essential being only through its knowledge. The gap between the subject and object thus conceived is so profound that there arises a question of how or whether our knowledge of the object in fact corresponds to the being of the thing in itself. Descartes turns to God to guarantee the correspondence; for Hume and Kant, the problem runs deeper.

Phenomenologists argue, however, that the divide between subject and object is in fact an *artificial product* of philosophical reflection rather than a problem that is based in reality: by reflecting on the question of what a subject is, modern philosophy actually *creates* a dichotomy between subject and object that is not initially there. This mistake is understandable: reflection objectifies and draws distinctions, and, when it is not self-conscious of this fact, it may take as inherent in reality distinctions that have in fact resulted from its own reflecting activity. Consider this analogous case: when we reflect upon knowledge, our reflection tends to distinguish the conceptual content from the sensory "data." But, at least according to the diagnoses of philosophers like Wittgenstein, Sellars, Ryle, and Merleau-Ponty, the notion of sense-data is really a fiction (ultimately incoherent) produced by our own reflection, rather than something really existing. Similarly, phenomenologists argue, modern philosophical reflection has *produced* the notion of the self-contained subject that is dichotomous with its object and can access that world only through its activity of knowing and judging. Modern philosophy goes wrong, then, in mistaking the *products* of its own reflection (i.e., the self-contained subject) for something that was there all along.

Phenomenology seeks to rectify this. Aware of the objectifying, distinction-drawing effects of reflection, phenomenology attempts what Merleau-Ponty has called a "radical reflection"—a reflection that articulates consciousness or human reality as it exists *before it reflects upon itself,* or in its *pre-reflective being.*[1] What it finds is that, pre-reflectively, we are not subjects *thinking* about a world beyond us, *judging* its meaning or essential being, and *actively* choosing how to act; we are, rather, beings perceptually caught up in, and *moved by,* an immediately meaningful world.

---

1. Merleau-Ponty introduces this notion of radical reflection in the preface of his *Phenomenology of Perception* (2003). The rest of the text can be read as an attempt to engage in such radical reflection.

This difference between the modern conception of the subject and the phenomenological conception of *being in the world* is nicely illustrated by the notions of mood or emotion that accompany each. On the modern conception of the subject, emotion is typically conceived as something fundamentally internal and subjective: it is conceived either as an inner feeling or as a subjective value attributed to things in the world on the basis of a set of personal ideas, desires, or evaluations.[2]

On the phenomenological account of *being in the world*, on the other hand, emotion and mood are to be found not *inside* a subject, as some introspectible feeling or set of beliefs and evaluations, but in the way that the world *presents itself to us*, in how things exist for us within our immediate perceptual inherence in the world.[3] When I am bored, for instance, everything I encounter in the world presents itself to me in a lackluster manner, and nothing moves me.[4] When I am happy, on the other hand, things stand out to me in their brightness and harmony, and I am buoyed by them. Rather than finding a bored or happy feeling within me, or perceiving things in the world and then judging that they are dull or buoying, I simply *find* myself caught up in a world that "means" to me in this way. In other words, the world, as it gives itself to us *in perception*, prior

---

2. The account that takes emotion to be an inner feeling has been called by some philosophers of emotion "the feeling theory of emotion," and Descartes is sometimes—though not without controversy—taken to hold such a theory. The latter account, where emotion is taken to be the result of an attribution of value, might be associated with Hobbes or Hume, or with certain contemporary versions of the propositional attitude theory of emotion where a modern conception of the subject is still at work.

3. Such an account can be found articulated in Sartre's *Sketch for a Theory of Emotion* (1962), and implied in much of Merleau-Ponty's work (see, for instance, 2003, part 1 chap. 6, and part 3 chap. 1, and 1964a). Here I am relying primarily on Heidegger's account of emotion and mood (see Heidegger 1996, §§29–30, and 40). Though Heidegger speaks primarily of moods (*Stimmung*, or *Befindlichkeit*, being attuned), the same basic account can, I believe, be given of particular emotions. Emotions are, I take it, relatively transient, charged, and directed forms of moods or attunement. See Heidegger 1996, 130–31, for the suggestion that there are various modes of attunement, and see section 30 for a discussion of what might be considered the particular emotion fear. (Though I will quote the Stambaugh translation, I will also provide the German pagination found in the margins of both the Stambaugh and the Macquarrie and Robinson translations. This pagination will be marked by putting a capital "H" before the numbers. For example, the previous citation would be [1996, 130–31 (H138–39)].)

Here, in the interests of space, I am concerned with giving only the briefest characterization of Heidegger's notion of mood and *Befindlichkeit*. For other, more sustained elucidations of Heidegger's notion of mood, see Bruce Baugh (1989), Charles Guignon (1984), David Weberman (1996), and Quentin Smith (1981).

4. Thus, Heidegger says, "Being attuned is not initially related to something psychical, it is itself not an inner condition which then in some mysterious way reaches out and leaves its mark on things and persons. . . . It is a fundamental existential mode of being of the *equiprimordial disclosedness* of world, being-there-with, and existence because this disclosure itself is essentially being-in-the-world" (1996, 129 [H137]).

to any thought or reflection about the world, is emotionally meaningful—and it speaks to us of *how* we are coming along in the world, or *how* we are situated within the world. Thus, Heidegger calls mood "*Befindlichkeit*," which might be translated as "how one finds oneself situated" (1996, 127 [H134]).

On the modern account, emotions are discovered through introspection, and are identified according to the *kind* of emotion that they are (anger, sadness, pride, etc.).[5] In the phenomenological account, labeling emotions in this way fails to do justice to the uniqueness of our personal emotional experiences, and a more honest access to emotions is found not by looking within, but by describing how the world currently "means" to us (cf. Collingwood 1958, esp. chap. 6; Campbell 1997, esp. chap. 2).

3. BODILY INTENTIONALITY

Implied in the phenomenological notion of *being in the world* is a notion of *bodily* intentionality. "Intentionality" is sometimes used (beyond phenomenology) to characterize a subject having *thoughts* or *propositional beliefs* about some particular mental object (its "intentional object"). Phenomenology is primarily interested, however, in the kind of intentionality that is at work *prior to* thoughts and judgment, in pre-reflective perception and action. In opposition to mind-body dualism, where the body is conceived as a mechanical being separate from and mysteriously directed by a consciousness, phenomenologists argue that the body must be understood as a perceiving body, sensitive to and meaningfully caught up in the world. Thus, below the level of our reflective engagement with and thoughts about the world, there lies a *bodily* intentionality.[6]

This bodily intentionality has two sides: on the one hand, we can consider it as it is lived pre-reflectively by the embodied being; on the other hand, we can consider it as it is perceived by other embodied beings. Bodily intentionality as it is *lived* is our ability to apprehend and take up meaning at a perceptual-motor level: it is, as Merleau-Ponty says (following Husserl), an "I can" rather than an "I think," or the "motor grasping of a motor significance" (2003, 159, 167; 1945, 160, 167; see also Heidegger 1996, 64 [H69]). Such bodily intentionality

---

5. Note the extensive classification of the different *kinds* of emotions in Hobbes (1994), Descartes (1975), and Spinoza (1992).

6. This line of thought is set out in the most thematic manner in Merleau-Ponty's work, and especially in his *Structure of Behavior* (1963) and his *Phenomenology of Perception* (2003 [*Phénoménologie de la perception* (1945)]). It is, however, also present (in more or less obvious ways) in Husserl's, Sartre's, and Heidegger's thought.

is evident in the precision and attunement of our habitual responsiveness to the world. If I am an experienced typist, for instance, when I type a document I need not think about where each letter on the keyboard is before I hit it with my fingers. Indeed, in composing this document, my concern is not with my fingers, but with what I am trying to say. And yet, my fingers *know* where to go. This "knowledge in the hands" cannot be a matter of lightning-fast thoughts directing my fingers, since, if I am asked to write out where each letter on the keyboard is, I find that I cannot remember exactly. My fingers know *better* than my own mind. But neither is this bodily knowledge simply a mechanical, conditioned reflex; for if I am given a much smaller keyboard, where my fingers need to travel very different distances in order to hit the letters, I very quickly find my way around it; I need not take the time to *recondition* all the movements that my fingers make. My hands know the keyboard not through conditioned mechanical movements, but in its gestalt or overall organization and thus in its meaningfulness and potential for expressing thoughts.[7] This example is just one among many that show that the human body is not a machine guided by the mind or constituted by reflexes, but an active sensitivity *oriented toward* the potential for meaning in its world, and *moved* to bring this meaning out. Bodily intentionality is the orientation of our bodily being toward meaning.

The orientation of our bodily being toward meaning in the world is not only pre-reflectively lived but is also *perceivable*. Against Descartes's supposition that we must *judge* that *that* is another person who is having an inner experience of the world, phenomenologists like Scheler, Sartre, and Merleau-Ponty argue that we actually *see* another person's *seeing* (Descartes 1993, Meditation Two; Scheler 1992; Sartre 1953, esp. 340–45; Merleau-Ponty 1964b, 169; 2003, part 2 chap. 4). When we see someone looking at something, for instance, we do not simply see a face that is positioned in the line of a certain thing and then infer that that person must be looking at that thing; rather than *mentally inferring an inner mentality,* we *perceive a perceiving body:* "I know unquestionably that that man over there *sees*, that my sensible world is also his, because *I am present at his seeing*, it *is visible* in his eyes' grasp of the scene. . . . A form that resembles me was

---

7. Similarly, Merleau-Ponty argues that an organist can play an instrument unfamiliar to her, and she does not need to spend the time that it would take to *recondition* her body to the new set up of this particular instrument. She takes only a short time to "settle into the organ as one settles into a house," and she does this not by drawing up a new mental plan of the organ, but by "incorporat[ing] within [her]self the relevant directions and dimensions . . . the stops, pedals and manuals are given to [her] as nothing more than possibilities of achieving certain emotional or musical values, and their positions are simply the places through which this value appears in the world" (Merleau-Ponty 2003, 168; 1945, 170). Cf. Heidegger (1996, §§14–18).

there, but busy at secret tasks, possessed by an unknown dream. Suddenly... its glance is raised and comes to fasten on the very same things that I am seeing" (Merleau-Ponty 1964b, 169).

In addition to perceiving others' perceiving, we see in others' bodily orientations toward their perceptual objects *something about these objects*. The meaning apprehended in the world by this other is not an inner meaning hidden in the privacy of her own mind; it is rather written all over her body.[8] Certainly, it may be that the meaning she finds in the world is not *perfectly* articulated in her bodily stance, and that it remains somewhat indeterminate or ambiguous. But nonetheless, it is not nothing. For instance, my companion's aghast stance toward the food on her plate prepares me to find there something horrifying. I may not yet know what, exactly, it is, but I do know that it is something that should not be there. And my interlocutor's stance of dismissiveness may not tell me for certain that I have said something unreasonable, but it raises the question for me and attunes me to what I have said, making the status of my words an issue for me. Even infants, as developmental psychologists have shown, look to their parents' bodily intentionality to help determine the meaningfulness of their environment: crawling across a glass surface, an infant will, when she encounters a ledge and drop under the glass pane (a "visual cliff"), glance at her mother. If her mother takes up the situation with a joyous or interested expression, the baby typically takes up the visual cliff as nothing to worry about, and continues crawling over the drop. If the mother looks fearful or angry, the baby similarly tends to take up the drop as to be feared or to be avoided, and halts in her tracks (Sorce et al. 1985). Thus, the other's bodily intentionality is not only visible; it also helps configure, for us, the meaningfulness of our situation.

To a significant extent, philosophers and psychologists thinking about our social engagements have failed to acknowledge such bodily intentionality and have continued to rely upon the idea that we *infer* what the other is experiencing.[9] This is no accident; in fact, it sheds light on how bodily intentionality works. For the most part, people's bodily intentionalities are *self-effacing*. That is to say, others' bodily intentionalities orient us not by being

---

8. "I do not see anger or a threatening attitude as a psychic fact hidden behind the gesture, I read anger in it. The gesture *does not make me think* of anger, it is anger itself" (Merleau-Ponty 2003, 214; 1945, 215). And: "The meaning of a gesture thus 'understood' is not behind it, it is intermingled with the structure of the world outlined by the gesture, and which I take up on my own account" (Merleau-Ponty 2003, 215; 1945, 216–17).

9. For a summary of the debates that have arisen within psychology because of a cognitivist bias in understanding our social relations (i.e., a bias that supposes that reading the other's experience is a matter of cognitive inference) see Zeedyk (1996).

thematic objects of perception, but in a more peripheral manner, by sweeping our attention toward their object of attention, and thus away from themselves. As a result, one may find oneself having assumed a stance complementary to the other's bodily intentionality without being explicitly aware of the other's intentionality (Bernieri and Rosenthal 1991). Others' bodily intentionalities are, then, *perceptual* directives that move us, referring us beyond themselves, and thereby effacing themselves. They are not thematically perceived objects implying some inner meaning, which is intellectually deciphered by us. The other's bodily intentionality *implicates* me, sweeps me up, and outlines for me what I am to find at the end of her gaze, or how I am to find it.

It is in large part this tendency of others' bodily intentionalities to implicate and inform our own that accounts for our experience of living in a shared reality. Were it the case that I had to *judge or infer* what the other is seeing, I would mostly never be sure that I share a reality with the people I encounter. For I could not know whether that which I infer the other is seeing is in fact what she sees unless she confirmed this with a linguistic avowal; and for the most part, people do not linguistically avow that they are seeing something. In seeing the other's seeing, however, our inherence in a shared reality is immediately confirmed. As Merleau-Ponty says, "The gesture which I witness outlines [*dessine en pointillé*] an intentional object. This object is genuinely present and fully comprehended when the powers of my body adjust themselves to it and overlap it. The gesture presents itself to me as a question, bringing certain perceptible bits of the world to my notice, and inviting my concurrence in them. Communication is achieved when my conduct identifies this path with its own" (Merleau-Ponty 2003, 215; 1945, 215–16). Through the co-implication of our bodily intentionalities, we are brought both to see new aspects of reality, and to confirm that we and others we encounter inhabit the same reality.

4. HOW OTHERS INDUCE EMOTIONAL TENSIONS IN OUR WORLDS

Intersubjective communication and a shared world is not, however, always successfully achieved. And in this fact lies, I believe, the impetus for our emotional metamorphoses. I have argued that we are implicated in others' bodily intentionalities, and moved by them to see the world in a certain manner. If, however, others' bodily intentionalities configure the world in a way that is incommensurable with our own habitual ways of taking up the world, there may arise a tension in our grasp of reality and a disturbance in our sense of our place

Multiple Implications × Friendship
Emotional Tensions

within reality. A child, for instance, may feel called upon to laugh with her uncle at a racist joke, while her longstanding friendship with someone of that race at the same time repels her from such a laughing stance. Thus, though she feels implicated in her uncle's configuration of the world, and called to confirm it, she also feels implicated in her friend and therefore unable to simply follow and endorse her uncle's orientation. She finds herself *multiply* implicated in the world, drawn in different directions, and unable to reconcile these two directions.

To be multiply implicated in this way is to be caught up in an *emotional tension*. Such emotional tension is not simply an inner feeling. It is, rather, a tension that arises within one's very experience of reality. It is the experience of having the meaning of reality put into question (is this a laughable thing or not?). And it is the experience of having *one's place within reality* put into question (am I my uncle's niece, or my friend's good friend? What is my proper place within this world?).

If we conceive of emotional tensions as merely inner, subjective feelings or thoughts, it is difficult to understand how they could have the kind of power over us that they often do. They would seem to be merely mental states belonging to and therefore ultimately under the control of the subject. The subject could, we suppose, set aside this subjectivity and focus on the rational, objective truth at hand. Thus we are inclined to be dismissive of emotionality ("stop being so emotional—be rational!"). If, however, we understand emotional tensions as a matter of putting *our very reality* into question, it makes sense that emotional tensions should so often be overwhelming. For our struggle with an emotional tension is a struggle not with some inner aspect of ourselves at odds with our grasp on reality, but with that very grasp on reality. We struggle to settle the meaning of this reality, and to find our place again within it, in a shared world. As I will argue later, this calls for a very different response than that of "be rational."

Others can, then, through their bodily intentionalities, configure situations in a manner that implicates us in different ways and induces an emotional tension in our own being in the world. In the next two sections, I will consider how our struggles with such emotional tensions can propel us toward existential transformations, and how, even within these struggles and transformations, other people play an essential role.

5. EMOTIONAL METAMORPHOSES: BECOMING "MAD"

At the beginning of this essay, I noted that emotion can lead to a kind of loss of self, wherein we seem to be taken over by an emotion and driven to act in ways that we would not normally endorse, or that we might even, retrospectively or from the outside, consider "mad." This possibility within our emotional lives has supported a traditional conception of emotion as an irrational force. In this section, I contend that such a conception of emotion is a serious misunderstanding and that, even though emotions may lead us to primitive, compulsive behaviors, they may still be in fact lived, embodied, and expressive attempts to make rational sense of our situation.[10] Furthermore, *others* may play an essential role in a person's becoming "mad." I advance these claims through a consideration of case studies, conducted by psychoanalyst Françoise Dolto-Marette, of jealousy or sibling rivalry in children of the age of about eighteen months. Informed by both Dolto-Marette's thoughts and Merleau-Ponty's, the interpretation I propose of these case studies is not the only interpretation possible; it is offered, rather, as a plausible interpretation that both puts to work, and lends support for, the phenomenological-existential conceptions of subjecthood, intersubjectivity, and emotion developed in this essay.[11]

Dolto-Marette seeks to understand the patterns of regression and often astounding development commonly observed in toddlers who are "jealous" of a new sibling. Such children tend to undergo regressions in potty training, language, and their ability for independent play, and they often show significant ambivalence and even aggression toward their new siblings. Strangely, if and when this jealousy is overcome, the child's apparent liberation from his jealousy is often accompanied by notable developments in motor skills and, especially, language acquisition.[12]

---

10. I refer to "madness" within quotes because implied within my criticism of the notion that emotions are irrational lies a latent criticism (informed by Laing and by Deleuze and Guattari) of traditional conceptions of madness as irrationality. On the one hand, I wish to suggest that what we commonly deem madness is often the effect of our social institutions, rather than some defect within the "mad" person, and that such "madness" often involves deep insights and creativity rather than defective or nonsensical ways of perceiving. On the other hand, I want to suggest that there is no clear line between those we tend to deem normal and those we tend to deem mad. All of us undergo a kind of loss of self at times, and even the most "mad" person, as Laing argues, is engaged in an attempt to make good sense of her world, given the real challenges with which she is presented and the resources with which her situation has left her.

11. Merleau-Ponty discusses Dolto-Marette's studies in his essay (based on a lecture course) called "The Child's Relations with Others" (Merleau-Ponty 1964a). My own reading of Dolto-Marette's work is informed by Merleau-Ponty, but also based on a careful reading of Dolto-Marette herself. To properly do justice to Dolto-Marette's account, I would need to lay out in much more detail her own conclusions and lines of reasoning. For the sake of brevity, I have not done that here, in this essay. See however, chapter 4 of my "On Being Moved: A Phenomenological Account of Emotion and Transformation" (2004).

12. For literature in developmental psychology on these general trends, see Sewall (1930); Dunn and Kendrick (1982); Griffin and De La Torre (1985). For Dolto-Marette's descriptions of her case studies, see Dolto-Marette (1947).

Dolto-Marette studies jealous behaviors closely in three boys, highlighting the interpersonal exchanges that are the context for significant developments. Because of her careful attention to the interpersonal context, Dolto-Marette's work gives us the resources (a) for reconceiving sibling rivalry as an interpersonally conditioned phenomenon rather than an irrational force getting the better of these children, and (b) for understanding our own responsibilities in others' emotional struggles.

In the first place, drawing on what we have said, we can understand the jealous behavior of these children as a result of an emotional tension that has developed in their world and which they are trying to resolve. Each child is initially the youngest child in the family. He is therefore accustomed to assuming his place within the world as the youngest of the family and as the one who is cared for by others. When the new sibling arrives, this is put into question. Not only are other family members now not oriented toward him as the youngest, but, in their behaviors, they also express an expectation that he take up a caring, responsible attitude toward another being, instead of being simply the recipient of such care. The child is thus torn, or in tension, between assuming his habitual place as the baby of the family and assuming a new, unfamiliar identity in answer to the solicitations present in the bodily intentionalities of others. He finds himself implicated in the world in two different ways.

Each boy's first way of dealing with this emotional tension seems to be to assume one side of it, and to assume the more familiar side: each becomes baby, regressing in his verbal accomplishments and his ability to control his own excretions. Though each boy gave up the bottle long ago, he compulsively seeks to drink out of a bottle again. He becomes passive and in need of help, where once he was an active, creative child. At the same time, he expresses aggression toward the baby, as if to try to remove her, so that he might more fully, tenably, assume the position of baby in the family.

From a moralistic stance, wherein one supposes a choosing subject free to behave rationally or to indulge in emotions, this kind of behavior would seem to be malicious—an indulgence in emotional behavior, when in fact the child "knows better." But such a moralistic stance cannot explain the following: *that the child, when offered a better way of assuming the situation, happily takes this up, and is momentarily liberated from his jealousy.*

In Dolto-Marette's studies, such liberations are relatively common occurrences. For instance, a boy named Gricha, clearly unhappy about the attention his baby sister is getting from his nanny, marches up to the baby, pretending to be a wolf, and proposes to eat her up. When, however, his nanny tells him that his baby sister is not afraid of him, and that in fact she is proud to have such a strong big brother, Gricha is immediately liberated from his hostile attitude and wants to help feed his sister. This liberation is so existentially penetrating that it manifests itself in other significant ways: for the first time, Gricha is able to call the baby by her proper name; he also regains his ability to control his excretions and shows notable advances in his vocabulary and motor capacities (Dolto-Marette 1947, 789–90).

Such an openness to a new way of configuring the situation suggests that Gricha is not initially being malicious; he is actually seeking a way of assuming a new place in this reality that includes a baby sister; he is trying to *make sense of* his situation. If Gricha wanted only to express irrational aggressive impulses toward the baby, the nanny's response would have been an obstacle to doing that. The fact that the nanny's response is instead taken up joyously as a welcome answer to the situation suggests that this is the kind of thing Gricha has been looking for all along—namely, a way of assuming a tenable position within this shared reality. The nanny has offered Gricha new resources, a new way of configuring the situation that makes better sense of it. She offers him a new identity as a big brother, and Gricha gladly takes this up as a more satisfactory answer than he has been able to find on his own. Prior to the nanny's suggestion, Gricha's own anxious behavior suggests that he, himself, can feel that becoming baby, and trying to get rid of the new baby, cannot totally resolve the tension he is experiencing. And yet, until he is offered a new way of taking on the situation, he is stuck with only these options; they seem to be the only resources available to him.

There is good reason to think, then, that Gricha's "inappropriate" behaviors are the result of a *lack of resources* for situating himself within and making sense of this new reality, rather than an indulgent outburst of irrational impulses. The inappropriate behaviors are, in other words, an attempt (albeit an inadequate attempt) to make his world more rational, instead of an abandonment of rationality.

The resources of which we speak here are *existential*, rather than merely intellectual resources; they are a matter not merely of how one thinks about an already clearly perceived world, but of how one perceives or makes sense of that world in the first place—how one settles ambiguities and tensions within it, and how one assumes oneself within that world. They are a matter of a *lived* logic, rather than a logic arrived at through reflection.

In order to understand Gricha's transformations, it may be helpful to consider, for a second, how existentialist thinkers have understood our capacity for truly existential transformations, or transformations in our lived logic. Kierkegaard,

Beauvoir and Hegel (if one reads Hegel as an existentialist) have noted that we tend to become entrenched in a certain lived logic, banging up against its contradictions. Beauvoir (1996), for instance, notes that the "serious" person bounces back and forth between the contradictions of the serious world, clinging first of all to an absolute value, and then, when this fails to give meaning to life, despairing in there being any values. One undergoes an existential transformation, according to Beauvoir and these others, when one learns to assume the world in terms of a lived logic that transcends and overcomes these contradictions. Thus, Beauvoir's serious person may transcend the contradictions of the serious world, and move into the realm of authentic freedom if she realizes that the options of "absolute values" or "no values" are false options, and that the source of a meaningful life lies in her own creative choices and her ability to take responsibility for them. She thereby moves to a new lived logic, in which she finds new resources for making sense of the tensions and difficulties that arise within her world.

It is just such a move, or existential transformation, that Gricha must undergo if he is to find a new, tenable place in reality alongside his new sister. He must cease to assume himself in those terms that are most familiar to him, and he must find a new way of assuming himself and his world. As it turns out, however, Gricha's liberation on the occasion of being offered, by the nanny, a position as "big brother" is not yet such an existential transformation. It is still caught up in the familiar terms of Gricha's situation, and thus it suffers from the contradictions of a logic inadequate to the complexities of being a unique person in relation with others. We see this when Gricha, after trying to inhabit the new role of "big brother" for a while, finds himself still in an untenable situation. The problem is that Gricha's only way of making sense of "being a big brother" is to copy his own big brother. He thus attempts to become his big brother. But since Gricha is in fact not the same person as his own big brother, and he lacks many of his big brother's abilities, he finds himself unable to be what he has assumed himself to be. In addition, Gricha's big brother resists Gricha's identification with him, telling him to stop copying him, and to leave him alone. Thus, this new resource ultimately fails Gricha, and he is thrown back into the situation of not knowing how to assume himself within this world newly reconfigured by the arrival of a new baby sister.

Now, however, Gricha's situation is worse than ever. For not only does he not know how to assume a meaningful place within reality, but also the only resources that he has found available to him (assume himself as the baby, or assume himself as the big brother) have proven to be failures. It should be no surprise, then, that Gricha now suffers his most severe regression, becoming more babylike than ever: he is unable to get out of bed, or even sit up; he insists upon being diapered and having a bottle, and soils his diaper; his speech regresses into the most inarticulate and monotone monosyllables, and so forth. On the one hand, this is a matter of Gricha suffering from the contradictions of his situation and, for lack of any other resources, being bounced back to his initial way of dealing with this situation (by being the baby). On the other hand, however, the increased severity of this regression expresses the newly experienced hopelessness and helplessness of Gricha's situation. Each time that he has attempted to make sense of his world (by becoming baby or becoming big brother), he has met with resistance in the world and in the behavior of others. He is therefore gradually robbed of even those resources he seemed to have for taking up this situation; his repeated failures at making sense lead to an increasing sense of the impossibility of finding his place within his family, and thus an increasing sense of desperation and hopelessness. His most substantial regression—where he seems to be most mad—is simply an expression of this severely constrained situation, a situation stripped of all resources.

On my account, then, our most "mad" emotional behaviors are not the result of an abandonment of reason and an indulgence in the irrational. They instead arise out of our own embodied attempts to *make existential sense of the world* and to *find our place in reality*.[13] When these attempts meet with *repeated failure*, a situation of experienced resourcelessness results. Compulsive behaviors are the expression of an extremely constrained being in the world, a being in the world stripped of all sense of possibility. It is, moreover, *other people* who help create this constrained situation for us, for it is in large part their bodily intentionalities and linguistically articulated attitudes that express resistance to our attempts at positioning ourselves.[14]

6. EMOTIONAL METAMORPHOSES:
SELF-OVERCOMING AND BECOMING A SUBJECT

In this section, I propose that becoming a subject is a matter of undergoing an existential transformation in one's lived logic, such that one moves beyond

---

13. See Calhoun (1992) for a discussion of forgiveness that is related to this point. In the context of arguing for different forms of forgiveness, Calhoun distinguishes between judging someone's behavior according to moral standards and understanding that behavior as an intelligible response in the context of their lives. It is the latter that I am arguing for.

14. Cf. Sue Campbell's defense of the claim that others can to an important extent *control* our feelings through their interpretations of our expressive acts (Campbell 1997, chap. 5).

the contradictions of one's previous situation and is able to make good sense (for now, at least) of one's world and one's place in it. Becoming a subject is, in other words, a matter of resolving the tensions that have disrupted one's world and put one's place in reality into question. Since those tensions can only be fully resolved and one's place in reality settled when others confirm one's new configuration of oneself and the world, this becoming-subject is realized in part through others. But furthermore, I contend that others lend us the existential resources for making new, better sense of our tension-filled situations in the first place. Thus, though (as we saw in the previous section) others can play an essential role in our compulsions and regressions, they may also offer us routes out of them. I argue for these claims through a consideration, once again, of Dolto-Marette's case studies.

I have noted that children who overcome jealousy often show, at the same time, substantial verbal developments. Both Merleau-Ponty and Dolto-Marette propose that this is not merely a coincidence. The verbal acquisitions, they argue, actually *express* or *realize* a new way of being in the world that is a solution to the situation of jealous tension. In other words, the linguistic developments are expressions of an *existential transformation,* rather than being merely intellectual acquisitions.

In Gricha's case, on the day when he seems to overcome, finally and totally, his jealousy, he acquires—in this *one* day—the use of the simple past (e.g., I was), the imperfect (e.g., *j'étais*),[15] the simple future (e.g., I will be), and future with the auxiliary "to go" (e.g., I am going to be). How are we to understand this sudden acquisition? Dolto-Marette and Merleau-Ponty argue that this new vocabulary reflects Gricha's move from a logic of absolutes to a logic of relativity.

Initially, Gricha lives by a logic of absolutes insofar as, from his point of view, either he is *the* baby of the family, or he is *the* big brother of the family—either he is *the* smallest, or he is *the* biggest. It makes sense that Gricha would operate with this logic, for, before the arrival of the baby, this is what he has known: he has been *the* baby, and his brother has been *the* big brother. But this logic is inadequate to Gricha's situation (and to any interpersonal situation), for it does not allow for the fact that one can be different things to different persons—that one could be big *relative to* the baby, and yet small *relative to* a bigger brother. In order to find his new place within the reality of his family, Gricha must

---

15. The French imperfect tense (*l'imparfait*) has no exact equivalent in English. It indicates an action in the past that is ongoing, or a repeated and incomplete action. For example, *je mangeais* = I was eating.

overcome this lived logic of absolutes for a lived logic of relativity. It is just this overcoming, and the embracing of a new logic that is expressed or realized in Gricha's new vocabulary.[16] He has come to assume himself in these new terms: I *was* the youngest, I *am no longer* the (absolute) youngest, and I *will become* the "oldest" (in relation to the new baby) (Merleau-Ponty 1964a, 110).[17] From now on, he uses quite fluently these verb tenses that reflect such relativity and repositioning. In addition, Gricha leaves behind all of his regressive behaviors, is cured of the stutter that set in when his baby sister arrived, and is consistently positively and responsibly disposed toward the new baby.

In this transformation, Gricha's reality has become richer, more flexible, more able to comprehend and give place to the imperatives of his world. Therein, Gricha seems to become the *subject* of his situation, instead of being captive of it, overcome by it. By finding the words to express his situation and—what is the same thing—realizing a new way of assuming himself and his situation, Gricha has achieved a certain freedom and autonomy within his situation. He can now deal smoothly and effectively with that which presents itself to him, rather than having himself put in question, torn apart, by it.[18]

It remains for us to ask how, exactly, Gricha is able to undergo such a transformation. How does he move from a situation of experienced helplessness and hopelessness to this new sense of being on top of things, and able to make good sense of them? How do any of us make such a move? I contend that we make this move by virtue of being implicated in others' bodily intentionalities,

---

16. Dolto-Marette characterizes this transformation as a transformation in the very logic that is lived by the child. She says it is "the liberation of autonomy and its moral corollary: a sense of [*le sens du*] the relative" (1947, 797 [all translations of this article are my own]). See, also, Merleau-Ponty (1964a, 111): "One might even say that what the child learns, in solving the problem of jealousy, is to relativize his notions. He must relativize the notion of the youngest and the eldest: he is no longer *the* youngest; it is the new child who assumes this role. He thus must come to distinguish the absolute 'youngest' from the relative 'youngest' which he now becomes. And in the same way he must learn to become the eldest in relation to the newborn child, whereas until now the notion of 'eldest' had only an absolute meaning." This is not an intellectual logical reconception of the situation; this is the achievement of a new *lived logic*—an *existential* logic.

17. Merleau-Ponty's own conclusion is significantly informed by another psychologist who studied Dolto-Marette's article: François Rostand. Rostand makes explicit the idea implied but not fully articulated in Dolto-Marette's article that Gricha's interpersonal situation played the role of "permitting the psychological establishment, simultaneously, of the *past* and the *future* around the *present*. The *past* and the *future* were *understood in terms of* the acceptance of being older" (Rostand 1950, 304). It is not just Gricha's affective relations with others that exist differently for him now; rather, time itself has been transformed, and where Gricha once lived out of a kind of eternal or absolute present, he now assumes the world in terms of a temporality articulated into past, present and future. "The acquired words are proof of the child's affective victory" (Rostand 1950, 306).

18. For an extended discussion of how finding expression for one's situation is a matter of gaining autonomy, or becoming a subject, see Collingwood (1958, esp. book 2).

and through them, being drawn into new ways of taking up the world and making sense of it. Others' intentionalities, as they are expressed in their behaviors and their linguistic articulations, lend us new resources.

In Gricha's case, there is good reason to think that it is through his implication in his big brother's way of taking up the world that he is drawn into new, more comprehensive, incorporative ways of taking up the world, and thus given the resources for overcoming his jealousy. On the day that Gricha finally overcomes his jealousy and acquires new verb tenses, he has spent the entire day playing with his older brother, Jean, and a boy named Serge who is older than the two of them. Despite the fact that Serge is bigger than Jean and able to do many things that Jean cannot do, and despite the fact that Serge shows a special fondness and care for the youngest, Gricha, Jean is not jealous. Jean accepts his own limitations, and also shows special care for Gricha. I have argued that others' behaviors or bodily orientations can orient us toward a situation, configuring the meaning of it for us. It is difficult to account for Gricha's sudden transformation on this particular day—his overcoming of his jealousy and his remarkable verbal development—except through this kind of interpersonal implication. By witnessing his older brother occupying the position of middle child, Gricha develops the existential resources for taking up his own situation as middle child; he grasps, not intellectually but at a *lived, pre-reflective* level, how to make sense of the world in terms of relative, rather than absolute positions. Because he has, in a lived manner, been asking the question of where his place in the world might be, Gricha is able to recognize this reconfiguration of the world as a way of resolving the tensions that have riddled his world up to now. He happily takes this up, and thereby his very world and his sense of his place in it are transformed. Gricha becomes a subject.

Thus, others seem to play an essential role in one's becoming a subject. Others can open us up to new ways of assuming ourselves by resisting our habitual and inadequate ways of trying to take up the world, and by simultaneously offering us new existential resources for making sense of our situation. They do this not primarily through intellectual instruction, but through the ways that they themselves live toward us and our shared world, through their bodily intentionalities.

7. CONCLUSION

In conclusion, I wish to spell out an ethical implication of this way of conceiving emotion and our emotional metamorphoses: allow me to point to the difference that it makes if we approach others (and ourselves) on the basis of the above conceptions of emotion and transformation, rather than on the basis of a moralistic conception of the self.

This essay has argued the following. Emotion is not an internal conscious event, but rather the experience of a tension within our reality that puts into question our place in reality. Expressions of emotion, correlatively, are not a matter of indulging in some irrational inner feeling or force, but rather a matter of trying to make sense of our situation, given the resources that we have. The compulsions and primitive behavior that sometimes result when emotions "escalate" or "spiral downwards" are to be explained not as merely irrational, but in terms of an increasingly constrained situation, where the emotional person finds herself increasingly stripped of the resources that she assumed she had for making sense of this situation. Other people play an essential role in producing such a constrained situation—and thus they play a role in the production of compulsions and regressions—for they resist attempts at configuring the situation, and therefore rule out certain potential resources as not viable. But at the same time, others can lend us new existential resources for making sense of our situation.

If this is right, then consider the effect of assuming a moralistic attitude toward others. A moralistic attitude supposes that the emotional person is abandoning her rationality in order to indulge in irrational forces. She is someone who "knows better than this" and is simply choosing to act badly. A moralistic attitude therefore simply condemns the person's behavior as bad, and calls on her to "do the right thing." In condemning the behavior, this attitude denies that there is even minimal validity to the resources being drawn upon.[19] Instead, then, of building on the limited resources already developed, the moralistic attitude strips the emotional person of whatever resources she does have. Thus, moralizing helps drive this person into an increasingly constrained state of hopelessness and resourcelessness, such that her behavior becomes increasingly compulsive and desperate and she becomes ever more incapable of mastering the situation and becoming a subject. The moralistic attitude, in other words, is likely to have the opposite effect of that which it intends.

This is precisely what Dolto-Marette finds in the case of a boy named Robert, when his parents respond by condemning his jealous behaviors. Robert begins, as Gricha did, by regressing and showing some aggression toward his new sibling. Unlike Gricha's nanny, however, Robert's parents respond by telling

---

19. Ronald de Sousa (1980) makes use of a similar notion of *minimal rationality*.

him that he is a bad boy, that he is doing ugly and mean things, and that he should know better. The result, in Robert's case, is that he becomes increasingly compulsive and desperate in his behaviors, and increasingly violent toward his sibling (he attempts to poke her eyes out with scissors, to push her off the table, etc.). It is only when, on Dolto-Marette's advice, the parents begin to respond to Robert in a way that acknowledges the difficulty of his situation that his behavior improves, he develops new resources for dealing with the situation, and he is eventually liberated from his jealousy and becomes a caring and responsible brother.

The problem with the moralistic attitude, then, is not that it resists others' configurations of reality—for sometimes it is important to resist ways of taking up the world that ultimately oppress or harm others. The problem with the moralistic attitude is that it is fundamentally dismissive of others' emotional expressions. It assumes that these ways of configuring reality are simply irrational, and that a person already knows better, or already has access to the "rational" response. It thereby neglects both the validity of a person's expressions (as expressions that do make sense of a situation, if only with limited resources) and the necessity, in a human life, of *learning,* or *developing* through intersubjective encounters, better resources for making sense of ourselves and our world. By treating emotion as irrational, the moralistic attitude—even as it exhorts us to be autonomous—stands in the way of genuinely becoming a subject. For it fails to see that far from opposing reason, emotion is that which propels our expressive attempts to make sense of, or to incorporate, the situations in which we find ourselves. Emotion is that which propels our becomings, and whether our emotions devolve into primitive, "mad" behaviors or evolve into epiphanies and genuine autonomy is in good part a function of whether or not others around us strip us of our expressive resources or help us develop them.

REFERENCES

Baugh, Bruce. 1989. Heidegger on *Befindlichkeit. Journal of the British Society for Phenomenology* 20:124–35.
Beauvoir, Simone de. 1996. *The Ethics of Ambiguity.* Trans. Bernard Frechtman. New York: Carol Publishing Group.
Bernieri, Frank J., and Robert Rosenthal. 1991. Interpersonal Coordination: Behavior Matching and Interactional Synchrony. In *Fundamentals of Nonverbal Behavior,* ed. R. Feldman and B. Rime. Cambridge: Cambridge University Press; Paris: Editions de la Maison des Sciences de l'Homme.

Calhoun, Cheshire. 1992. Changing One's Heart. *Ethics* 103:76–96.
Campbell, Sue. 1997. *Interpreting the Personal: Expression and the Formation of Feelings.* Ithaca: Cornell University Press.
Collingwood, R. G. 1958. *The Principles of Art.* New York: Oxford University Press.
Deleuze, Gilles, and Félix Guattari. 1983. *Anti-Oedipus: Capitalism and Schizophrenia.* Trans. Robert Hurley, Mark Seem, and Helen R. Lane. Minneapolis: University of Minnesota Press.
———. 1987. *A Thousand Plateaus: Capitalism and Schizophrenia.* Trans. Brian Massumi. Minneapolis: University of Minnesota Press.
Descartes, René. 1975. The Passions of the Soul. In *The Philosophical Works of Descartes,* trans. Elizabeth S. Haldane and G. R. T. Ross, 329–428. Cambridge: Cambridge University Press.
———. 1993. *Meditations on First Philosophy.* Trans. Donald Cress. Indianapolis: Hackett.
De Sousa, Ronald. 1980. The Rationality of Emotions. In *Explaining Emotions,* ed. Amélie Rorty, 127–52. Berkeley and Los Angeles: University of California Press.
Dolto-Marette, Françoise. 1947. Hypothèse nouvelle concernant les réactions dites de jalousie à la naissance d'un puîné. *Psyché* 7:524–30; 8:788–98.
Dunn, Judy, and Carol Kendrick. 1982. *Siblings.* Cambridge: Harvard University Press.
Griffin, E. Wilson, and Christina De La Torre. 1985. New Baby in the House: Sibling Jealousy. *Medical Aspects of Human Sexuality* 19:110–16.
Guignon, Charles. 1984. Moods in Heidegger's *Being and Time.* In *What is an Emotion?* ed. Cheshire Calhoun and Robert Solomon, 230–43. New York: Oxford University Press.
Heidegger, Martin. 1996. *Being and Time.* Trans. Joan Stambaugh. Albany: State University of New York Press.
Hobbes, Thomas. 1994. *The Leviathan.* Ed. Edwin Curley. Indianapolis: Hackett.
Laing, R. D. 1971. *Self and Others.* Toronto: Penguin.
———. 1990. *The Divided Self: An Existential Study in Sanity and Madness.* Toronto: Books.
Maclaren, Kym. 2004. On Being Moved: A Phenomenological Account of Emotion and Transformation. Ph.D. diss., Pennsylvania State University.
Merleau-Ponty, Maurice. 1945. *Phénoménologie de la perception.* Saint Amand: Gallimard.
———. 1963. *The Structure of Behavior.* Trans. Alden Fisher. Pittsburgh: Duquesne University Press.
———. 1964a. The Child's Relations with Others. Trans. William Cobb. In *The Primacy of Perception,* ed. James Edie, 96–158. Evanston: Northwestern University Press.
———. 1964b. The Philosopher and His Shadow. In *Signs,* trans. Richard C. McCleary, 159–81. Evanston: Northwestern University Press.
———. 2003. *Phenomenology of Perception.* Trans. Colin Smith. London: Routledge.
Rostand, François. 1950. Grammaire et affectivité. *Revue française de la psychanalyse* 14:299–310.
Sartre, Jean-Paul. 1953. *Being and Nothingness.* Trans. Hazel Barnes. New York: Washington Square Press.
———. 1962. *Sketch for a Theory of the Emotions.* Trans. Philip Mairet. London: Methuen.

Scheler, Max. 1992. *On Feeling, Knowing, and Valuing: Selected Writings.* Ed. Harold Bershady. Chicago: University of Chicago Press.

Sewall, Mabel. 1930. Two Studies in Sibling Rivalry. *Smith College Studies in Social Work* 1:6–22.

Smith, Quentin. 1981. On Heidegger's Theory of Moods. *The Modern Schoolman* 58:211–35.

Sorce, J. F., R. N. Emde, J. J. Campos, and M. D. Klinnert. 1985. Maternal Emotional Signaling: Its Effect on the Visual Cliff Behavior of 1-year-olds. *Developmental Psychology* 21:195–200.

Spinoza, Baruch. 1992. *Ethics, Treatise on the Emendation of the Intellect, and Selected Letters.* Trans. Samuel Shirley. Ed. Seymour Feldman. Indianapolis: Hackett.

Weberman, David. 1996. Heidegger and the Disclosive Character of the Emotions. *Southern Journal of Philosophy* 34:379–410.

Zeedyk, M. Suzanne. 1996. Developmental Accounts of Intentionality: Toward Integration. *Developmental Review* 16:416–61.

TWO

RACIAL GRIEF AND MELANCHOLIC AGENCY

Angela Failler

This paper reflects on how the relationship between embodiment and agency might be illuminated through developments in psychoanalytic theory on racialization and racism. A recent interdisciplinary study by Anne Anlin Cheng (2000) titled *The Melancholy of Race: Psychoanalysis, Assimilation, and Hidden Grief* serves as the primary example toward this aim. Ultimately, an argument is made for the value of a psychoanalytic approach that highlights the less visible or less tangible workings of racial identity, workings that historicist and poststructuralist accounts obscure in their focus on the body and its markers as material or discursive effects. In other words, this paper insists on acknowledging the ways in which unconscious meanings that are produced in relation to experiences of embodiment play a key role in shaping possibilities for agency.

Although psychoanalysis is perhaps best known for understanding embodiment through the axis of sexual difference, numerous efforts have been made to bring psychoanalysis to bear upon questions of "race" and racial difference. These efforts include explorations of racial identification (e.g., Fuss 1995; Cheng 2000; Eng and Han 2003), internal motivations for racial prejudice (e.g., Fanon 1952; Allport 1954; Young-Bruehl 1996), broader patterns of race relations and ethnic hatred (e.g., Freud 1930/1978; Žižek 1998), constructions of race (including whiteness) in forms of cultural representation such as film and literature (e.g., Pellegrini 1996; Johnson 1998; Tate 1998), constructions of race within the discourse and practice of psychoanalysis itself (e.g., Shepherdson 1998; Seshadri-Crooks 2000; Brickman 2003), and the possibility that recognizing racial identification as central to the formation of sexual subjectivity requires the revision of some of psychoanalytic theory's basic tenets (e.g., Abel et al. 1997; Eng 2001; Walton 2001). Such efforts make use of the attention of psychoanalysis to unconscious desires and fantasies of the self in relation to others, while simultaneously challenging the primacy of sexual difference as *the* organizing principle in our experiences of embodiment and relationality.

Building on the accomplishments of this work, my paper poses a specific question: what are the implications of psychoanalytic accounts of racialization and racism for conceptualizing the relationship between embodiment and agency? Or, how might possibilities for conceptualizing agency be opened up through a psychoanalytic reading of embodiment and racial identification? In posing these questions, I first want to suggest that agency conceived of within a psychoanalytic framework picks up where agency conceived of in a sociopolitical framework leaves off. That is, where agency in much social and political theory is seen as contingent on an individual's access to and recognition by formal, institutional structures whereby he or she is granted the freedom to exert willful, self-conscious action, psychoanalysis would argue that the "freedom" implied in agency is contingent on unconscious structures and nonrational activity as well. Christopher Lane (1998) makes this distinction, observing that "political and psychical liberation are nonidentical" as, for example, "a country's independence from colonial rule does not in any simple way translate into freedom for its citizens" (4). Lane's example not only points to the inability of formal equality or liberation to unequivocally guarantee substantive changes in people's daily lives, but to the reality that people do not simply or easily let go of *feeling* the effects of having been colonized. Put differently, even once officially "freed," people do not automatically shed their identifications with the subordinate positions they previously held.

Similarly, the complex process of racialization cannot be explained by a theory of socialization that posits the raced subject as the outcome of cultural-discursive practices and historical-material conditions alone (a theory that seems to offer little potential for agency, particularly if the subject already has limited access to the legitimizations of official or discursive power). Psychoanalysis would suggest, instead, that racialization is simultaneously achieved through the ways in which we become *imaginatively* attached to fantasies that organize meanings of racial identity and physical markers of race. In this sense, to borrow again from Lane, individuals cannot be considered "simply the imprint of their national and symbolic structures" (Lane 1998, 3–4). It is more accurate to say, rather, that symbolic structures intermingle with and are intersected by psychical structures in the formation of our racial identifications, and that it is precisely at these intersections where negotiations of agency occur.

Psychoanalysis is not being offered up in this paper as a corrective to sociological, historicist, or poststructuralist accounts of race, but rather as a supplement that attends specifically to the less palpable, interior projections of racialization and embodiment. My distinction between these different approaches, then, does not suggest their incompatibility but just the opposite: there is an interimplication between psychical life and social life that makes working at the nexus of psychoanalytic theory and cultural theory especially fecund; that is, reading psychical life as it is implicated both in and by sociopolitical life allows for a more nuanced interpretation of the relationship between embodiment and agency than a focus on either psychical life or sociopolitical life might on its own. This methodological strategy adheres to Shoshana Felman's (1987) well-known distinction between *implication* and *application* in bringing psychoanalysis to bear on phenomena in social research. Felman argues that thinking in terms of implication in this context helps to avoid the kind of reductive, unidirectional cause-and-effect formulations that a straightforward application of theory-to-object tends to promote (49).

Cheng's (2000) study *The Melancholy of Race* is an effective example of theoretical interimplication as she considers how psychical dynamics of race are integral to the historicity of race and vice versa. In particular, she responds to the problem of how to think about agency for minoritized subjects; for while minoritized subjects suffer from specific losses or injuries within a systematically racist and sexist culture, they also actively participate in the construction of their own identities and the racialized/gendered categories they inhabit. This problem has been raised elsewhere by feminist theorists including Wendy Brown (1995, 2001) and Patricia Elliot (1991), who are wary of efforts that seek retribution for disenfranchised persons by way of establishing their victimhood or powerlessness as a basis for politics. Such efforts, they maintain, reinforce the so-called victim's status as a non-agent, and eclipse experiences, including emotional or psychical affect, that may *not* reflect total powerlessness. By paying attention to how race is negotiated psychically, that is, in giving a theory of racial subjectivity not entirely determined by social or political apparatus, Cheng offers a different view for agency amid ongoing legacies of colonialism and racism. Further, by paying attention to how race and the racialized body become meaningful not only through social or public discourses of race but also in how the psyche assigns meaning to the body and its experiences, she locates the potential for agency beyond formal avenues of grievance in the imaginative space between the psyche-soma and the social where both racial grief and racial identifications are played out.

Extending Freud's concept of melancholy into an analysis of racial identification and race relations, Cheng argues that racial identity in contemporary America is underpinned by internalized loss or "hidden grief" for both the dominant white culture and racialized others. By shifting melancholy from a strictly psychical concept to one that implicates the circulation of power in the broader context of the social, she manages the difficult task of understanding psychical life as always, already influenced by social life, and vice versa. Moreover, by suggesting that *both* dominance and otherness come at a loss, she calls into question the simplistic division between power and powerlessness in race relations (Cheng 2000, xi)—a move that is crucial for reenvisioning possibilities for agency.

Critical of understanding racialization as simply the imposition or inscription of social meaning onto docile bodies, Cheng is interested instead in how racial categories are imaginatively supported; that is, how we as individuals become attached to the racial identities we occupy, and how these attachments, in turn, are expressed in cultures of race relations. For Cheng, our attachments to racial identities and our relationships to (racial) others are mediated by the dynamics of loss and identification. Psychoanalytically speaking, identification is an internal or unconscious response to the loss of a beloved object (potentially a person, idea, or thing). According to Freud in his account of melancholia, when the pain of losing a beloved object is unbearable, the ego, in an attempt to cover over or compensate for its wound, sets up an identification with that object, retaining it inside, as it were, as co-existent with the self. He writes: "[by assuming] the features of the object, [the ego] is forcing itself, so to speak, upon the id as a love-object and is trying to make good the id's loss by saying: 'Look, you can love me too—I am so like the object'" (Freud 1923/1978, 30). With the object turned inside or incorporated as such, the ego is able to postpone the painful recognition of its loss. The loss, in other words, is withdrawn from consciousness (Freud 1917/1978, 245). At the same time, however, the process of mourning is stalled, since with the lost object now buried within the self, it cannot be let go. This is to say that in melancholy the bereaved has trouble moving on to establish meaningful attachments to new, available objects. Instead, he or she remains psychically "stuck" to the lost one.

To complicate matters further, in melancholy the ego's relationship to the lost object is fraught with ambivalence: in its absence, the object is not only beloved and missed, but also felt to be abandoning and therefore hated. Hence, when the object is incorporated or taken inside, ambivalence, too, is turned inward, and feelings of hatred meant for the lost object become *self*-reproaches in their place (Freud 1917/1978, 248). When the self comes to replace the lost object as the object of reproach in this way, the subject's own body becomes a site upon which this rejection is often reenacted. Put differently, the bereaved may invest his or her body with the ambivalence and hatred meant for the lost object as a way of sidestepping the psychical conflict or guilt resulting from hating what was also once loved. In this case, the body's meaning for the subject reflects not only the way in which bodies are assigned meaning culturally, but also how psychical negotiations with loss are "written on" or "worn by" the body (Grosz 1992, 38).

But how does melancholy shed light on the formation of racial identity and race relations, in particular? What is "lost" in the process of becoming a raced subject? How does race or racial embodiment, specifically, emerge as an expression of or compensation for loss in this context? And finally, where does the possibility for agency lie given this apparently stultifying dynamic?

In Cheng's account, the formation of racial identity in America is characterized by melancholy or internalized loss for both the dominant white culture and racial others—but differently so. For the dominant culture, she explains, white identity is secured through the simultaneous exclusion and consumption of racialized others. That is, while socially sanctioned practices such as racial profiling and segregation ensure that minorities and nonwhite immigrants never quite belong to the nation, the nation depends on possessing and exploiting these "others" to support its social and economic hierarchies, as well as its fantasies of itself as a multicultural, democratic state (Cheng 2000, 10). In order to retain these others both literally and imaginatively to feed America's ego, America must also refuse to acknowledge that it is indeed founded upon their use and abuse. Analogous to Freud's account of the melancholic individual who refuses to relinquish the (already lost) object in order to sustain a fantasy of him- or herself as unscathed by its loss, Cheng observes of the white nationalist ego that its "racist institutions . . . do not want to fully expel the racial other" (Cheng 2000, 12). That is, rather than excluding racial minorities altogether, they are retained for the purposes of propping up its white, capitalist authorities.

Further to this, and again analogous to Freud's account of melancholy wherein the reality of the object's loss is withdrawn from consciousness, Cheng suggests that the denial of nonwhite subjectivity is so deeply incorporated into white America's cultural imagination that it does not begin to recognize what is lost by way of its exploitive and degrading treatment of racial minorities. That is, while feeding off or consuming these "others" serves to nourish the nation's ego on the one hand, on the other it proves impoverishing since, as one reviewer puts it, the "nation [is] thus deprived of some of the most vital energies of its citizens" (Johnson, 2006). However, this particular loss, America's loss of some of the most vital energies of its citizens, fails to be either recognized or articulated *as a loss* in the culture at large since, crucially, the exclusion and exploitation of minorities and immigrants is required to maintain existing hierarchies of power.

This melancholy dynamic of exclusion and consumption (loss and incorporation), along with its mechanisms of denial, obviously has implications for the formation of nonwhite subjectivity as well. For if the nonwhite other *is* the melancholic white culture's lost object—simultaneously excluded and consumed—the loss for this other is the impossibility of being an inviolable or unassailable subject (Cheng 2000, 175), that is, of living without the threat of exclusion and/or exploitation. Racial melancholy for the nonwhite other, then, functions as the internalization of this vulnerability to racial violence and, simultaneously, an identification with the (albeit unattainable) racial ideal of whiteness. Identifying with whiteness or the ideals of white America, in this case, serves as a kind of psychic "holding on" to the fantasy of inviolability, or to the desire of remaining intact despite its loss. In other words, for racial minorities, identifying with whiteness may preserve some sense of safety or fitting in.

By identifying with whiteness, however, the racial other is caught in a logic of assimilation whereby the pressure to measure up and the longing to belong continuously haunts his or her sense of self as a subject (Cheng 2000, 80–81). This haunting is made torturously clear in Cheng's retelling of an unforgettable scene from Maxine Hong Kingston's *The Woman Warrior: Memoirs of a Girlhood among Ghosts* (1975). In the scene, the story's protagonist-narrator verbally and physically attacks another young Chinese American girl in their school bathroom. Her own hurt feelings at not fitting in, of not being "American feminine" enough, are acted out as violent taunts and prods at this other girl whose physical features, in particular, become the target of the narrator's aggression:

> I looked into her face so I could hate it up close. . . . She wore black bangs. . . . I thought I could put my thumb on her nose and push it bonelessly in, indent her face. . . work her face around like a dough. . . . I hated her weak neck. . . . I wished I was able to see what my neck looked like from the back and sides. I hoped it did not look like hers. . . . I grew

my hair long to hide it in case it was a flower-stem neck. I walked around to the front of her to hate her face some more. (Kingston 1975, 175–76)

What Cheng notes about this scene, in particular, is that the narrator's disgust at the other girl's body reveals an anxiety about her own, racialized body (2000, 74). That is, the narrator does not hate this girl's face or body dispassionately, but in a simultaneous recognition and denial of the fact that it resembles her own. By homing in on those features read stereotypically as Asian or Asian-feminine—a "boneless" nose, a "flower-stem" neck and, elsewhere in the scene, a "China doll hair cut" (Kingston 1975, 173)—the narrator projects onto the other girl a similar kind of racialized rejection or denigration that she describes elsewhere as having experienced herself.

Included in her exhaustive list of complaints about the other girl's physical embodiment (she hates the girl's "papery fingers," her pastel cardigan, the way she folds wax paper from her lunch bag, and "the wheezes that came out of her plastic flute" [Kingston 1975, 173–77]), the narrator is exasperated by her quietness. She has heard her talk outside of school, yet at school, we are told, the girl merely whispers, "as soft as if she had no muscles" (173). Infuriated by this sign of weakness, the narrator corners her in the empty bathroom one day after school, pinches her skin, pulls her hair, and screams at her, "Come on! Talk! Talk! Talk!" (180). The girl does not speak, however, expelling only tears, sobs, and snot. No words. The narrator, on the other hand, invokes the voice of white authority and assimilation, insisting that she is trying to help the girl to fit in by forcing her to speak American-like: "'You don't see I'm trying to help you out, do you? Do you want to be like this, dumb (do you know what dumb means?), your whole life? Don't you ever want to be a cheerleader? Or a pompom girl?' . . . 'I'm doing this for your own good.' . . . 'Talk.' . . . 'Just say, "yes," or, "O.K.," or, "Baby Ruth"'" (Kingston 1975, 180–81). But still, she elicits no words.

The narrator's idealization of the cheerleader or pompom girl in this dialogue makes obvious the way in which identifying with patriotic white American femininity functions for her as a means of coping as a Chinese American girl in a masculinist, white nationalist context. In other words, identifying with the figure of the cheerleader allows her, at least in these moments in the bathroom, to *dis*identify with the designation of "other" and the social unpopularity or alienation attached to it. However, it also suggests, as Cheng points out, that "the denigrated body comes to voice . . . only by assuming the voice of authority" (Cheng 2000, 75). That is, only by identifying with or mimicking the very authoritative, racist structures that have designated both her and the other girl who resembles her as abject subjects in the first place, does the narrator assume agency as a speaking subject. Put differently again, only by assuming the position of perpetrator in relation to this silent other does the narrator feel *unlike* a victim. Yet, in the end, torturing her did not help her fit in, nor did it allow the narrator to escape her own feelings of violability in the world beyond the bathroom. In fact, despite being the aggressor, the narrator suffers in this incident too, exposing the scene of racial bullying as simultaneously her own trauma: "I was getting dizzy from the air I was gulping. Her sobs and my sobs were bouncing wildly off the tile, sometimes together, sometimes alternating" (Kingston 1975, 181).

But what alternatives are there? That is, what other routes to agency are there for racially marginalized subjects that do not involve the taking in and acting out of assimilatory ideals? According to Cheng, one of the conditions that maintains the desirability and fantasy of assimilation for racial minorities is the failure of legal or formal procedures of grievance to exact reparation for injuries associated with histories of racist and colonial violence. Since the legal framework for grievance is based on "the promise of acquiring public recognition," she argues, it does not necessarily guarantee agency for the griever: to be recognized upon the grounds of racial injury means to be recognized as an "other," and thus is still to inhabit the position of object rather than subject (Cheng 2000, 174). At best, in other words, the recognition accorded racialized subjects via formal avenues of grievance is the status of victim.[1] But the status of victim, in turn, reinforces a view of racialized minorities as inherently wounded or injured and in need of a so-called legitimate authority (the state or the law) to bestow subjecthood upon them. Paradoxically, notes Cheng, the "gesture of granting agency through formal grievance confers agency on the one hand and rescinds it on the other" (Cheng 2000, 175). That is, previously denied agency is only "restored" to the racially injured plaintiff upon the condition that he or she reiterates his or her position as a violable being.[2]

Along with Cheng, political theorist Wendy Brown considers it a tricky strategy to use victimization as the basis for restoring agency to disenfranchised persons. Brown is concerned with both legal procedures of grievance and the efforts of identity-based political movements working on behalf of particular

---

1. At worst, however, as feminist cultural critic bell hooks notes in her essay "Representations of Whiteness in the Black Imagination" (2000), grievances made by racial minorities often draw the accusation of "reverse-discrimination," effectively silencing attempts by people of color to articulate the experience of being terrorized by whites/whiteness (176).

2. And at the same time, by this gesture of granting agency, the dominance of white authority reasserts itself in having the power to do so. Thanks to Letitia Meynell for this observation.

groups of socially injured persons. For Brown, basing a politics on injury, specifically, comes at the cost of having to repeatedly demonstrate this injury, thereby further entrenching the designations of "perpetrator" and "victim." In other words, to found a politics on an identity based in injury, the relationship between identity and injury needs to be continually reiterated or "re-staged" (Brown, 2001, 55). As a result, the identities of *both* the injured (victims) and the injuring (perpetrators) become fixed as social positions, thereby limiting possibilities for imagining ambiguity or repositioning between these two distinct yet interdependent "states of injury" (Brown 1995, 27).

Moreover, even though formal or public avenues for grievance may offer disenfranchised persons the opportunity to finally speak out, these avenues are not necessarily equipped to respond to that which is "incommensurable and unquantifiable" about racial grief (Cheng 2000, 175). Put differently, since justice based on grievance and compensation relies on calculable and tangible evidence, it cannot attend to those internal reverberations of loss, those effects of racism that are most insidious precisely because they are unrepresentable or unspeakable. "Grief is the thing left over after grievance has had its say" (172), Cheng writes, drawing attention to the fact that the psychical residues of racial injury remain long after racism is publicly named. If we are to think, for example, of Kingston's narrator's tirade against her classmate as a kind of "speaking out" wherein the language of authority is taken up in an attempt to legitimate her complaints about the other girl, we cannot help but also notice its inexpressible "leftovers"; for even after she has "had her say" at this other girl's expense, grief returns to land the narrator in bed with a mysterious illness for the next eighteen months (Kingston 1975, 181–82).

How then might agency be imagined within this condition of racial melancholy where it seems that loss cannot be adequately articulated and therefore mourned due, simultaneously, to psychical incorporations and social disavowals? In her aptly named paper "After Loss, What Then?" (2003), Judith Butler considers this dilemma. She suggests that certain losses, including those owing to practices of colonization, racism, and genocide, are often so devastating that the very thought of them, let alone "working through" or "getting over" them, is negated or made impossible (Butler 2003, 468). Thus, the more pertinent question is not how do we "get over" loss once and for all but, instead, how does what follows from loss bear its trace? (468–69). In other words, does the grief that ensues from loss have a vice grip on our potential for connection and creativity, or could it serve instead as a resource for the future? Given that we cannot reverse or get rid of the past, including the history of our losses, literary theorist Mari Ruti (2004) suggests that we aim to create a more "imaginatively supple" relationship to it, that we find ways to live the past in the present as a site of possibility.³ But what would this look like for those suffering from losses associated with continuing histories of colonial violence and racial exclusion? How can healing occur if the conditions that perpetuate loss do not substantially shift but are instead invoked over and over again?

Cheng proposes that in order to see the productive potential for agency within the conditions of racial melancholy, melancholy itself must be interpreted as an integral, perhaps even necessary, response to loss, that is, part of an ongoing process of mourning that is neither finally a failure nor a success, but a sign of the "constant negotiation between loss and recollection" (Cheng 2000, 96). For instance, rather than counting an identification with assimilationist ideals simply a failure to preserve a coherent "ethnic self" in the face of white hegemony, Cheng sees it as a strategy in response to racism, a mode of defense that emerges to stave off further violation and to build a sense of self-security. Her reading of the narrator from *The Woman Warrior* illustrates this point. She does not resign the narrator to being an agency-less victim whose melancholy is entirely an effect of the racist social context within which she lives; instead, by acknowledging the complex ways in which the narrator negotiates her experiences and identifications (with her classmate, voices of authority, the figure of cheerleader) as an embodied, racialized subject, Cheng renders her a "subject of possibility" (to borrow the phrase from Elliot 1991, 240). In doing so, her work offers us a valuable example of the way in which psychoanalysis might be pressed into the service of social critique and a creative vision for agency. That is, by drawing attention to how the psychic life of power (to borrow the phrase from Butler's 1997 title) is inextricable from those historical-material and discursive relations that keep racial hierarchies intact, this approach opens up new possibilities for conceptualizing the relationship between agency and embodiment.

REFERENCES

Abel, Elizabeth, Barbara Christian, and Helen Moglen, eds. 1997. *Female Subjects in Black and White: Race, Psychoanalysis, Feminism*. Berkeley and Los Angeles: University of California Press.

---

3. My reference to Mari Ruti here is based upon a public lecture at which she presented ideas from her recently published book *Reinventing the Soul: Posthumanist Theory and Psychic Life* (2006).

Allport, Gordon W. 1954. *The Nature of Prejudice.* Cambridge, Mass.: Addison-Wesley.
Brickman, Celia. 2003. *Aboriginal Populations in the Mind: Race and Primitivity in Psychoanalysis.* New York: Columbia University Press.
Brown, Wendy. 1995. *States of Injury: Power and Freedom in Late Modernity.* Princeton: Princeton University Press.
———. 2001. *Politics Out of History.* Princeton: Princeton University Press.
Butler, Judith. 1997. *The Psychic Life of Power: Theories in Subjection.* Stanford: Stanford University Press.
———. 2003. After Loss, What Then? In *Loss: The Politics of Mourning,* ed. David L. Eng and David Kazanjian, 467–73. Berkeley and Los Angeles: University of California Press.
Cheng, Anne Anlin. 2000. *The Melancholy of Race: Psychoanalysis, Assimilation, and Hidden Grief.* Oxford: Oxford University Press.
Elliot, Patricia. 1991. *From Mastery to Analysis: Theories of Gender in Psychoanalytic Feminism.* Ithaca: Cornell University Press.
Eng, David L. 2001. *Racial Castration: Managing Masculinity in Asian America.* Durham: Duke University Press.
Eng, David L., and Shinhee Han. 2003. A Dialogue on Racial Melancholia. In *Loss: The Politics of Mourning,* ed. David L. Eng and David Kazanjian, 343–71. Berkeley and Los Angeles: University of California Press.
Fanon, Frantz. 1952. *Black Skin, White Masks.* Trans. Charles Lam Markmann. New York: Grove, 1967.
Felman, Shoshana. 1987. *Jacques Lacan and the Adventures of Insight: Psychoanalysis in Contemporary Culture.* Cambridge: Harvard University Press.
Freud, Sigmund. 1917/1978. Mourning and Melancholia. In *The Standard Edition of the Complete Psychological Works of Sigmund Freud,* vol. 21, ed. and trans. James Strachey, 237–58. London: Hogarth Press.
———. 1923/1978. Ego and the Id. In *The Standard Edition of the Complete Psychological Works of Sigmund Freud,* vol. 21, ed. and trans. James Strachey, 3–66. London: Hogarth Press.
———. 1930/1978. Civilization and Its Discontents. In *The Standard Edition of the Complete Psychological Works of Sigmund Freud,* vol. 21, ed. and trans. James Strachey, 59–145. London: Hogarth Press.
Fuss, Diana. 1995. *Identification Papers.* New York: Routledge.
Grosz, Elizabeth. 1992. The Body. In *Feminism and Psychoanalysis: A Critical Dictionary,* 35–40. Oxford: Blackwell.
hooks, bell. 2000. Representations of Whiteness in the Black Imagination. In *Black Looks: Race and Representation,* 165–78. Toronto: Between the Lines.
Johnson, Barbara. 1998. *The Feminist Difference: Literature, Psychoanalysis, Race, and Gender.* Cambridge: Harvard University Press.
———. 2000. Book cover blurb for Anne Anlin Cheng, *The Melancholy of Race.* Oxford University Press.
Kingston, Maxine Hong. 1975. *The Woman Warrior: Memoirs of a Girlhood Among Ghosts.* New York: Vintage Books, 1989.
Lane, Christopher, ed. 1998. The Psychoanalysis of Race: An Introduction. In *The Psychoanalysis of Race,* 1–37. New York: Columbia University Press.
Pellegrini, Ann. 1996. *Performance Anxieties: Staging Psychoanalysis, Staging Race.* New York: Routledge.

Ruti, Mari. 2004. Reinventing the Soul: Posthumanist Theory and Psychic Life. Public lecture at the Ontario Institute for Studies in Education, Toronto, Ontario.
Seshadri-Crooks, Kaplana. 2000. *Desiring Whiteness: A Lacanian Analysis of Race.* New York: Routledge.
Shepherdson, Charles. 1998. Human Diversity and the Sexual Relation. In *The Psychoanalysis of Race,* ed. Christopher Lane, 41–64. New York: Columbia University Press.
Tate, Claudia. 1998. *Desire and the Protocols of Race: Black Novels and Psychoanalysis.* Oxford: Oxford University Press.
Walton, Jean. 2001. *Fair Sex, Savage Dreams: Race, Psychoanalysis, Sexual Difference.* Durham: Duke University Press.
Young-Bruehl, Elisabeth. 1996. *The Anatomy of Prejudices.* Cambridge: Harvard University Press.
Žižek, Slavoj. 1998. Love Thy Neighbor? No, Thanks! In *The Psychoanalysis of Race,* ed. Christopher Lane, 154–75. New York: Columbia University Press.

THREE

A KNOWING THAT RESIDED IN MY BONES: SENSUOUS EMBODIMENT AND TRANS SOCIAL MOVEMENT

Alexis Shotwell

1. INTRODUCTION

"Knowledge for social movements must move us," writes Avery Gordon; it must be "sensual and magical" (2004, 62).[1] I find this an evocative and intuitively compelling call to action. What might happen when we take our conceptual experience of social worlds to interact with and be conditioned by our embodied experience? How are socially situated materialities epistemically important? I want to extend Gordon's categories to seriously consider sensuousness as material, embodied understanding that structures our experience and capacities for action.

We can see the significance of sensuous knowledge in the disciplinary formations Foucault unpacks in *Discipline and Punish* (1995), among other works. For example, we might have a sophisticated theoretical and emotive understanding of the futility and brutality of the prison industrial complex, but that understanding acquires a different depth if we are in jail. The strictures governing how we move through space, how we behave socially, how we feel comfortable manifest themselves on conceptual, affective, and

---

1. "Knowledge" is often understood to name a subject's (S's) true and justified belief that something (p) is the case. Thus "S knows that p" if and only if S is justified in her belief that p, and p is true (perhaps with appropriate responses to Gettier problems). Within those terms "sensuous knowledge" may strike some readers as a misnomer: sensuousness makes no propositional claims about the world. In much of the discussion below I use the term "sensuous understanding" to acknowledge debates around nonrepresentational content in experience, and to assert the epistemic salience of socially situated embodiment. I also use "sensuous knowledge" out of respect for my archive: the writers and activists I engage use the terms "knowing" and "knowledge" in their work in ways that contest a definition of knowledge as limited to an epistemic subject's propositionally mediated relationship to the world.

sensuous levels. The importance of our bodily comportment is highlighted perhaps when we step outside norms of "normalcy," and those of us who are negatively racialized, fat, disabled, or gender ambiguous, for example, step outside those norms without moving a toe. In other words, the importance of the sensuous dimension is sometimes most visible when it is least liberatory.

In this paper, however, I want to make visible the liberatory dimensions of sensuous understanding. I argue for the importance of sensuousness for social movements, focusing on transliberationist and genderqueer social movements as both object and theoretical wellspring for this work. Implicitly, I set sensuousness against a liberal model of personhood. Susan Babbitt has argued that the standard liberal, Rawlsian conception of individual rational choice leaves out a kind of nonpropositional knowledge—"knowledge people possess in the form of intuitions, attitudes, ways of behaving, orientation, and so on" (Babbitt 1996, 50). If we were to understand the decision to transition from a liberal standpoint, we would have to radically flatten the ingredients of that transformation—centrally, its implicit, felt aspects. In what follows, I argue that trans flourishing depends on transformations of the world—and, as Babbitt points out, often people have to transform themselves in order to access resources for full human flourishing (Babbitt 1996, 46). Sensuous knowledge is precondition, ingredient, and result of a mutual transformation of the self and social worlds. The account I offer of sensuous knowledge is indebted to Babbitt's articulation of relational, multiple, and contingent personhood (Babbitt 1996, 2001).

In section 2 I begin by introducing the threads this essay braids together: sociological theory on the materiality of social movement practice; debates within transsexual and transgender theory; and some problems of position and language I face in writing this at all. In section 3 I draw on Eli Clare's rich and important work to explicate the sensuous knowledge that interests me. I then investigate the trope of being at home in one's body to indicate that sensuous understanding is relational and often political. I argue the desire to feel at home in one's body can be a key, though often under-acknowledged, aspect of social movements. Attending to the fact that people point to how their bodies feel as an indication of political or social movement spaces they want to pursue, I conceive of sensuous knowledge as the motor, impetus, or reason for social movement. In section 4 I examine the importance of sensuous knowledge to our theorization of social movements, arguing for a reciprocal and energizing relationship between social movements and sensuous knowledge. The experience of participating in social movements—attending a strike, direct action, or mass demonstration, for example—can evoke an anti-authoritarian understanding of one's situation. Political, relational, and social movement situations can and do open sensuous spaces in people's experience of their lives: politically and relationally situated embodiments that call for or result from social change. Reciprocally, the role of socially situated embodiment in trans social movement shows us that nurturing sensuous understanding as a practice of freedom is crucial to social movements more generally.

2. SITUATING SENSUOUSNESS

In *Ghostly Matters: Haunting and the Sociological Imagination,* Avery Gordon examines the experience of cultural haunting and the relationship between unacknowledged history and power. She situates sensuous knowledge as "receptive, close, perceptual, embodied, incarnate. It tells and it transports at the same time. Sensuous knowledge is commanding: it can spiral you out of your bounds. . . . Sensuous knowledge always involves knowing and doing" (Gordon 1997, 205). Gordon's understanding of sensuous knowledge involves pleasures and pains, sensations we can name and ones we have no language for, and ways of being constrained or freed in the world. Sensuousness names a socially situated experience of one's embodiment. It is a "different kind of materialism, neither idealistic nor alienated, but an active practice or passion" (Gordon 1997, 205). Sensuous knowledge opens possibilities for embodied transformation.

I share Gordon's interest in knowledge *for social movements:* a kind of understanding or way of being that has a purpose. Such knowing is good for something, which here means that it does some good for someone. It is not, that is, extractable from its context. The knowledge that comes out of socially mediated embodiment is situated, invested, directed toward something; knowledge for social movements is knowledge in favor of social transformation and also knowledge that aims to be useful to social movements. It is a specific style of knowledge, carrying an imperative. It *must move us.* The knowledge Gordon cares about here is not only invested in some kind of social transformation, it is itself transformative of its knower. To know in this way, or to know these things, is to be moved. The knower may be affected, as in response to a moving story, and so this understanding relates to our affective and emotional relations with the world. Knowledge that moves us is both affective and transformative, complexly emotional and political. This is a kind of knowing that, in Sandra Bartky's words, "transforms the self who knows, a knowing that brings into being new sympathies, new affects as well as new cognitions and new forms of intersubjectivity" (Bartky 2002, 71–72).

Gordon's notion of sensuous knowledge can be usefully situated in the terrain of feminist activism and texts, queer spaces and folks, and transliberationist movements. Second-wave feminist theory placed importance on the role and liberation of the body. Queer activists and theorists, especially those working against a gender-binary system, offer complex accounts of heterodox sensuousness. Much transgender and transsexual memoir and theory offers rich analysis and accounts of a liberatory politics co-constituted between a lived bodily experience and a political community.

I read this politics in terms of sensuousness. A notion of "the body," of the politics of socially embedded embodiments, and of a bodily way of knowing has been put forth in these overlapping fields of discourse, practice, and activism. It is too easy to mine trans stories, in particular, to back up academic points; I am leery of participating in the ongoing academic-hip concern with trans issues, stories, and (sometimes) actual people. I am not trans, and I am conscious of some of the dangers associated with writing about trans memoirs in support of an argument about sensuous knowledge.[2] No number of trans friends and lovers can mitigate those dangers. But it is important that how I think about sensuousness, and a reason that it is a compelling analytic category for me, is a result of reading and talking to trans writers and activists. I mean what examples and analysis I offer as a form of respect. This discussion is also completely embedded, as are many trans narratives themselves, in feminist and queer thinking—categories I occupy with less difficulty.

Language is important here, and an additional source of hesitation for me. Our language indicates political stakes, lived contradictions, and networks of dialogue. In the preceding paragraphs, for example, I quickly slipped from the phrase "transgender and transsexual" to the floating prefix "trans." Terminologies carry histories. In this chapter, I follow the fraught use of "transsexual" to name people who were assigned one gender and sex at birth and have or are transitioning to another through changes in their bodies, social interactions, or appearance. The term "transsexual" is freighted with

---

2. These dangers include essentializing, exoticizing, capitalizing, co-opting, flattening, tokenizing, totalizing, etc.; C. Jacob Hale (1997) outlines some of these.

medical histories that have enabled, constricted, and torqued transsexual gender expression. Read in these histories, transsexual people have completed gender reassignment surgery—by implication meeting the Harry Benjamin Standards of Care, fulfilling accounts of a psychological gender dysmorphia as laid out in the DSM IV, and having a particular orientation to gendered genitalia.[3] My use of the term, however, includes self-identified transsexuals/ transexuals who do not necessarily enact the strict medical sense of the definition.[4]

"Transgender" has, since 1996 or so, been framed as an umbrella term, encompassing a range of gender crossers—from people who experience discomfort with how people expect them to express their gender, to cross dressers, to genderqueers who explicitly reject a gender binary system, to transsexuals, to other gender variant people. Transgender, in this usage, is contested by theorists and activists who argue against a conflation of transgender and transsexual experience. Viviane Namaste, for example, strongly critiques what she sees as a reduction of transsexual embodied experience to transgender-qua-queer, arguing that to read "transgender" together with "queer" makes invisible transsexual people who identify as straight. Further, Namaste—writing in a Québécois context—examines the Anglocentrism implied in the use of a term virtually unique to English (Namaste 2000, 2005).

The question of language is tied to a deeper question of embodiment and debates in trans circles on language and labels. For example, much trans theory and memoir expresses contending analyses of the narrative of being trapped in the wrong body. Jay Prosser, for example, writes: "My contention is that transsexuals continue to deploy the image of wrong embodiment because being trapped in the wrong body is simply what transsexuality feels like. . . .

---

3. Henry Benjamin authored the first major study of sex reassignment and transsexuality, *The Transsexual Phenomenon* (1966). In 1979 an organization named in honor of his work established the Harry Benjamin International Gender Dysphoria Association, which produced Standards of Care that regulated both doctors who provide sex-reassignment surgery and "consumers" who want to transition using surgery, among other tools. These standards of care now intersect with the *Diagnostic and Statistical Manual of Mental Disorders* of the American Psychiatric Association, in which Gender Identity Disorder is included. Some people have been able to leverage a GID diagnosis to get their insurance companies to pay for their transitions. Many critiques have been leveled at the DSM's classification of GID, and at the Benjamin Standards of Care: the first can be seen as pathologizing what is a non-psychiatric medical situation (the wish for hormonal or surgical intervention in gender expression) and the latter a rigidly heteronormative gender narrative. There is also substantial critique from many points of view of a perceived reification of genital surgery as the be-all and end-all of trans happiness.

4. Though "transsexual" is typically thought to be "correct" English, the spelling "transexual" is also common in activist circles and marks a refusal of medicalized sex-change identity.

The image of wrong embodiment describes most effectively the experience of pretransition (dis)embodiment: the feeling of a sexed body dysphoria profoundly and subjectively experienced" (Prosser 1998, 69). Sandy Stone argues, contrary-wise, that we have not

> taken the step of problematizing "wrong body" as an adequate descriptive category. In fact "wrong body" has come, virtually by default, to *define* the syndrome. . . . So long as we, whether academics, clinicians, or transsexuals, ontologize both sexuality and transsexuality in this way, we have foreclosed the possibility of analyzing desire and motivational complexity in a manner which adequately describes the multiple contradictions of individual lived experience. (Stone 1997, 353)

My account attempts to bridge competing explanations for the "wrong-body" narrative. As Prosser argues, we do ill to dismiss the felt, embodied experience of "wrongness" or "rightness": some bodily experience is always with us, and sensuousness attempts to name this. At the same time, I offer sensuous knowledge as a name for that experience of contingent freedom that comes with a socially situated embodiment, where being in the "right body" has more to do with our social world than with any individuated experience of our body. That is, we might feel like we're in the wrong body because there is a problem with our world.

Finally, a note on transliberation as social movement. As a social movement, I see transliberation to both partake in a long history and be still very much in process. I am thinking of trans social movement as collective political work to change existing social relations, even when this work shows up on a relatively small scale. Identifying as trans, or being identified as gender nonconforming, doesn't make a person a social movement of one. Individual actions do, though, contribute to the kind of collective work that makes up social movements. Trans movements in the United States, even with Namaste's caution against flattening trans people into one huge transgender community, clearly demonstrate some classical social movement markers. There are trans marches, organized direct action, political lobbying, health initiatives, grassroots education, and solidarity organizations. These actions relate to and create the possibilities for new forms of socially situated embodiment. These social movement activities come out of and craft what Avery Gordon calls *sensuous knowledge for social movements*. And crafting sensuous knowledge for trans social movement, to reprise Naomi Scheman, recognizes that "transsexual lives are lived, hence livable" (Scheman, 1997).

3. SENSUOUS KNOWLEDGE AS MOTIVATION FOR SOCIAL MOVEMENT

How we live is important. The threat of death and beating palpably attends being read as gay, lesbian, trans, or genderqueer, and this is important to everyday living almost everywhere: it shapes the texture and possibilities of everyday life. If you are not clearly read as a recognizable gender, for example, you can die; and in this world, now, you will suffer to one degree or another. In other words, even when gender variant people are not killed or assaulted, they experience the torquing, friction, discomfort, and disfiguration involved in resisting norms of gender binary straight whiteness, among other things, just by living. Even people who transition and pass seamlessly bear the history of this work. The most obvious, and least speakable, result of trans and queerphobia is the production of social worlds in which trans and genderqueer people suffer radically impoverished possibilities for flourishing, a felt sense of group vulnerability, and comparatively desolate conditions for the expression of dignity. This is a sensuous problem: living well involves a socially contingent comfort in one's body. In this context, flourishing without fitting established norms requires a transformation of the world so that living is more possible. In this section, I illustrate the kind of embodiment I have in mind through Eli Clare's multiaxial writings. His work takes seriously the givenness of the feel of things: sensuousness marks a complicated embodiment, related to the social world we inhabit and offering a resource for struggle.

In the following passage from *Exile and Pride: Disability, Queerness, and Liberation,* Clare evokes a complex relation between embodiment and the social and interpersonal practices involved in the experience of "knowing gender":

> [O]ur bodies are not merely blank slates upon which the powers-that-be write their lessons. We cannot ignore the body itself: the sensory, mostly non-verbal experience of our hearts and lungs, muscles and tendons, telling us and the world who we are. My childhood sense of being neither girl nor boy arose in part from the external lessons of abuse and neglect, from the confusing messages about masculinity and femininity that I could not comprehend; I would be fool to claim otherwise. But just as certainly, there was a knowing that resided in my bones, in the stretch of my legs and arch of my back, the stones lying against my skin, a knowing that whispered, "not girl, not boy." (Clare 1999, 129)

Clare figures a knowing that is both socially crafted and emerging from an experienced body. This knowing whispers ambiguity: a gender that is trans, but not stably "between" or "crossed over": a verb rather than noun. This knowing comes from a body that contributes to and initiates understanding, that communicates. The "sensory, mostly non-verbal" experience of our embodiment tells us who we are, and, on Clare's account, it tells the world who we are. This telling is thoroughly related to the external lessons and messages from our social worlds about, for example, gender. But the impetus for knowing arises from the interrelation between one's body, its communication, and the political arenas it moves through.

In Clare's work, what we might be tempted to read as an essentializing call to the feel of the body is always nuanced and deepened by his deeply intersectional account of what it is to be embodied—in his case, a queer, transgendered, disabled, white, mixed-class, childhood sexual abuse survivor, butch embodiment. Moreover, this embodiment incorporates nonbody things as part of itself; Clare writes that "at 13, my most sustaining relations were not in the human world. I collected stones. . . . Those stones warm in my pockets, I knew them to be the steadiest, only inviolable parts of myself" (1999, 124). In the realm of the sensuous, there are always stones, landscapes, radically other-than-ourselves ingredients in the "body." This body is never singular, simple, one-dimensional, or reducible to its materiality, though its bodily being is also not abstract. As Clare writes: "The stolen body, the reclaimed body, the body that knows itself and the world, the stone and the heat which warms it: my body has never been singular. Disability snarls into gender. Class wraps around race. Sexuality strains against abuse. *This* is how to reach beneath the skin" (137). The sensuous knowledge I see Clare articulating is clearly embedded in political realities that make bodies and worlds feel the way they do. It also motivates transformation of those very worlds.

What would a gender theory look like that is not abstracted from experience?[5] Many trans memoirs hold out a far less determined sense of what was "wrong," and what would be "right" about gender, or even of what gender one was and what gender one longs to be than the standard medical model

---

5. I take this question from Leslie Feinberg's statement that "Today, a great deal of 'gender theory' is abstracted from human experience. But if theory is not the crystallized resin of experience, it ceases to be a guide to action. I offer history, politics, and theory that live and breathe because they are rooted in the experience of real people who fought flesh-and-blood battles for freedom. And my work is not solely devoted to chronicling the past, but is a component of my organizing to help the future" (Feinberg 1996, 9).

of trans experience provides. Genderqueer and gender non-conforming accounts complicate and contradict the telos implied in a nostalgia for a fixed-gender-one-wasn't, opening the possibilities for yet unnamed gender positions. This is difficult work, since it involves living in ways that may not yet be articulable.

For example, in a chapter called "Stones in My Pockets, Stones in My Heart," Eli Clare unpacks some of the nonbinary, still inchoate, work of gender, in this mode:

> I want to enter as a non-girl-not-boy transgendered butch—gendered differently than when I first came out, thinking simply, "*This* is how I'll be a woman," never imagining there might be a day when the word *woman* was too small; differently from the tomboy who wanted to be a hermit; but still connected to both. Enter with my pockets and heart half-full of stone. Enter knowing that the muscled grip of desire is a wild, half-grown horse, ready to bolt but too curious to stay away. (Clare 1999, 138)

I quote this passage in part for Clare's metaphorical richness. But more, it's important to see how sometimes words are too small, roles too small— entering *differently from* the tomboy, the hermit, the woman—but how self-formation can be still intimately connected to frames of meaning that don't accommodate a way of being. Clare searches for ways to write "not about the stones, but the body that warmed them, the heat itself" (Clare 1999, 124). But writing about the body that warms the stones turns out to be impossible without writing about the stones as well. The stones in his pocket and the stones in his heart become the sign of splitting off from his body in order to live in the face of childhood sexual abuse, in the face of queerphobia and ableist bigotry. At the same time, crucially, the stones also signal a hope for nonreductive, complex embodiment. And so when Clare writes: "the stones rattling in my heart, resting in my pockets, were my one and only true body," I reach to understand the path toward reclaiming an embodiment "full of pride and pleasure" that includes the pleasure of stones warm against skin. This self-formation includes picked-up stones as part of one's being, *and* crafting a heat that can warm them.

Sensuous knowing in Clare's text carries the sense of knowing "what feels right"—complexly and transformatively. It is "knowing that whispered 'not girl, not boy'" "wanting to enter . . . gendered differently." Sensuousness is centrally tied to the interaction with others and the world.

Audre Lorde theorizes a similar space, which she calls "the erotic": "an internal sense of satisfaction to which, once we have experienced it, we know we can aspire. For having experienced the fullness of this depth of feeling and recognizing its power, in honor and self-respect we can require no less of ourselves" (Lorde 1984, 54). For Lorde, the erotic carries a sense of working in concert with others to "pursue genuine change within our world" (Lorde 1984, 59).

Bodies, understood as politically situated, show up a lot in writing about a political transformation of our way of existence, particularly in queer and trans narratives. And the notion of being at home in one's body, of refusing to "live outside ourselves . . . on external directions only" (Lorde 1984, 58) is important. Many people write about the work of making their bodies homeplaces, though the explanations for how this happens vary from needing to make the outer body match a coherent inner self to needing to find social spaces for ambiguous, queered bodily expression of gender. Throughout, though, I find a sensuous indication of the enmeshment of bodies and politics, well exemplified in the language of the body-as-home.[6] I draw an example, once again, from Clare.

Clare, writes about the different "homes" a body can be, articulating the deep enmeshments that produce these homes. Clare looks at a relation between the physical worlds he moves through and the social worlds of a political queer community: "My queer body: I spent my childhood, a tomboy not sure of my girlness, queer without a name for my queerness. I cut firewood on clearcuts, swam in the river, ran the beaches as Battle Rock and Cape Blanco. When I found dykes, fell in love for the first time, came into a political queer community, I felt as if I had found home again" (Clare 1999, 10). Clare's body is queered largely through ambivalence—being a tomboy not sure of girlness, queer without a label. His ambivalence is figured through activity: cutting firewood, swimming, running. And somehow, finding a political queer community feels like finding home *again*. Even when you've never been sure of home, finding it returns as though it were a memory. Clare's queer body arises as such out of the clear-cuts, the rivers, the beaches and years of going without a name. It finds a home. But this body is complex—it is a home only in the context of a relationality, a

---

6. Jay Prosser fruitfully examines Leslie Feinberg's *Stone Butch Blues*, illuminating this yearning for "home." He looks at the "emergence of transgender on the fault lines and tensions between transsexual and queer" and argues: "Within this project, home may prove a powerful organizing trope"—though not always in the same ways for everyone (Prosser 1998, 177).

community. It can only be home if we understand that "bodies are never singular, but rather haunted, strengthened, underscored by countless other bodies . . . that place and community and culture burrow deep into our bones . . . that language too lives under the skin" (Clare 1999, 10–11). This is what it is for a body to be sensuous as the ground for liberation: completely irreducible to any simple or asocial body, but also completely material in its effects and realities. Clare tells stories about bodies in this complex register—the sentence closing his book calls for more "bold, brash stories about reclaiming our bodies and changing the world" (136). Trans stories offer a lodestone for some ways of being where in order to reclaim a body, the world has to change—and where in order to change the world one has to complexly incorporate a body. Being-at-home always involves other people, and can involve whole networks of sociality.

For example, Gavriel Alejandro Levi Ansara writes: "I tried to be happy as a butch woman, but the woman part just wasn't me. . . . I am transitioning because I feel most comfortable when people refer to me in male terms and because I feel most comfortable and liberated in my body as a man" (Ansara 2004, 92–93). These accounts articulate the felt body in relation to succeeding or failing to be comfortable, to be at home. Being-at-home is explicitly an achievement; it is also always socially embedded. For Ansara, comfort comes as much from how other people relate to him ("when people refer to me in male terms") as from a particular experience of embodiment ("I feel more comfortable and liberated in my body as a man"). In Clare's sense, he enters as a man, and this constitutes a significant part of his being-at-home.

The feeling of "being at home" marks one way that personal and political experience are inextricably enmeshed. The embodiment that can feel like home doesn't have to be stably gendered, or completely accepted in the social world. Juan-Alejandro Lamas writes about "genderfusion"—a kind of other-genderedness. For Lamas, refusal to settle on being a man or woman did not preclude having top surgery (double mastectomy and chest reconstruction)— "it was seeing myself on the outside how I do on the inside" (Lamas 2004, 118)—though this surgery was not in the mode of gender reassignment. Still, this reshaping has sensuous effects. Lamas:

> Why, if I cut them off, must I choose male? Why must it be gender reassignment? Why must I choose anything? "Top surgery," mastectomy, whatever you want to call it—I cut my breasts off. No therapy, no permission, no regrets, no sadness. Only joy, and a feeling of pure ecstasy,

freedom, and connectivity with my body that I had never felt before. Today I love my body and it feels right to me, it feels mine—a really weird thing for a person like me to say, believe me. (Lamas 2004, 120)

This felt body is clearly politically placed—it is called to manifest as legible within a gender binary system, with social, medical, and legal frameworks to back it up. So Lamas's feeling of ecstasy, freedom, body connectivity, makes a political call back to those systems—a sensuous experience that requires political change. In this case, the political change necessary would create a space other than the gender options now available (even relatively transgressive options like "gender reassignment"). Lamas's sensuous experience grounds the question "why must I choose anything?" and thus it is the impetus and motor for political change. Sometimes the experience of sensuousness arises from the kind of freedom Lamas feels, sometimes it arises as resistance or rebuttal to felt structures of domination.

Toni Morrison offers the metaphor of home as a space of resistance to racist structures; without reducing gender structures to racial formations, I read her account as usable by analogy. In her article "Home," Morrison writes that several questions have troubled her work: "How to be both free and situated; how to convert a racist house into a race-specific yet nonracist home. How to enunciate race while depriving it of its lethal cling? They are questions of concept, of language, of trajectory, of habitation, of occupation" (Morrison 1997, 5). We can put these questions into conversation with some others: How to "have" gender in ways that acknowledge its socially stabilized nature, destabilize it, and yet be safe enough? How to find comfort within or despite a gender binary system that one is awkwardly situated in relation to? How to find deep, physical comfort in transitioning and passing yet fight gender-normativity? Michelle O'Brien writes, for example, about her transition: "I began to realize that if I was going to be a part of a revolution, I'd have to begin by figuring out myself. I'd have to begin with an understanding of this body that exceeds my words, that eludes their categories, that demands a world beyond my imagination" (O'Brien 2004, 3). Making the "house" we've been given "home," claiming that it can be home, involves understanding one's present situation clearly, transforming it, and finding the possibility of always contingent joys. As Jay Prosser argues, "home is, on some level, always a place we make up, [and] belonging is ultimately mythic—for all of us perhaps unreachable without some act of sweet imagination" (Prosser 1998, 205).

4. SOCIAL MOVEMENTS AND THE CREATION OF SENSUOUS KNOWING

Social movements are a good place to think about sensuous knowledge in part because they show up the centrality of this thread in the fabric of our experience. They are sites of sweet imagination, where sensuousness involves thinking hopefully. Moreover, social movements promise to create circumstances that transform our sensuous knowledge; they can create new knowledge or give us a way to organize our felt politics differently. When political actions and the creation of new ways of being are successful, they articulate and show that a number of people share some intersecting analysis of a problem. These analyses don't have to be coherent: all they have to do is overlap enough that people are moved to come to the action, write a letter, and so on. As much as any theoretical or intellectual work many oppositional manifestations (demonstrations or direct actions) "happen" in our emotions and our bodies. There is an element of social movement activity that is deeply affective and sensuous. People feel connected, inspired, alienated, angry, loved, loving, confused, righteous, scared, empowered, bored, and much more. And many of these responses are created in the action itself.

The kind of episodic experience of a mobilization, march, and so on is woven into a fabric with more duration and thicker social interconnections than a onetime action or speech makes visible. In the context of long-term organizing, or when activists understand ourselves as inheritors of histories of struggle, these kinds of onetime experiences acquire resonance and texture. Accounts of the U.S. queer liberation movements highlight pivotal marches, interactions with police, and direct actions as episodically significant in transforming people's felt sense of their political topographies. Taken together and narrated, these onetime experiences become part of the process of placing oneself, as a social being, in relation to history.

Cultivating sensuous knowledge for social movements implies changing our habitus, what feels natural to us and what places us in a social realm. Such transformations involve an integrated reconstruction of our cognitive, affective, and sensuous knowledges. Eli Clare, answering the question *how to write about my body reclaimed* writes:

> In queer community, I found a place to belong and abandoned my desire to be a hermit. Among crips, I learned how to embrace my strong, spastic body. Through feminist work around sexual violence—political activism, theoretical analysis, emotional recovery—I came to terms with the sexual

abuse and physical torture done to me. And somewhere along the line, I pulled desire to the surface, gave it room to breathe. Let me write not about the stones, but the heat itself. (Clare 1999, 134)

Most tangibly, transformations in sensuous understanding involve a shift in how we identify and follow *longings*, in Gordon's terms—a cultivation of the subjective factor such that our felt responses line up along new priorities. And lining up along these lines requires, as well, new objective conditions—the work of sensuous knowledge is political and motivated. Clare's capacity to write about a reclaimed body, covalent with the capacity to reclaim that body, comes out of queer and disability rights and feminist social movement work. This is, as Gordon notes, a transformation of worldview, of our way of existence.

If sometimes sensuous understanding calls for a political transformation, then, social movement and political spaces also create or nurture new sensuous knowledges. The *social*-sensuous practices we participate in are significant for how we see and feel our own sensuous experience. Eli Clare's feeling of finding home comes significantly out of finding a political queer community—it was not perfect, but it opened a space for feeling differently. Sometimes a single person can open that space—for many people Christine Jorgensen's 1950 gender reassignment surgery, and the extraordinary media storm that surrounded it, opened a public discourse about transsexuality.[7] This discourse, of course, was for the most part extremely transphobic and implicitly mobilized against transgendered yearnings. Still, as Leslie Feinberg writes about Jorgensen: "Just as her dignity and courage set a proud example for the thousands of transsexual men and women who followed her path, she inspired me—and who knows how many other transgendered children. . . . Christine Jorgensen's struggle beamed a message to me that I wasn't alone" (Feinberg 1996, 7). Feinberg goes on to draw out the importance of spaces like gay bars in the early 1960s to forming oppositional genders and sexualities—even for people who did not identify as genderqueer, gay, or lesbian. Having these collective spaces—discursive and actual—fuels individual and collective political transformation. They become the space into which we can *enter as* someone we feel at home being, and without which we cannot craft the joy and connectivity Lorde theorizes as the erotic. The work of writing memoirs and histories likewise situates what could otherwise seem like isolated struggle in wider context—and even knowing

---

7. Joanne Meyerowitz (1998) offers a detailed account of the relation between media attention and a public space for trans imaginings.

that others have walked a path makes it seem possible and workable to take it, yourself. This is one sense in which social movement spaces nurture new sensuous understandings.

Desire is important here—an erotics of indeterminacy, intensely curious, embodied. Avery Gordon calls for a felt knowledge of worlds beyond what we now know, while noting that we as yet *lack* the craft experience to produce this embodied knowledge. The sensuous experience of worlds conducive to freedom and happiness might be more limited than cognitive or affective experience of their potential. Perhaps one result of life under current social relations is that it is easier to imagine or long for worlds beyond what we know today than it is to sensuously know those worlds; the body experiences in the present moment, and this present moment is limited, at least, by the world-as-it-is.

There are, though, felt experiences of embodied freedom; anecdotal reports range from the feeling of bringing one's entire living room set into the street for a Reclaim the Streets party to the goodness of harvesting one's own potatoes. Robin Kelley, asking how social movements "actually reshape the dreams and desires of the participants," describes attending a conference on the future of socialism during which "a bunch of us got into a fight with an older generation of white leftists who proposed replacing retrograde 'pop' music with the revolutionary 'working-class' music of Phil Ochs, Woody Guthrie, preelectric Bob Dylan, and songs from the Spanish Civil War. And there I was, comically screaming at the top of my lungs, 'No way! After the revolution, we STILL want Bootsy! That's right, we want Bootsy! We need the funk!'" (Kelley 2002, 10–11). On the one hand, the fact that we'll still need the funk after the revolution is about recognizing the importance of imagining current pleasure as part of a longed-for future (you can dance to it). On the other, I take Kelley to make the deeper point that in thinking about social justice movements intellectuals do ill to minimize explorations of freedom and love. Sensuousness is one part of an experience of a radically transformed future that includes experiences of embodied, thus contingent, freedom and love.

5. SENSUOUSNESS AS CRUCIAL TO POLITICAL TRANSFORMATION

When people say they are working at "building a new world within the shell of the old" I think they are pointing toward the kind of sensuousness Avery

Gordon calls a utopia that is precisely not a "no place." Rather, this utopia is a "longing for nonsacrificial freedoms and exuberant unforeseen pleasures," a sensuous excess and evasion of structures of domination. Gordon sees this utopia in the "things we are and do that exceed or are just not expressions of what's dominant and dominating us" (Gordon 2004, 129). This utopia is sensual—*a way of living in the here and now*—and it is daily, and it is ongoing. And there is both joy and discomfort in such dailiness. I read the domain of joy in sensuousness—not evacuated of politics or fundamentally inexpressible, but rather a reason why it feels good to struggle.

Sensuous knowing offers a way to think about knowledge that moves us, and that calls for movement—knowledge that moves others. The formation we call gender ripples recursively between individuals and their social-political ontologies. Gender has thus been one of my optics in trying to think practically about the sensuousness and how it might show up in people's actual lives and struggles. This is because gender is a mode that can also reveal a nondualistic experience of mind and body, unfixity, and collective joy—though of course it usually, overwhelmingly, fails to fulfill these roles. Sensuous knowledge for social movement, then, shows up as one site of creating a livable world—a complex home without guarantees. It is a resource for change, a site of praxis, an unspeakable but deeply political social and ethical mode of being. Sensuousness, then, is one way to talk about joy as a resource for social change.

Trans narratives of being-at-home underscore the fact that this sensuous joy, or the erotic, is often a socially mediated achievement. The conditions for flourishing are at root a freedom-from—freedom from gender-based harassment, assault, murder. They are also a freedom-to—a relational uptake of transitioning, of genderqueer narratives, of new or other pronouns. Transgender, transsexual, and genderqueer living partakes of relational agency, in which autonomy is contingently crafted through things like being addressed by one's pronoun of choice. Feeling good in one's body and the world is further dependent on broader political change, on having access to what hormones and procedures bring one's bodily experience into line with one's projected self, on the basic physical and psychic safety that many people take for granted. Sensuousness, stitching together sociality and embodied experience, names one aspect of the complex, agentful living implicit in flourishing. If we are to do justice to this living, we must take into account its affective and embodied aspects, and pay attention to sensuousness as a measure for multifaceted, complex transformation.

REFERENCES

Ansara, Gavriel Alejandro Levi. 2004. Transitioning or What's a Nice Dyke Like Me Doing Becoming a Gay Guy? In *From the Inside Out: Radical Gender Transformation, FTM, and Beyond*, ed. Morty Diamond, 91–93. San Francisco: Manic D Press.

Babbitt, Susan E. 1996. *Impossible Dreams: Rationality, Integrity, and Moral Imagination*. Boulder, Colo.: Westview.

Bartky, Sandra Lee. 2002. *Sympathy and Solidarity and Other Essays*. Lanham, Md.: Rowman and Littlefield.

Benjamin, Henry. 1966. *The Transsexual Phenomenon*. New York: Julian Press.

Clare, Eli. 1999. *Exile and Pride: Disability, Queerness, and Liberation*. Cambridge, Mass.: South End Press.

Feinberg, Leslie. 1996. *Transgender Warriors: Making History from Joan of Arc to RuPaul*. Boston: Beacon Press.

Foucault, Michel. 1994. *Discipline and Punish: The Birth of the Prison*. Trans. Alan Sheridan. New York: Vintage.

Gordon, Avery F. 1997. *Ghostly Matters: Haunting and the Sociological Imagination*. Minneapolis: University of Minneapolis Press.

———. 2004. *Keeping Good Time: Reflections on Knowledge, Power, and People*. Boulder, Colo.: Paradigm Publishers.

Hale, C. Jacob. 1997. Suggested Rules for Non-Transsexuals Writing about Transsexuals, Transsexuality, Transsexualism, or Trans ____. Sandy Stone: Would You Like Theory with That? http://sandystone.com/hale.rules.html (accessed October 4, 2006).

Kelley, Robin D. G. 2002. *Freedom Dreams: The Black Radical Imagination*. Boston: Beacon Press.

Lamas, Juan-Alejandro. 2004. Genderfusion. In *From the Inside Out: Radical Gender Transformation, FTM, and Beyond*, ed. Morty Diamond, 113–22. San Francisco: Manic D Press.

Lorde, Audre. 1984. *Sister Outsider: Essays and Speeches*. Trumansburg, N.Y.: Crossing Press.

Meyerowitz, Joanne. 1998. Sex Change and the Popular Press: Historical Notes on Transsexuality in the United States, 1930–1955. *Gay and Lesbian Quarterly* 4(2): 159–88.

Morrison, Toni. 1997. Home. In *The House That Race Built: Black Americans, U.S. Terrain*, ed. Wahneema Lubiano, 3–12. New York: Pantheon Books.

Namaste, Viviane K. 2000. *Invisible Lives: The Erasure of Transsexual and Transgendered People*. Chicago: University of Chicago Press.

———. 2005. *Sex Change, Social Change: Reflections on Identity, Institutions, and Imperialism*. Toronto: Women's Press.

O'Brien, Michelle. 2004. New Flesh, New Struggles. Deadletters, http://www.deadletters.biz/kink.html (accessed October 5, 2006).

Prosser, Jay. 1998. *Second Skins: The Body Narratives of Transsexuality*. New York: Columbia University Press.

Scheman, Naomi. 1997. Queering the Center by Centering the Queer: Reflections on Transsexuals and Secular Jews. In *Feminists Rethink the Self*, ed. Diana Tietjens Meyers, 124–62. Boulder, Colo.: Westview.

Stone, Sandy. 1997. The Empire Strikes Back: A Posttranssexual Manifesto. In *Writing on the Body: Female Embodiment and Feminist Theory*, ed. Katie Conboy, Nadia Medina, and Sarah Stanbury, 337–59. New York: Columbia University Press.

FOUR

THE PHRENOLOGICAL IMPULSE AND THE MORPHOLOGY OF CHARACTER

Rebecca Kukla

1. INTRODUCTION

I open with a particularly bizarre passage from Rousseau's *Confessions:*

> If there is one incident in my life which plainly reveals my character, it is the one I am now going to describe. . . . I entered a courtesan's room as if it were the sanctuary of love and beauty; in her person I felt I saw the divinity. . . . "This thing which is at my disposal," I said to myself, "is Nature's masterpiece and love's. Its mind, its body, every part is perfect. . . . Either my heart deceives me, deludes my senses and makes me the dupe of a worthless slut, or some secret flaw that I do not see destroys the value of her charms and makes her repulsive to those who should be quarrelling for possession of her." I began to seek for that flaw with a singular persistence. . . . Just as I was about to sink upon a breast which seemed about to suffer a man's lips and hand for the first time, I perceived that she had a malformed nipple. I beat my brow, looked harder, and made certain that this nipple did not match the other. Then I started wondering about the reason for this malformation. I was struck by the thought that it resulted from some remarkable imperfection of Nature and, after turning this idea over in my head, I saw as clear as daylight that

---

This research has been supported by the Social Sciences and Humanities Research Council of Canada and the Greenwall Foundation. I am grateful to the librarians at the Library of the Institute for the History of Medicine at Johns Hopkins University for their excellent assistance with this research. Thanks to members of the Carleton University Philosophy Department, the University of California at Santa Cruz History of Consciousness Program, and the International Society for Phenomenological Studies for helpful conversations about earlier oral versions of this paper. Thanks also to Letitia Meynell and an anonymous reviewer for excellent comments on an earlier draft.

instead of the most charming creature I could possibly imagine I held in my arms some kind of monster, rejected by Nature. (Rousseau 1953, 300–301)

Rousseau claims to be able to read the character of the courtesan from a single, morphological aberration, even as he claims that his own character should be read instead from an elaborate narrative "incident." This static, fleshy mark must be there for a *reason,* he claims, and it becomes for him the privileged measure of the courtesan's spirit. Rousseau's interpretation of the nipple is of course ludicrous—rooted in a kind of magical thinking that confuses arbitrary metaphorical interpretations of bodily marks for characterological evidence.

Yet this logic is not unique to Rousseau. We have a long history of attempting to read character off of the surface of the body. Seventeenth-century theories of the maternal imagination held that we could read newborn bodies as direct testimonials to the inner passions of their mothers. William Sheldon developed his theory of "somatotypes" in the middle of the twentieth century, and claimed that there was a "+80% correlation between morphological types and their temperamental correlates" (Sheldon 1942, 11–12). Readings of fat bodies as lazy and unproductive and Jewish noses as mercenary have deep roots in our cultural imagination (Lebesco 2004; Gilman 1998, respectively). The *Journal of the American Society of Plastic Surgeons* reports that in a recent study, in which photographs were digitally altered so as to produce the appearance of facial deformities on normal subjects, "Patients with abnormal facial characteristics were rated as significantly less honest, less employable, [and] less trustworthy... than were the same patients with normal facial appearances" (Widgerow 2004, 2006–10).

In this essay, I am interested in how we read the outer form of the body as a characterological text in scientific, medical, and popular discourse. However, my purpose is not primarily to document or critique such readings. Instead, I want to ask a question that I don't think has been asked directly since Hegel did so in his little-discussed, detailed critique of phrenology in the *Phenomenology of Spirit* (1977, §§309–46): how did our attempts to read the body as manifesting character become so absurd and problematic in the first place? For we might well wonder, where in the world would character be manifested, except the body? Surely it is with our bodies that we enact cruelty and kindness, avarice and empathy. It is our body that speaks and gestures. Why should we believe in a character trait that exists "inside" someone, completely independently of her embodied behavior? Normally, our character is manifested and incarnated in our bodily comportment. In her article "The Look and Feel of Virtue," Nancy Sherman describes the "locked eye gaze and firm handshake" characteristic of military character at its best (2005, 60). Our gaze and our handshake are living expressions of character that manifest our attentiveness to and confidence around others; they do not have the arbitrary, superstitious quality of Rousseau's monstrous nipple or the anti-Semite's mercenary nose. Why, then, are we tempted to develop implausible, elaborate morphologies for reading inner character off of the body's outer marks and shapes, given that we seem to be perfectly capable of observing character directly in the living body?

I will follow Hegel in arguing that this temptation—which I will call the *phrenological impulse*—is born out of our desire to understand the relationship between body and character once a less problematic ancient view of this relationship has been banished. Since ancient times, our ontology of character has transformed from an ontology of *virtues and vices,* defined in terms of skills and propensities for right and wrong *action,* into an ontology of *inner traits,* understood as stable features of an internal entity such as an independent soul or mind. The phrenological impulse is the drive to win back our ability to read character off of the body once we have adopted such an ontology of stable inner traits. In this paper I will argue that the phrenological impulse, if it cleaves closely to its own motivating principles, is incoherent: it is driven by an ontology and an epistemology that render invisible the very thing it seeks to make visible, namely character. Furthermore, I will try to show that given an initial phrenological picture, our best efforts to understand the nature of character and its relation to the body actually give rise to something quite different: a romantic, teleological picture of the self as fully realized only through the active harmonization of the inner soul with the outer body. After showing how phrenological logic helped to drive nineteenth-century science, I will turn to the contemporary medical and popular discourse surrounding cosmetic surgery and body modification. Such discourse provides a vivid case study in how the phrenological impulse still captures our imagination and constitutes our implicit ontological understanding of the embodied self.

One caveat before I launch in: even though the history of phrenology is inextricably bound up with the history of racism, I will not focus directly on race, or, for that matter, gender in this paper. The raced and gendered body is deeply infected with moral and social meanings, and moored in our imagination to notions of raced and gendered characters. Exactly how this complex intertwining works is a matter of political and scientific debate and passion. But precisely because gender and race are such vexed notions along exactly the lines I am exploring, they add layers of complexity that I want to step back from here. I want to show how thorny our implicit metaphysics is, even when we focus our attention on traits that do not so clearly inhabit the contested borderlands between the bodily and the characterological, in part so that we can return to questions about the ontology and politics of gender and race with new clarity.

2. THE BIRTH OF THE PHRENOLOGICAL IMPULSE

For the Greeks, the body *at work* expressed character, and the cultivation of character was the cultivation of a body that could see rightly and work well. Aristotle persistently drew an analogy between the development of virtue and the mastery of a craft; both, for him, must be grounded in *ethos,* or habit (cf. Aristotle 2006, 1103a20). In *De Anima,* he called the soul the form of the living body (Aristotle 1976, ii 1, 412a–b). That is, for him the soul was not a separate entity that *used* or was *housed in* the body, but rather the very thing that was actualized in purposive bodily activity. As he put it, body and soul are no more separable than the axe and its sharpness (Aristotle 1976, ii 1, 412a–b). In the *Republic,* Socrates offered a detailed plan for cultivating virtuous character through the cultivation of the body, through feeding, gymnastics, musical training, and other mundane practices. Proper moral education in boys, according to Socrates, would produce men who have mastered "the appropriate silence of younger men in the presence of older ones, making way for them and rising, care of parents . . . and, as a whole, the *bearing of the body*" (Plato 1994, 425a–b, my emphasis). Plato and Aristotle understood character as that which is directly expressed in bodily performance, decorum, and practice. The goal of moral education was not to shape the brute form of the body in order to indirectly shape a separate character, but instead to teach the body to comport itself excellently and justly. Correspondingly, the observation of someone's character did not involve the discernment of something inner by way of something outer, but rather the direct perception of virtues and vices manifested in her actions and comportment.[1]

---

1. Clearly, I gloss over the complexities of the ancients here; Plato, at least, certainly allowed for some pretty sharp separations between body and soul. However, he still understood character as composed of living virtues rather than stable traits, and he believed that in normal cases, the body served as a direct living expression of the soul.

In the *Phenomenology of Spirit,* Hegel follows the Greeks in insisting that character is directly manifested, and indeed finds its reality, in *work, speech,* and *deeds*—that is, what the body creates, says, and does. But, he claims, the Stoics found themselves unable to tolerate the moral luck that this entailed. To the extent that character is manifested in bodily accomplishment, it is at the mercy of the contingencies of the concrete world and the fallibility of the flesh, and intentions do not fully determine the meanings of actions. I might *intend* to act magnanimously, or to display heroism, but my body might not be up to the task, circumstances may thwart my plans, or society might not appreciate my efforts. Stoic spirit preferred to retreat into an inner self whose character was independent of its deeds—a character that could remain pure even when its actions were polluted by the contingencies of the external world. As Kant put it in one of his more infamous moments, "Even if, by a special disfavour of fortune or by the niggardly provision of a stepmotherly nature, [the] will should wholly lack the capacity to carry out its purpose—if with its greatest efforts it should yet achieve nothing . . . —then, like a jewel, it would still shine by itself, as something that has its full worth in itself" (Kant 1997, 8). According to this picture, the body does not stand as reliable testimony to the nature of the true, inner self. Nietzsche would soon make much of this historical separation of an independent, inner "doer" from its deeds in the *Genealogy of Morals* (1989).[2] This move not only reified and internalized the self, but also went out of its way to alienate this internal self from its outer bodily manifestations.

Meanwhile, according to a by-now familiar narrative, the rise of mechanistic science during the Enlightenment transformed our understanding of nature and subjectivity, and our standards for knowing either one. In interpreting nature as brute matter governed by strict, mathematically expressible causal laws, we elevated self-standing, perceptually accessible objects defined by their causally efficacious properties into the gold standard for metaphysical reality, while enumerative induction based on such properties became the corresponding gold standard for explanation and prediction. Values, meanings, and goals retreated into the inner space of the soul or mind. Because there was no place for narrative or teleology in this picture, which recognized only measurable properties as naturalistically legitimate, these notions lost their

---

2. "For just as the popular mind separates the lightning from its flash and takes the latter for an action, for the operation of a subject called lightning, so popular morality also separates strength from expressions of strength, as if there were a neutral substratum behind the strong man, which was free to express strength or not to do so. But there is no such substratum; there is no 'being' behind doing, effecting, becoming; 'the doer' is merely a fiction added to the deed—the deed is everything" (Nietzsche 1989, First Essay, Section 13).

scientific respectability. In such a picture, there is no room for the virtuous body on either side of the inner/outer divide. When the body is understood as a brute material object governed by blind causal laws and individuated by its inherent properties, its living, purposive activity will not show up.

Hegel does not criticize phrenology for its commitment to the idea that we can read the character from the body—indeed, this is for him the great *insight* that phrenology reveals only in a partial and distorted form. Rather, phrenology's great flaw, for Hegel, is its commitment to an underlying ontology and set of epistemological and explanatory standards that makes these readings vacuous. The phrenological impulse demands that we win back our ability to know the character through the body—to render empirically accessible, according to Enlightenment standards of knowledge, the very inner self that has been alienated from the body and banished from the natural order, but with a sharply attenuated observational tool box. In trying to reclaim the empirical accessibility of character, we cannot simply return to viewing bodily deeds, work, and speech as meaningful manifestations of character. Only brute physical *marks* on the body now count as scientifically respectable observables from which character might be inferred. Accordingly, characters must be understood as composed of discrete inner traits that were the right sorts of determinations to be isomorphic to and covariant with such marks.[3] Such character traits have a fundamentally different ontology from the lived virtues.

The phrenologist, broadly construed, seeks such a morphological metric of character. Phrenology sought to turn the art of discerning character into a *science* with the mechanistic, naturalistic trappings demanded by the Enlightenment: a science "by which all the powers of the Intellect, Affections and the Will can be thoroughly and accurately *measured*," as one practitioner put it (Merton 1899, iii). The phrenological methodology that I am identifying extends well beyond phrenology itself. It includes any attempt to find systematic correlations between inner traits and discrete, inherently meaningless, value-free observable properties of the body, whether these are genetic codes, patterns of brain activity accessible through imaging technology, or any other such markers that meet the standards of Enlightenment naturalism.[4]

---

3. For example, John Casper Lavater, the father of physiognomy, insisted that "each external trait . . . correspond[s] exactly and invariably to a timeless disposition of the detached and self-consistent soul" (Stafford 1987, 185–92).

4. In his book, *The New Phrenology: The Limits of Localizing Cognitive Processes in the Brain* (2003), William Uttal gives an excellent reading of much of contemporary cognitive science as analogous to (pseudo-) scientific phrenology. His work is compatible with my own, although his rhetoric, sources, and targets are quite different. With a few exceptions, however, philosophers

3. THE PARADOXES OF PHRENOLOGY

Hegel argues that any such phrenological project is self-undermining, as it attempts to heal a split between body and character that was itself produced by an ontology specifically designed to uphold and protect this split. According to him, phrenology transforms the body into a *picture* rather than an *organ* of the soul. Phrenology understands the body as "a wholly *immobile* reality, which is not on its own a *speaking sign*, but . . . a mere Thing" (1977, §323). The skull is a particularly rigid and static body part, and hence its status as a privileged signifier for phrenologists is telling. "It is *not* with the skull that we murder, steal, write poetry, etc. . . . nor does it in the least betray such deeds by a *change of countenance* so that the skull-bone would become a speaking gesture" (§328). Since the phrenological body does not *speak,* its outer marks become mere symptoms of inner character traits, rather than their direct expression. Hegel wants us to notice the irony in our transforming the body into something that does not speak—for what speaks if not bodies? It is only by abstracting the speaking self away from the body and artificially reducing the body to something meaningless that we can derive this picture, and this is a bad start if our goal is to use the body as our medium for knowing the self it houses. For if character traits are isomorphic with mute marks on the body, then character itself must be conceived as a "solid, inert thing"—a "dead thing." Availing himself of fortuitous language, Hegel accuses the phrenologist of *ossifying* character.

To drive home the contrast between direct readings of the body and the contorted and indirect readings produced by the phrenological impulse, Hegel turns from the immobile skull to the much suppler hand. Imagine trying to read whether a man has a businesslike character from his hand. We could proceed in either of two ways. If we are willing to acknowledge that we can perceive meaningful and purposive actions as such, then reading it is no great trick: we can perceive that his hand is signing a document, greeting a colleague, pointing at where a file belongs, and so forth. Here, Hegel says, "we may say of the hand that it *is* what a man *does*" (1977, §315). But, he claims, when we try to read the hand under the governance of the phrenological impulse, we abstract away from its purposive activity and reduce it, like the skull, to a set of static marks that are symptoms of separate, correlated character traits (fig. 1).

---

and philosophical psychologists have all but ignored phrenology in general and its relationship to contemporary psychology in particular. Indeed, Hegel's critique of phrenology is one of the chapters of the *Phenomenology of Spirit* that has received the least attention.

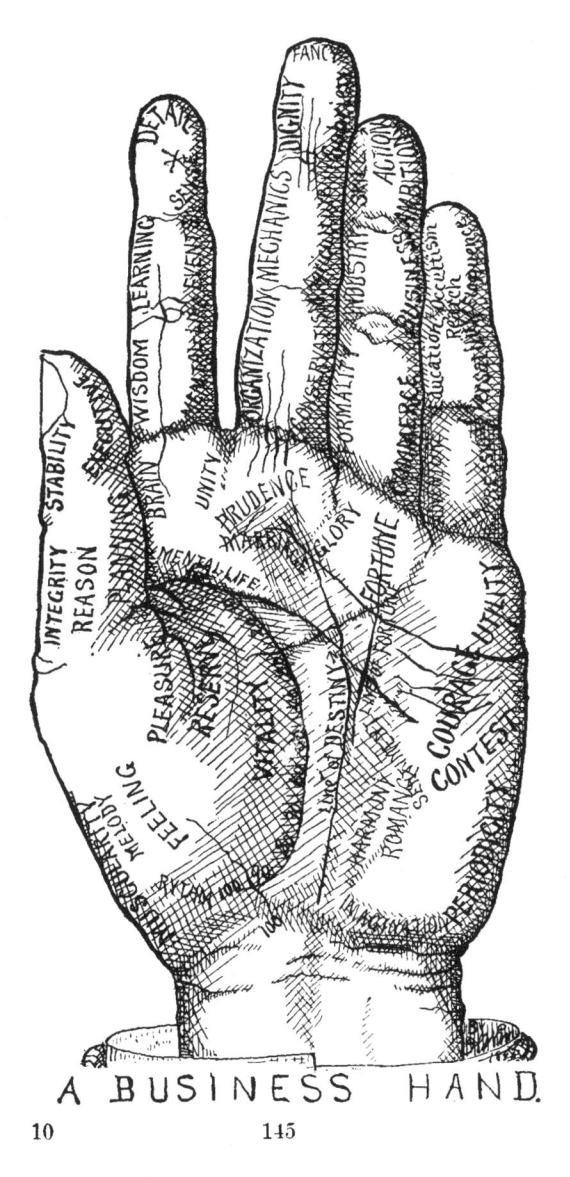

Fig. 1 "A Business Hand," from Holmes W. Merton, *Descriptive Mentality from the Head, Face, and Hand* (Chicago: A. F. Seward, 1899), 145.

Once in the grip of the phrenological impulse, how are we to decide which bodily traits are correlated with which character traits? Hegel identifies two possible methodological paths. On the one hand, we can read bodily marks as *meaningful* signs with representational content. This is the path of the physiognomist, who, like Rousseau in my opening quotation, takes the body as a representational text that mirrors the character within. For the physiognomists, a piglike nose indicates a piglike character, red hair a fiery character, and so forth. The Fowler brothers, who were the most prominent phrenologists in nineteenth-century America, do not shy away from such hermeneutic readings of the body. In their hands, every bodily detail—hair, skin, voice, eyes, walk, and so forth—becomes representational. Their readings draw liberally on social meanings and ethnic stereotypes, as well as their own metaphoric and metonymic fancies. For instance, they write: "Flat noses indicate flatness of mind and character. . . . The Roman nose indicates a martial spirit, love of debate, resistance, and strong passions, while hollow, pug noses indicate a tame, easy, inert, sly character, and straight, finely-formed Grecian noses harmonious characters" (Fowler and Fowler 1846, 38–39). Indeed, in their hands even the spatial layout of the skull itself has representational content. The back of the head becomes a sequestered space housing parental love and domesticity, or the organ of "philoprogenitiveness" as the phrenologists called it. Women with small domestic spaces in the back of their heads are supposedly unmotherly. Not only does this arrangement mimic the concrete arrangement of social space, but their drawing of the trait of philoprogenitiveness, which the caption describes as "situated above Amativeness, in the back part of the head," literally *is* a drawing of a domestic space (see figs. 2a and 2b).

Hegel dismisses all such physiognomic readings on two grounds. First, by investing bodily marks with meaning in order to read them, we betray the very naturalistic principles that inspired the need for such readings in the first place, for *meanings* have no place in a brutely causal science of nature. Second, he insists that once we construe inner character as a separate entity from the body, only a superstitious belief in "pre-established harmony" (1977, §335) could support our faith that the signs on the body and the traits of the inner character *match*. This is the magical thinking that underwrote Rousseau's reading of the courtesan's nipple.

The second option is truer to the naturalism that originally motivated the phrenologists. Here the marks on the body are conceived as intrinsically meaningless, bearing only a contingent connection to their characterological correlates, and the scientist's job is to discover these correlations through

2. PHILOPROGENITIVENESS.

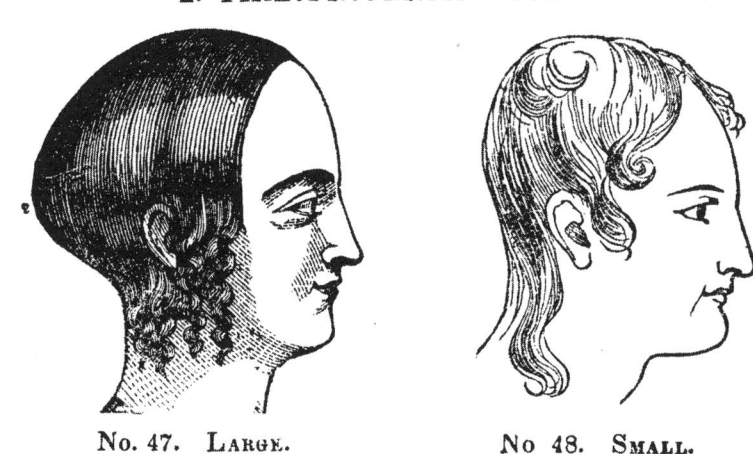

No. 47. LARGE.   No 48. SMALL.

Fig. 2a "Philoprogenitiveness," from O. S. Fowler and L. N. Fowler, *The Illustrated Self-Instructor in Phrenology and Physiology* (New York: Fowler and Wells, 1857), 54.

2. PHILOPROGENITIVENESS.

DEFINITION—Love of children, animals, pets, and horses.
LOCATION—Philoprogenitiveness is the second social organ, and is situated directly above Amativeness, in the back part of the head, and is number two in the Symbolical Head.

Fig. 2b "Philoprogenitiveness," from Lydia F. Fowler, *Familiar Lessons on Phrenology* (New York: Fowler and Wells, 1847), 31.

enumerative induction based on observations of constant conjunctions. The phrenological body is "a language whose sounds and sound-combinations" are linked with what they represent by "arbitrary combination" (Hegel 1977, §314), because "from the standpoint of observation, a *particular* determinateness of Spirit is indifferent to a *particular* formation of the skull" (§335).

For example, British phrenologist George Combe insisted that "the only legitimate and philosophical method of investigation is that which is pursued by phrenologists, namely, observing the laws which regulate the union of the mental and corporeal parts of man, without pretending to discover the essence or modus operandi of either" (Combe 1925, iv). Combe insisted on cleaving to the strict inductive method, free from any theoretical glue that would assign intrinsic meaning to body parts. For, as he insists, "Physiologists . . . have dissected the brain, in the hope of discovering in its texture an indication of the functions which it performs in relation to the mind; but success has not hitherto crowned their efforts. When we examine, with the most scrupulous minuteness, the *form, colour, and texture* of the brain, no sentiment can be perceived slumbering in its fibers; nor half-formed ideas starting from its folds" (Combe 1925, x).

But if we are only allowed to use observed constant conjunctions between contingently related outer body marks and inner character traits in order to develop our morphology of character, then how can we ever observe the inner half of the conjunct? The phrenological impulse sought to *make* the inner empirically accessible by way of observations of the outer body, plus a set of correlative principles. But in this case, we clearly can't use observations of the inner character as part of the inductive basis for forming these principles. And indeed, the phrenologists specifically denied that introspection counted as a scientifically legitimate empirical method—rather, the mind could become an object of empirical investigation only through the medium of the body.[5] It was precisely because the mind, character, or soul had become something separate from the body and hidden from the scientific eye that we needed phrenology in the first place. Hence this strict inductive method is doomed from the start.

Thus, although the point of phrenological science is to render the inner empirically accessible, Hegel argues that at best it does this indirectly, by *positing* inner character traits as the theorized cause of both external behavior

---

5. For example, Merton opens his phrenology textbook with the claim, "In the first place, then, the Human Mind . . . cannot, *by itself,* become an object of philosophical investigation. Placed in a material world, it cannot act or be acted upon, but through the medium of an organic apparatus" (Merton 1899, i).

and external marks (1977, §339). But, he claims, if character traits are merely such theoretical posits, then, in order for them to bear the relevant explanatory relationships, we have to understand them as *dispositions* to produce the external signs they are designed to explain. As he puts it, phrenology takes the "real self" as a "*presumed* inner. It is not the murderer, the thief, who is to be recognized, but the *capacity to be one*" (1977, §320). Once we understand the character as such a theoretically posited collection of dispositions, we have two options. Either inner traits *always* manifest themselves in outer signs, or else they merely *tend* to do so, but can be unrealized, unfulfilled, or interrupted for one reason or another. If they correlate perfectly with outer signs, then they serve no theoretical purpose. There's no point to believing in or appealing to an inner self, if this self is no more than an exact shadow of its outer manifestations. The more interesting option is the second one. On this view, the character trait of magnanimity, for instance, essentially *tends* to manifest itself in magnanimous acts. But it may fail to do so if the magnanimous person is too poor to have anything to give or too weak to act on his magnanimous impulse, or if this character trait is overwhelmed in a particular case by a competing one, such as jealousy. This kind of dispositional account requires that we understand character traits *teleologically*, as *properly* manifested on the body in distinctive ways, but not as *necessarily* so manifested.

Something like this picture feels quite commonsensical, and it accords well with the original Stoic desire to understand character as robust across the contingencies of the body. But Hegel argues that even though it seems to be the phrenologist's only real option, his own standards of knowledge, strictly maintained, would render this dispositional account empty and unfalsifiable. By the phrenologist's methodological standards, the *proper* manifestation of character can be inferred only from outer marks on the body, as these have the sole claim to the status of legitimate naturalistic evidence. Thus, the phrenologist can always explain away an apparent mismatch between character and body in terms of an unrealized disposition. Hegel writes, "When observing the skull, it might be said that this individual *really ought* to be what, according to the law, his skull proclaims him to be, and that he has an *original disposition*, but one that has not been developed: this quality is not present but it *ought to be present*.... If the *reality* is not present, the *empty possibility* serves equally well" (1977, §337). Outer marks now become the measure of the "true self," *regardless* of whether the inner manifests itself in behavior as it *ought* to. But, Hegel rejoins, "If anyone said, 'you certainly act like an honest man, but I see from your face that you are forcing yourself to do so and are a rogue at heart,' without a doubt, every honest fellow to the end of time ...

will retort with a box on the ear" (§322); indeed, "the retort here would, strictly speaking, have to go to the length of beating in the skull of anyone making such a judgment." (§339). The violence of Hegel's response has a point; if we were to take his interlocutor seriously, the way to *change his mind* would be to *beat in his head* and change its physical shape.

On Hegel's reading, then, the Stoic reification of character as an inner space alienated from the body, combined with an Enlightenment imperative to reduce the real and the knowable to observationally accessible objects with stable properties subsumable under causal laws, together gave rise to the phrenological impulse and its paradoxes. We render character unobservable by alienating and ossifying it, and then attempt to earn back our access to it by finding nomological connections between observable bits of the body and corresponding characterological dispositions. But any such method will only be able to comprehend the inner in terms of the inherently meaningless and mute outer marks that were merely supposed to contingently indicate it. In the meantime, the purposive, speaking body is lost from view.

4. THE NATURAL ORDER OF THE BODY

For my purposes, one of the most important consequences of this dispositional understanding of character is that it opens up the notion of a proper *fit* between inner character and outer body, conceived as two independent entities. A self whose inner dispositional character matches her outer body is one whose various components are properly harmonized. But a self whose parts can be understood as fitting together can also be understood as fractured by a lack of fit: inner dispositions may remain unrealized potentials, or, since body and character are only contingently related entities, a character might even find itself saddled with the wrong body altogether. An essentially magnanimous self may find itself trapped within a body with a covetous face or skull, or unable to develop its inherent characterological potential.

These normative notions of proper and improper fit suggest a romantic vision of the achievement of our full potential through the harmonization of mind and body. In this vision, it is *proper* that character display itself on the body: according to the Fowler brothers, "nature compels all her productions to proclaim their inner virtues—their own shame even—and hoists a true flag of character at their masthead, so that he who runs may read" (Fowler and Fowler 1846, 54). At the same time, this fitting relationship may not hold if either the body or the character is improperly maintained and developed. The Fowlers freely offer recommendations for how to "cultivate" or "restrain" various bodily and characterological traits in order to harmonize the parts of the self. Their rhetorical emphasis is on self-improvement and self-realization through the development of our essential character traits, as revealed to us through phrenological readings.

According to the Fowlers, the causal relations between body and character run in both directions: not only does the inner character tend to manifest itself on the exterior of the body, but the care of the body also has characterological repercussions: "It is [our] *physiological* conditions and habits, that cause nine tenths of human depravity. Are not both children and adults depraved when cross, and cross because sick, that is, rendered sinful by being unwell? Who does not know that drinking engenders depravity—makes the best of men bad? *But why, and how?* By disordering the body" (Fowler and Fowler 1846, 8). This passage makes manifest a normative conception of the proper order of the body, as well as the presumed right of the phrenologist to prescribe bodily changes and to critique bodily practices. Most of the original phrenological texts are shot through with such teleological rhetoric, even as they strive to establish phrenology as a bona fide naturalistic science. In them, natural laws do not remain blind and descriptive, but become prescriptions whose transgression is immoral. Indeed, from the Enlightenment onward, through Sheldon's somatotype theory, the medicalization of obesity and more, attempts to make character accessible through a brutely naturalistic science of the body get mixed up with their opposite, namely the moralizing of the observable exterior of the body and the demand that we modify the body for purposes of self-realization. The quantificational rhetoric of inches and angles intertwines with a moralistic rhetoric of the proper care of body and soul guided by principles of order and harmony.[6]

This teleological vision permeated nineteenth-century morphologies of character, both inside and outside the domain of phrenology narrowly construed. For instance, the influential educational theorist Daniel Moritz Schreber, father of the notorious paranoiac Judge Schreber, shared with the phrenologists the belief that character could be read off of the body: an upright posture displayed an upright character while a forward slump indicated "dumbness and cowardice," and so forth (Schatzman 1973, 38).

---

6. John van Wyhe comments, "Gall's system was a rich combination of the external examination of physiognomy, an Enlightenment orderly Nature and positivist rhetoric, an innate faculty psychology, and the Romantic concept of organic unity of plan" (van Wyhe, 2002, 40).

But Schreber's primary interest was in developing techniques for altering the form of the body so as to produce proper character. In addition to prescribing various exercise routines and other bodily regimens, he invented a series of braces and other tools for the external manipulation of bone and muscle that were specifically designed to form the character and the will by remaking the body. His core idea was that specific bodily forms, no matter how produced, would support and enable specific character traits by concretely determining which inner dispositions were possible. Although he insists that "Our very self, our inner personality, the innermost kernel of our self consciousness" is "something different from the body" (Schreber 1859, qtd. in Schatzman 1973, 63), he followed Rousseau in seeing the content of the will as driven and constrained by the automatic inclinations of the body to move and respond in certain ways. His system of bodily training and modification "*completes* and *perfects* the whole development of the body ... while laying the necessary foundation for the development of the mind" (Schreber 1855/1899, 1).

Philosophers have long been fond of telling a clean story of the hegemonic rise of the Enlightenment conception of blind nature and nomological science. However, when we look at how the concept of nature has actually been employed in scientific practice and popular discourse over the last three hundred years, the reality has always been murkier and more multivalent than this. The conception of nature proper to mechanistic Enlightenment science is appropriately contrasted with the *supernatural* or the divine: that which stands outside the system of causal law. More commonly, however, we contrast the natural, not with the supernatural, but with the *artificial;* that is, with that which has been intentionally made or altered by human hands. The natural/artificial distinction is orthogonal to the natural/supernatural distinction.

Yet a third sense of the "natural" is just as pervasive as the first two, if far less crisply defined. We often mark as "unnatural" that which is disfigured, deformed, hybrid, or monstrous, in contrast to that which we deem to be ordered as it "naturally" should be. This is the sense, presumably, in which Rousseau took the courtesan with the deformed nipple to be "rejected by nature"; surely he did not think that she was either supernatural or artificial. Because naturalness here serves as a teleological ideal, it is consistent with artifice: we can *make* something natural by imposing order on it. Thus gay adolescents are shipped off to camps designed to "correct" their "unnatural" sexuality and to create "natural" desires in them, and children with ambiguous genitalia or facial deformities are surgically altered so as to remove their "unnatural," aberrant features.[7] Likewise, while Schreber clearly had no opposition to *artificial* bodily interventions, he at the same time viewed the *natural* as a normative standard to be realized through interventions that would eliminate "unnatural . . . excesses of all kinds" (Schreber 1855, unpag. preface). Naturalness, on this third conception, is measured by aesthetic criteria such as harmony, proportion, symmetry, and fit. This inherently normative notion of the natural is hard to make precise. Such judgments of naturalness and unnaturalness are generally grounded in intuitive standards of proper order that are to at least some extent culturally specific, and hence they are especially historically malleable and ripe for social critique. This teleological conception of the natural, which contrasts with the deformed, is of course quite ancient. It was explicit in the hands of Aristotle, for whom natures could be thwarted or realized. While the mechanistic sciences of the Enlightenment tried to banish it and to cleave to a nonnormative conception of the natural, we see the reemergence of this conception of nature in romantic discourse, albeit in a changed form: in the wake of the alienation of the inner from the outer self, and the emergence of an ontology of character traits as opposed to virtues, the "natural" harmonization of body and soul becomes a teleological project in its own right.

As we have seen, this romantic, teleological conception of the proper order of the body flourished along side of and in messy entanglement with the "blind," scientific conception of the natural. This is not surprising, given that this romantic conception is ironically fertilized from *within* mechanistic science itself. Earlier we saw Hegel's argument that it was the attempt to discover nomological relationships between meaningless marks on the body and inner character traits that demanded a particular dispositional account of character. In turn, this dispositional account demanded a notion of the "proper fit" between inner and outer. This notion of "proper fit" suggests a picture of the fully realized self as one whose inner and outer traits are well matched. The resulting romantic picture of the relationship between body and character echoes the lost ancient picture, insofar as both invoke a teleological, normative conception of nature, and both treat the cultivation of the properly ordered body as a primary method for cultivating moral character. However, whereas the link between these projects was direct for the ancients, in the

---

7. I have defended in detail the claim that Rousseau saw the "natural" as something that could be cultivated or produced, rather than being simply given or originary, in several places. See in particular *Mass Hysteria: Medicine, Culture, and Mothers' Bodies* (Kukla 2005, chap. 2) and "Making and Masking Human Nature: Rousseau on the Aesthetics of Education" (Kukla 1998, 228–51).

wake of the separation of inner character traits from the outer body we get the specifically romantic notion that the inner and outer self are potentially mismatched and ought to be harmonized. Hence during the late eighteenth and the nineteenth centuries, the development of a naturally *fitting* self—as opposed to a monstrous, deceptive, mismatched self—became a central goal of moral education and physical discipline.

5. THE PHRENOLOGICAL IMPULSE IN CONTEMPORARY BODY MODIFICATION DISCOURSE

I believe that the phrenological impulse continues to mark the implicit ontology that underlies our popular, medical, and scientific understandings of body, character, and the relationship between them. For the rest of this paper, I will use cosmetic surgery as an example of the contemporary life of the phrenological impulse, and the impact of this impulse upon our cultural and medical judgments of appropriate and inappropriate body management practices.

Our discourse surrounding cosmetic surgery apparently fluctuates between several different folk ontologies. According to one common story, modifying the body *changes* the character, providing us with a new, custom-made personality and identity. An introverted young woman who doesn't seem to be good at much of anything gets a nose job and breast implants and is transformed into a talented extrovert. "Reconstruct a face; change a life," runs the rather Frankensteinian slogan of the World Craniofacial Organization (www.worldcf.org, accessed October 29, 2008). According to a second story, modifying the body can *reveal* or *mask* the true character within, depending on whether it is an authentic harmonization or an inauthentic deception. Transsexual surgery, for instance, is often interpreted as revelatory, while surgery to remove racially distinctive traits is often interpreted as deceptive, as is surgery designed to "normalize" the appearance of children with Down syndrome. One surgeon recently entreated, "Do we not have a responsibility to *produce* patients *according to their own individual characteristics* and not to create . . . impostors?"[8] (Widgerow 2004). An advertisement for a plastic surgery practice suggests, "Any disharmony between body and soul can be tackled earlier when . . . it is easier to obtain more natural-looking results" (Bordo 1998, 204).

---

8. Virginia Blum documents the tendency for surgeons to accuse one another of this flaw in *Flesh Wounds: The Culture of Cosmetic Surgery* (2003).

These two apparently contradictory stories find some reconciliation in a third, teleological story that echoes the romantic rhetoric of the nineteenth century. We afford cosmetic surgery the power to create a body that enables the unrealized potential of the inner self to develop and express itself. A recent episode of ABC's "reality" TV show, *Extreme Makeover*, documented a series of surgical procedures performed on an awkward eighteen-year-old girl. When the show revealed her new look after a month of interventions and recovery, her surgeon commented that she had "begun an adolescent" at the start of the month but was now "very much a woman"—her undeveloped potential had been quickly brought to fruition under the knife.

Behind such purported power lies a phrenological ontology according to which characterological traits have identifiable *proper looks*. In "Physical Beauty: Only Skin Deep?" bioethicist and M.D. Medard Hilhorst writes of the farmer and the fisherman, "A white, untanned and unwrinkled skin would simply not *fit* them. We expect the features of their bodies to tell a different story. Suppose someone introduces himself as a man who has been a farmer all his life, but he has the looks of a fashion model. We would not trust him; we might even consider him *creepy*. For we see someone who does not fit the image to which we know a farmer *should* correspond" (Hilhorst 2002, 20; emphasis added). Here Hilhorst not only takes the body as a meaningful, readable text that can lie or tell the truth about the character within, but she accepts the normative principle that it is *proper* that body and character should correspond. Invoking the aesthetics of the "creepy," she holds the fisherman himself accountable for this mismatch—this person would not be *trustworthy*, presumably in virtue of the inauthenticity of his body.

We count as acceptable only those body modifications that supposedly make people look like they "naturally should." Reality television shows such as *Extreme Makeover* and *The Swan* certainly do not fetishize the *given* body, but they still draw heavily upon the idea that they are making people look the way they are *supposed* to look. Advertisements and reality TV shows promise their patients "natural beauty." One measure of the authenticity of a modification is that it fits with our ideologically infected intuitions about what sorts of looks might count as teleological realizations of a proper, natural order. We accept that a woman may need breast implants, liposuction, and a face-lift to look as she "naturally" should, but we do not accept that someone's "proper" look might call for butt hair implants, cellulite injections, the performance artist Orlan's surgically constructed largest technically possible human nose, or other monstrosities that offend our entrenched pictures of "naturally" orderly bodies (www.orlan.net, accessed October 29, 2008). Achieving a "natural" fit between body and character is thus a normative project, where the measure of the natural embeds unthematized, intuitive aesthetic ideals that are by no means socially innocent.

In her study of women's reasons for seeking cosmetic surgery, Kathy Davis quotes one patient, seeking breast reduction, who comments, "I know a lot of people think big breasts are sexy, but I'm just not that kind of person. I'm basically a small-breasted type. That's just who I am" (Davis 2003, 77). Virginia Blum claims that such comments "suggest the experience of a radical split between the 'I' who feels and the 'I' who appears in the mirror" (Blum 2003, 56–57). Now it seems to me that this patient's comment lends itself to two different readings, one of which saddles her with a problematic phrenological ontology, and one of which leaves her sounding quite sensible. We cannot tell, from her comment, whether she locates the mismatch between her "self" and her physical breasts in a failure of correspondence between her "inner self" and her body, or between her body and her lived, social identity. Blum presupposes the former. If this reading is correct, then such a comment not only splits the inner from the outer self, but at the same time demands their reunification by suggesting that the inner "I" has *virtual* physical characteristics that ought to be realized in external physical traits. Notice that there is nothing strange about not feeling at home in a large-breasted body, if we locate this alienation in a mismatch between this body, its projects and desires, and its social reception; large breasts may impede the most dearly held projects of a living, embodied self (running, dancing, receiving professional respect, being a "tomboy," etc.). But there is something strange indeed about splitting the body into an essential, small-breasted inner version and a large-breasted outer version. I argued earlier that it was only when character was alienated from the body and internalized that its relation to the body became so problematic. This patient's comment seems absurd only when we are tempted to read her as suggesting that her "inner self" has small breasts, if only we could see them.[9]

---

9. As I was proofreading this paper, CBC radio was interviewing a man who was an advocate for the "body modification [piercing, tattooing, branding, etc.] community." He claimed that the goal of his group was to ensure that "everyone could have an external image that matched their internal image" (Canadian Broadcasting Corporation, 2006).

6. THE CASE OF THE SNAGGLETOOTH KILLER

I want to end by looking at the case of Ray Krone, the so called "snaggletooth killer." In 1991 Krone, a thirty-four-year-old mailman with no previous record, was sentenced to death in Arizona for the murder of Kim Ancona, a cocktail waitress who worked at a bar he frequented. The definitive piece of evidence against him was the pattern of bite marks on Ancona's body, which an expert witness testified matched the distinctive pattern of his teeth. He was exonerated and released in 2002, when new DNA evidence provided solid proof that Kenneth Phillips, a convicted violent sex offender, had committed the murder. In February 2005 *Extreme Makeover* aired an episode featuring Ray Krone undergoing multiple cosmetic procedures, including cosmetic dentistry, laser eye treatment, hair transplantation, neck liposuction, plastic surgery on his skin, brow and eyelids, and an intensive diet and exercise plan supervised by a personal trainer (American Broadcasting Corporation 2005). The episode received some media attention, and Krone has since launched a career as a motivational speaker and a spokesperson for various human rights and legal advocacy groups.

What interests me about Krone is how the media represented the relationship between his two sets of looks, his character, his presumed guilt, and his innocence, both before and after his makeover. Krone's media-created nickname, the "snaggletooth killer," elevated the physical evidence built into his body into an entire identity. Like Cinderella's foot and O. J. Simpson's hand, Krone's teeth came to stand as the privileged measure of his character in virtue of their physical match with an external object. Although the shape of his teeth was the only physical trait used against him in court, media descriptions of Krone stressed that he had the overall "look" of a stereotypical criminal. A newspaper article that appeared the day after the airing of the *Extreme Makeover* episode proclaimed, "People who followed Krone's trials and exoneration knew him for more than his teeth. He was balding, but what hair he had flowed to his shoulders. He had acne scars, and his face had . . . a 'scowl'" (Boekel 2005). We don't know the extent to which Krone's general "criminal look" was held against him by the jury that convicted him, nor, likewise, the extent to which his trademark snaggleteeth became imaginatively emblematic of his criminal body during the trial. Legally speaking, though, Krone's snaggleteeth served as evidence against him, not in virtue of their *moral meaning* or their *characterological significance,* but rather in virtue of their brute physical shape. However, since his exoneration much of the media coverage has focused on the tragedy of an innocent man who *looked like* a criminal and hence was treated as one. On this reading, Krone was wrongfully convicted, not so much because the justice system misused a specific piece of physical evidence, but because his *own body* betrayed him by serving as a deceptive characterological text. The narrow legal meaning of Krone's bite pattern expanded in the retellings and representations of his story, taking over Krone's entire body and infusing it with characterological meaning.

This reading dominated the *Extreme Makeover* episode, during which the show's doctors and producers sought, as they put it, to "decriminalize Ray's looks" (iEnhance 2005). In attributing to Krone's teeth a deceptive moral meaning that he deserves to have erased, the show at no point marks a distinction between the meaning of his teeth as signs of his internal character, and the meaning of his teeth as evidence based on their physical relationship to the crime scene. Using the objective connection between his body and his fate as a springboard, the episode freely implicates Krone's entire aesthetic appearance in his perceived criminal identity. During the course of the show, Krone not only receives a dental workover to remove the snaggleteeth that had testified against him, but a top-to-bottom "decriminalization" designed to remove all the classic markers of socioeconomic hardship. An advance press release for the show put out by the network stated, "Now Ray wants to get an extreme makeover to take away that snaggletooth face of a killer. . . . When people see him, they see a criminal. His teeth continue to get worse, his hairline is receding, and his once athletic body is now withered."[10] At the end of the episode a voice-over announces triumphantly that Ray "no longer sees the face of a killer" in the mirror.

But of course, Krone never was a killer, so if he saw the face of a killer in the mirror before his makeover, presumably he saw a face that was *not actually his own*. Somehow his innocent soul was saddled with the *wrong face*. Thus construed, the *Extreme Makeover* team is not merely providing him with the gift of better looks as a consolation prize for his unjust suffering. Rather, they are *giving him the face that is rightfully his,* his *natural* face. One contributor to Law Professors Blog Network commented, "I just saw Ray on *Extreme Makeover* and he looks great. Now his outer beauty matches his inner beauty." What

---

10. *Extreme Makeover* Web site at http://www.tvguide.com/tvshows/extreme-makeover/100144, accessed October 29, 2008.

makes the makeover a fitting gift, from this point of view, is that Krone's looks *really do* signify criminality.

So were Krone's body and character simply mismatched, according to the mythos of the show? Was he just a virtuous, good-looking, straight-toothed soul trapped in a criminal body? Not quite. According to the voice-over, cosmetic dentist "Dr. Dorfman will erase the worst part of Ray's *life* . . . and finally remove his pain when he looks in the mirror." So the alteration of his body apparently has the power to erase memory, and hence to reconstitute and not just reveal the inner. Some of the follow-up coverage picked up on this theme, claiming that now that Krone has a new look, he will have to build a new identity for himself (cf. Boekel 2005). In fact, during the episode various people claim that they are erasing not just the criminal *look*, but "the criminal" from Krone, as though he had a criminal stain on his character that subsists independent from any of his actual actions—a stain he has earned the right to have removed by virtue of his good behavior and his unjust suffering. Through surgery and other physical interventions, Krone not only achieves a natural fit between body and soul, but also removes a disfigurement from his character itself, and completes his redemption.

The phrenological impulse thus drives much of our contemporary discourse surrounding cosmetic surgery. Such discourse is premised on a historically specific alienation and reification of soul and body, and its companion drive to contingently reunite them via morphologies that let us read character traits off of static physical properties of the body. Both are uneasily partnered with a romantic, teleological conception of the natural fit between the inner and outer self as a prescriptive ideal to be achieved through the cultivation and manipulation of the body. Behind 250 years of narratives of criminal teeth, mercenary noses, depraved nipples, devout head bumps, and righteous postures lies an obscured picture of character as directly embodied and the living body as directly meaningful and normatively contoured—a picture that will not fit coherently into our lay metaphysics as long as we are in the grip of the phrenological impulse and its motivational underpinnings.

REFERENCES

American Broadcasting Corporation. 2005. *Extreme Makeover*. Episode 3:13. February 10.
Aristotle. 1976. *De Anima*. Trans. D. W. Hamlyn. Oxford: Clarendon Press.
———. 2006. *Nicomachean Ethics*. Trans. C. C. W. Taylor. Oxford: Clarendon Press.

Blum, Virginia. 2003. *Flesh Wounds: The Culture of Cosmetic Surgery.* Berkeley and Los Angeles: University of California Press.
Boekel, Teresa Ann. 2005. Who's That Guy? *York Daily Record,* February 11.
Bordo, Susan. 1998. Braveheart, Babe, and the Contemporary Body. In *Enhancing Human Traits,* ed. E. Parens, 189–221. Washington, D.C.: Georgetown University Press.
Canadian Broadcasting Corporation. 2006. *Subcultures.* CBC Radio 1. July 20.
Combe, George. 1925. *A System of Phrenology.* 2nd ed. Edinburgh: John Anderson Jr.
Davis, Kathy. 2003. *Dubious Equalities and Embodied Differences: Cultural Studies of Cosmetic Surgery.* Lanham, Md.: Rowman and Littlefield.
Fowler, O. S., and L. N. Fowler. 1846. *Phrenology: A Practical Guide to Your Head.* N.p.: n.p.
Gilman, Sander. 1998. *Creating Beauty to Cure the Soul: Race and Psychology in the Shaping of Aesthetic Surgery.* Durham: Duke University Press.
Hegel, Georg W. F. 1977. *Phenomenology of Spirit.* Trans. A. V. Miller. Oxford: Oxford University Press.
Hilhorst, Medard. 2002. Physical Beauty: Only Skin Deep? *Medicine, Health Care, and Philosophy* 5:11–21.
iEnhance. 2005. *Extreme Makeover* press release. Episode 3:13. http://www.ienhance.com/extreme-makeover/extreme-makeover-s3e13.asp.
Kant, Immanuel. 1997. *Groundwork of the Metaphysics of Morals.* Trans. M. Gregor. New York: Cambridge University Press.
Kukla, Rebecca. 1998. Making and Masking Human Nature: Rousseau on the Aesthetics of Education. *Journal of the British Society for Phenomenology* 29(3): 228–51.
———. 2005. *Mass Hysteria: Medicine, Culture, and Mothers' Bodies.* Lanham, Md.: Rowman and Littlefield.
Lebesco, Kathleen. 2004. *Revolting Bodies? The Struggle to Redefine Fat Identity.* Amherst: University of Massachusetts Press.
Merton, Holmes. 1899. *Descriptive Mentality for the Head, Face, and Hand.* Philadelphia: McKay.
Nietzsche, Friedrich. 1989. *On the Genealogy of Morals.* Trans. W. Kaufmann and R. J. Hollingdale. New York: Vintage Books.
Plato. 1994. *Republic.* Trans. Robin Waterfield. New York: Oxford University Press.
Rousseau, Jean-Jacques. 1953. *Confessions.* Trans. J. M. Cohen. London: Penguin.
Schatzman, Morton. 1973. *Soul Murder: Persecution in the Family.* New York: Random House.
Schreber, Daniel Moritz. 1855/1899. *Medical Indoor Gymnastics.* Trans. R. Greaffe. London: Williams and Norgate.
———. 1859. *The Wonderful Structure of the Human Organism, Its Life and Its Health Rules. An Easily Comprehensible Whole Picture of Human Nature for Teachers, Students, and Everyman who Strives after a Thorough Education and the Health of the Body and Soul.* N.p: n.p.
Sheldon, William. 1942. *Varieties of Temperament.* New York: Harper.
Sherman, Nancy. 2005. The Look and Feel of Virtue. In *Virtue, Norms, and Objectivity,* ed. Christopher Gill, 59–82. Oxford: Clarendon Press.
Stafford, Barbara M. 1987. Peculiar Marks: Lavater and the Countenance of Blemished Thought. *Art Journal* 46:185–92.

Uttal, William. 2003. *The New Phrenology: The Limits of Localizing Cognitive Processes in the Brain*. Cambridge: MIT Press.

van Wyhe, John. 2002. The Authority of Human Nature: The *Schädellehre* of Franz Joseph Gall. *British Journal for the History of Science* 35:17–42.

Widgerow, A. 2004. First Signals. *Journal of the American Society of Plastic Surgeons* 113(7): 2206–10.

FIVE

PERSONAL IDENTITY, NARRATIVE INTEGRATION, AND EMBODIMENT

Catriona Mackenzie

1. INTRODUCTION

Debates about personal identity in the philosophical literature often center on thought experiments, such as teletransportation, fission, brain/body transplants, and so on, that involve imagining, from a first- or third-person point of view, radical physical or psychological changes to a person. Such changes are usually brought about by bizarre science fiction technologies, and the imaginative acts we must perform in order to play along with these thought experiments require us to suspend many of our ordinary beliefs about the world and the conditions of human existence within it.[1] Within this literature, much less attention has been paid, however, to ordinary, everyday cases of personal change over time. Such cases include change arising from physical or psychological trauma or illness, where the initiating cause of the change is due to factors outside the person's control, as well as significant changes of heart or mind, whether arising from the exercise of the person's own agency or from external factors. In referring to persons, including ourselves, who have undergone such changes we often use locutions such as "She is not herself any more" or "She is (or I am) no longer

---

1. For important critiques of the use of science fiction thought experiments in the personal identity literature, see especially Kathleen Wilkes (1988) and Tamar Szabo Gendler (1999).

Earlier versions of this paper were presented at the conference of the Australasian Association of Philosophy, Sydney, July 2005; the Royal Institute of Philosophy conference on "Narrative and Understanding Persons," University of Hertfordshire, July 2005; and the conference of the Canadian Society for Women in Philosophy, Dalhousie University, September, 2005. Thanks to audiences at all three conferences for helpful comments. Thanks also to Philippa Byers, Sue Campbell, Steve Matthews, Peter Menzies, Diana Meyers, Cynthia Townley, and an anonymous reviewer for this collection for helpful comments on earlier drafts.

the same person." But what exactly do we mean in using such locutions? And do they tell us anything of philosophical or practical interest about personal identity?[2]

In her book *The Constitution of Selves*, Marya Schechtman argues that expressions such as these are not merely metaphorical and that they disclose the nature of our real, practical interests in questions of personal identity (Schechtman 1996, 88).[3] These practical interests, which are focused on issues such as moral responsibility, self-interested concern, survival, and compensation, are obscured rather than illuminated by standard philosophical approaches to personal identity because these approaches conflate two distinct questions that require distinct kinds of answers. The first question, the question of reidentification, is concerned with the logical relation of identity and with specifying the necessary and sufficient conditions for a person at one time being the same numerically identical person at a later time. The answer to this question must be determinate and cannot admit of degrees. It thus has a different logical form from the second question, of characterization, which is concerned with questions such as which psychological features of the person are central to, or truly expressive of, her identity and how the person conceives of herself in a first-personal sense. These questions, Schechtman argues, are focused on psychological, rather than logical, relations, and the answers to them can and must admit of degrees.

Schechtman argues that philosophers have construed our concerns about personal identity as concerns about reidentification and have sought to address these concerns via criteria for reidentification. Since many of our practical concerns are focused on the issue of characterization, however, it is not surprising that these criteria prove unsatisfactory. Schechtman argues that bodily continuity theories do not provide an adequate account of what matters to us about identity, because they are not sufficiently responsive to our intuitions about the importance of psychological continuity for survival, moral

---

2. As Susan Brison points out, it is noteworthy that while philosophers have reflected endlessly on the implications of outlandish science fiction thought experiments for conceptions of personal identity, there has been virtually no reflection on the philosophical implications of trauma survivors' experiences of loss of identity, or the sense of having "outlived" oneself (Brison 1997).

3. In a more recent paper, Schechtman (2001) argues that ordinary cases raise essentially the same issues about psychological change and survival as the science fiction cases, but in a more complicated and controversial way. Whereas in the science fiction cases we are more inclined to think radical changes do bring about change in identity, in the ordinary cases we tend to interpret talk of loss of identity as metaphorical. She also argues that personal survival in cases of radical psychological change requires not only narrative continuity but also empathic access to, or identification with, one's past self.

responsibility, self-interested concern, and compensation. On the other hand, psychological continuity theorists cannot account for the importance we attach to numerical identity, collapsing the distinction between some past or future person *being* me and some past or future person being *like* me.[4] As an answer to the question of reidentification, psychological continuity theories ultimately founder in incoherence because psychological continuity is not a relation of identity.

Schechtman's solution to the problem is to argue that intuitions supporting the bodily continuity criterion of identity are in fact responsive to the question of reidentification and that bodily continuity is the appropriate metaphysical and epistemic criterion to use when answering this question. Thus, when trying to determine, for example, whether the decomposing body found in the mountains is numerically identical with the cross-country skier who went missing during a blizzard last winter, we seek evidence, such as that obtained from DNA sampling, that will enable us to establish whether or not the decomposing body is one and the same bodily continuant as the missing skier. On the other hand, intuitions supporting the psychological continuity criterion are responsive to the question of characterization. It is to identity in this sense that we are referring when we say of a person who has undergone significant psychological or psycho-physical change that she is no longer herself, or that a person subjected to prolonged psychological abuse or sexual assault has been robbed of her identity.

Schechtman's view is that although questions of reidentification do have practical import, what matters most to us is identity in the sense of characterization. Further, our concerns about continuity of identity in this sense are focused on what it is that constitutes a person as the same temporally extended subject, that is, with how to characterize the relations between a temporally extended subject and her past and future actions, desires, beliefs, and character traits. These concerns, she proposes, are best answered by a theory of narrative self-constitution.

I agree with Schechtman that our practical interest in identity is best articulated in terms of a theory of narrative self-constitution, and in the following section of the paper I discuss this view and adduce some considerations in support of it. I shall argue, however, that Schechtman's approach to the body is still caught, to some extent, within the terms of the traditional stand-off between bodily continuity and psychological continuity theorists and gives too much credence

---

4. See the discussion of "the extreme claim" in Schechtman (1996, 52–54).

to intuitions elicited by science fiction thought experiments. For this reason, she understands our practical interest in the body almost entirely in third-personal terms as an interest in reidentifying other persons' bodies, overlooking the first-personal significance of the body in the constitution of identity.

In the third section of the paper I develop this critique of Schechtman. I also explain why, if narrative is an organizing principle for understanding one's history and future possibilities, as Schechtman argues, then developing an integrated and ongoing narrative of one's embodied subjectivity is central to the activity of self-constitution. This narrative, I contend, is not separate from but interwoven with, and dialectically constituted in relation to, a person's self-conception. I use the notion of a "bodily perspective" to refer to this narrative and argue that a person's bodily perspective is an essential part of the background interpretive context in terms of which her actions, emotions, beliefs, desires, values, and character traits are intelligible both to herself and to others.

In the final section of the paper I briefly consider the implications of experiences of alienated embodiment for my account of bodily perspective.

2. PERSONAL CHANGE AND NARRATIVE INTEGRATION

Geraldine Brooks's historical novel *March* interweaves two overlapping, first-person narratives centering on one man's experiences during a year of the American Civil War and recounted retrospectively from the perspective of the protagonist, Mr. March (Brooks 2005).[5] One narrative explains March's decision to enlist as a chaplain with the Union forces, by reconstructing his life up to the point of his decision. Having started out at the age of seventeen a "callow Connecticut peddler" determined to make his fortune, March becomes by turns, a very wealthy industrialist, the young husband of the feisty abolitionist Marmee and father of their four girls, and an impoverished but proud chaplain, convinced that the loss of his fortune has made him a better man. The other narrative tells the story of his experiences during the year of his enlistment, a year in which his ideals are shattered, his faith in himself is undermined, and he gradually becomes emotionally disconnected from his wife and children. Their once central place in his affections is displaced by

---

5. The story of March is Brooks's fictionalized narrative of the war experiences of the absent father in Louisa May Alcott's *Little Women*.

his rekindled love for Grace Clement, a former slave. March had fallen in love with Grace twenty years earlier while working as a young peddler. He chances upon her again during the war when she is tending the wounded in the field hospital that has been set up in the now run-down house of her former master. March's chance meeting with Grace sets up a chain of events that results in him working in the South on a cotton plantation for most of his enlistment. His sense of emotional disconnection from his family is bound up not only with his renewed feelings for Grace, but with his guilt and sorrow over the premature and violent deaths of the black men, women, and children with whom he had formed a strong emotional bond while working on the plantation. The final third of the novel is recounted mainly from the perspective of his wife, Marmee. Physically and emotionally transformed and nearly dead from fever, March has been taken to a Washington hospital where Grace is now working as a nurse. March feels himself to be a different person from the man who left for war a year ago, emotionally unable to return home, while Marmee, reunited with him at the hospital, feels that her marriage has been "shattered into shards" and the pieces "shifted and sorted into something I did not recognise" (Brooks 2005, 296).

From the metaphysical point of view the story of March's personal transformation is perhaps uninteresting. His body is barely recognizable either by himself or by others, but it has not been replaced by a qualitatively identical replica.[6] He is flooded with traumatic memories, but they are clearly his own and not someone else's quasi-memories.[7] And although he no longer regards himself as the same person he once was, he does not imagine he is Napoleon.[8] However his story raises the most fundamental of our practical concerns about identity and about our lives as temporally extended subjects. How can March resume his old life while at the same time accepting responsibility for actions, both over the course of the last year and over the course of his adult life, that have harmed others? How can he come to terms with the traumatic experiences he has undergone, and integrate them into an ongoing life? How can he reestablish emotional connections with his wife and children while not disavowing the

---

6. I am referring here of course to the famous teletransportation examples from Derek Parfit's *Reasons and Persons* (1984).

7. The theory of quasi-memory was originally developed by Sydney Shoemaker (1970) and later adopted by Parfit (1984). Both Schechtman (1994) and Richard Wollheim (1984) have questioned the coherence of the notion of quasi-memory.

8. The example of imagining oneself to be Napoleon was originally discussed by Bernard Williams (1973a). Williams's example is also discussed by Parfit (1984) and by David Velleman (1996).

emotional significance of his relationships with the former slaves with whom he worked, most of whom who are now dead? How can he come to terms with the way his values, ideals, and sense of self-worth have been challenged and reordered? What kind of future can he envisage for himself and his family? Is there a way of reunifying the scattered shards of his life and marriage?

Schechtman argues that these kinds of questions go to the heart of our practical concerns about identity because the focus of these concerns is how to make sense of oneself as a persisting temporal subject and as an agent. To be a persisting subject is to be a subject whose present experiences are shaped by the past, which exerts a cognitive and affective influence on the present, even if it is not always remembered, and whose present actions are directed toward an anticipated future.[9] To be an agent involves integrating one's diverse and sometimes conflicting values, desires, experiences, goals, and character traits into some kind of unified identity.[10] The kind of crisis of identity that March experiences, is a crisis because he cannot achieve this kind of integration. He cannot reconcile the different aspects of his past, which are pulling him in different and conflicting emotional directions; the future he once anticipated has lost its meaning, but he does not have a sense of what an alternative future might look like, or how he might bring it about; as a result he does not know how he should act in the present. Such crises illuminate the role of autobiographical narratives in the constitution of identity, for it is our narrative self-conceptions, Schechtman argues, that give rise to the sense of ourselves as persisting subjects and that enable us to organize and make sense of our experience. When these narrative self-conceptions break down, so too do the intelligibility and significance to us of our emotions, experiences, desires, values, and beliefs.

Schechtman's analysis of narrative self-constitution is subtle and complex, and I cannot provide a full account of it here. What I want to emphasize are two central aspects of this analysis: the first is the role of narrative as an implicit

---

9. Schechtman's account of the cognitive and affective influence of the past on the present, and of the role of this influence in giving rise to the sense of oneself as a temporally persisting subject, is indebted to Wollheim's work, particularly *The Thread of Life* (1984).

10. There are clear resonances between Schechtman's account of the kind of agency involved in narrative self-constitution and the work of Harry Frankfurt (1988; 1999) and Christine Korsgaard (1989; 1996; 2002). In a recent article, Schechtman (2005) contrasts agency-based approaches to the unity of personhood, such as those of Frankfurt and Korsgaard, with metaphysical approaches to psychological continuity, such as those of Parfit. She argues that being a unified agent may well be a condition of experiencing oneself as a unified subject over time, and vice versa. The account of narrative self-constitution developed in *The Constitution of Selves* (1996) could aptly be characterized as an agency-based account of temporal subjectivity.

organizing principle for understanding one's history and future possibilities; the second is the social dimensions of narrative personhood.

2.1. Narrative as Self-Interpretation

Narrative theories are often criticized on the grounds that they assume our lives are more coherent, structured, and intelligible than they really are.[11] Much of our day-to-day lives is after all quite mundane and involves countless routine and quickly forgotten actions that have no ongoing meaning or significance. Even when we think of lives as a whole, people's lives can be quite haphazard, comprising numerous different and disconnected sequences of actions and events. Further, what we do in and with our lives is shaped by all sorts of unexpected contingencies that can derail even the most carefully planned life. Narrative theories, it is argued, which represent lives as though they have the structure of a plot, with a beginning, a middle and an end, gloss over all this randomness and contingency and assume a degree of authorial control over the story that we simply don't have in our lives.[12] A more formal statement of this kind of criticism is that the events and experiences of a person's life do not take the form of neat causal sequences, nor does a life have the teleological structure of a plot.[13]

Such criticisms arise from a misunderstanding of the central claims of narrative theories, such as Schechtman's. Narrative theories do not claim that we should think self-consciously of our lives as stories that we write as we live them or of ourselves as characters in these stories.[14] Nor are they claiming that each minute action or event in a life must be somehow essential to the overall story of one's life. The claim is rather that the lives of persons cannot be thought of as a series of discrete, disconnected experiences or events but rather have an implicit narrative form. What characterizes the form of a narrative is that the different episodes and happenings and the relations among the characters are meaningful by virtue of the role they

---

11. Galen Strawson (1999; 2004) makes this point in the context of a broader critique of narrative theories. For an insightful and incisive critique of Strawson's conception of the self, see Kathleen Wilkes (1999). For a response to Strawson's critique of narrative identity, see Schechtman (2007).
12. For a statement of this kind of criticism, see Samantha Vice (2003).
13. For a critique along these lines, see John Christman (2004).
14. Samantha Vice (2003) mistakenly interprets narrative theories in this way. She criticizes the narrative view on the grounds that we neither do think of ourselves as if we were characters in the story of our lives, nor ought we to, since doing so is likely to lead to bad faith and to mistaking life for art.

play in the overall narrative sequence. Narrative is an organizing principle or a structure for interpreting the events and characters that makes sense of what happens, and makes the sayings and doings of the characters intelligible.[15]

Schechtman's claim is that we are persons and our lives are intelligible to us only to the extent that we exercise these same narrative or interpretive capacities. To be a person is to constitute oneself as a persisting subject by developing a self-conception that makes one's history, and one's actions, emotions, desires, beliefs, character traits, and so on psychologically intelligible, both to oneself and others. This persisting subject is not a separate metaphysical entity, a further fact, nor is its identity fixed and awaiting discovery; rather, it is continually constituted in an ongoing and dynamic process of self-interpretation.[16] Nevertheless, part of what is involved in constituting oneself as a persisting subject is to create an identity that has a degree of permanence and coherence. This identity takes the form of character or a set of relatively stable and integrated traits, habits, dispositions, and emotional attitudes.[17]

Schechtman argues that we create our identities and shape our characters by appropriating our past, anticipating our future actions and experiences, and identifying with or distancing ourselves from certain characteristics, emotions, desires, and values. In constituting ourselves as particular persons we therefore distinguish those aspects of our histories and character that are attributable to us but with which we do not identify, from those that are central to our

---

15. Peter Goldie (2003) argues that there are three essential characteristics of successful narratives. First, a successful narrative must be coherent in the way that a chronicle or list need not be; that is, it must reveal causal connections between the events described. Second, it must be meaningful; that is, it must enable the audience to make sense of the sayings and doings of the characters, to understand their reasons, or their internal perspectives. Third, a successful narrative reveals the narrator's evaluation of and emotional response to the perspectives of the characters and the events described in the narrative.

16. Parfit argues that the only alternative to reductionism about persons is to be committed to some kind of "further fact" view of persons; that is, the view that personhood involves a further metaphysical fact, or the existence of a separately existing metaphysical entity, over and above the existence of the brain and the body. Korsgaard (1989) contests the claim that these are the only two alternatives, arguing that a practical, or agency-based, account of persons is neither reductionist nor committed to a separately existing metaphysical self. Mark Johnson (1997) argues that personal identity does involve further facts over and above the existence of the brain and body, but these are ordinary facts, not "superlative facts," that entail no substantive metaphysical commitments and that are quite consistent with ontological reductionism.

17. Schechtman's account of the importance of character to our sense of ourselves as temporally persisting subjects echoes Paul Ricoeur's (1992) discussion of character as central to *idem* identity, or sameness, or the "what" of identity, which he distinguishes from *ipse* identity, or selfhood, or the "who" of identity.

self-conceptions.¹⁸ This is why personal identity in the characterization sense admits of degrees, just as moral responsibility, self-interested concern, survival, and compensation admit of degrees. After significant personal change we can be like our former selves in some ways but not in others; our actions may be expressive of our characters or quite out of character; it may be more important to us to fulfill some desires and goals than others, or to be rewarded for some achievements or compensated for some sacrifices than for others.

As Schechtman makes clear, however, the development of a narrative self-conception is a complex process. The psychic effects of past events or periods in our lives may shape our present outlooks and emotional stances more than we realize; characteristics from which we distance ourselves may be more central to our identities than we acknowledge; and we can be self-deceived or just plain mistaken about the kind of person we are or the significance of our actions. March's wife, for instance, tells a somewhat different, and less rosy, story than his about the effects of the loss of his fortune on his family's welfare. Thus, Schechtman distinguishes a person's *explicit* from her *implicit* self-narrative or self-conception. Although an *explicit* self-narrative need not be explicitly articulated, and most often is not, it is capable of being articulated to others as an account of oneself. In giving such an account, or in asking others to account for themselves, one is not, of course, accounting for one's self-conception per se. Rather, one accounts for those aspects of one's self-narrative that are relevant in the context, explaining, for example, why one has acted or responded emotionally in a particular way, why one values a particular friendship or spends one's time engaged in certain activities. An *implicit* self-narrative, in contrast, is one of which the person is unaware and which cannot be consciously articulated but that nevertheless shapes her understanding of herself and her relations to others. Schechtman gives the example of a man whose behavior and emotional responses toward his brother evidences an implicit narrative of hostility, of which he fails to be aware (Schechtman 1996, 115–16). Because this implicit script explains so much about the man's motivations, actions, and emotions not only in relation to his brother but more generally, it forms part of his narrative self-conception. However, because he is unable to articulate and reflect upon the role it plays in his history and present attitudes, the behaviors

---

18. In a recent paper, Schechtman (2001) seems to suggest that those aspects of our history and character that are attributable to us, but with which we do not emotionally identify or sympathize, do not in some sense survive in our present selves. I think the language of survival is not helpful to Schechtman's aims in this paper, because it is so entrenched in metaphysical approaches to personal identity, whereas Schechtman's concerns are more centrally focused on the activities involved in constituting oneself as a unified agent over time.

to which it gives rise are not intelligible to him, and perhaps not even noticed by him, so he cannot integrate this implicit script into his self-conception.

There are two points to be made about the distinction between explicit and implicit self-narratives. First, I think Schechtman is right to highlight the role of such implicit scripts in the explanation of our own and others' behavior. The notion of an implicit self-narrative also helps to make sense of the way in which retrospective reflection can disclose reasons and motives that were perhaps not salient or accessible to reflection at the time, but that from the present perspective enables one to better understand one's past actions, behaviors, or emotional responses.[19] The process of coming to an understanding of, appropriating, and trying to achieve some degree of emotional closure with respect to one's past self, however provisional, thus seems to involve the becoming explicit of an implicit self-narrative. Nevertheless, the contrast between explicit and implicit self-narratives is perhaps not as clear cut as Schechtman makes it out to be. For even with explicit self-narratives, it would be naïve to assume we have complete motivational self-transparency; rather, the extent to which we understand ourselves is a matter of degree and may change over time. Although some repressed implicit narratives may never become explicit, even explicit narratives may never be fully explicit.[20]

Second, Schechtman's claim that those strands of one's self-narrative that are implicit should be considered less a part of one's identity than those strands that are explicit and therefore capable of articulation, conflates autonomy and identity. It is certainly true that the man in Schechtman's example is not autonomous with respect to his emotions of hostility toward his brother, since these emotions are not accessible to reflection. However, these emotions may be integral to his character and to the emotional schemas in terms of which he understands and responds to the world and other people, even if they clash with his self-conception, or his professed values and beliefs.[21]

---

19. Thanks to Philippa Byers for bringing this point to my attention. As I discuss below, such processes of reflection cannot be achieved by introspection alone, but are crucially dependent on input from others.

20. Thanks to an anonymous reviewer for helping me to clarify this issue.

21. Ronald de Sousa (1987) argues that emotions function as conceptual schemas that frame our practical engagement with the world, making salient certain reasons and certain features of our situation while pushing others into the background. On this account, emotional schemas, even if they are not always accessible to rational reflection, are the background conditions for cognition. Further, understanding the emotional schemas in terms of which an agent interprets the world and his interactions with others may be more important for understanding what motivates him (and who he is) than his professed beliefs and values.

2.2. Personhood as a Social Concept

While acknowledging that articulacy and intelligibility are matters of degree, Schechtman argues that the ability to articulate our self-conceptions and to make them intelligible both to ourselves and to others functions as one important constraint on the process of self-constitution. The other important constraint is that our self-conceptions cohere with reality, that is, that they are not delusional, psychotic, or paranoid, based on gross factual errors about the world, or resistant to revision in the light of evidence. Both the articulation and the reality constraints arise, she argues, from the intrinsically social character of personhood. Personhood is social in two interconnected senses. First, the very concept of personhood is social in the sense that what it means to be a person in a particular culture is governed by a complex network of social institutions, norms, practices, conventions, expectations, and attitudes. In order to constitute herself as a person, an individual needs to be able, as Schechtman puts it, "to grasp her culture's concept of a person and apply it to herself," that is, to be able to lead the life of a person within that culture (Schechtman 1996, 95). Among other things, this involves, for example, constituting oneself as a morally responsible, rational, self-aware agent. Secondly, one's self-conception must be capable of being made intelligible to others; it must make sense with reference both to the social norms of personhood and to the broad narrative of one's life that others would tell. When a person's self-narrative violates the social norms of personhood or is contradicted by other people's narratives of the person, as occurs, for example, in various forms of mental illness, her capacity for personhood is diminished. Schechtman's point then is that in order to be intelligible to ourselves we must be capable of making ourselves intelligible to others.

Schechtman's focus on the second- and third-personal dimensions of narrative self-constitution is important. We cannot make sense of our lives from the first-personal perspective alone, nor is introspection always the best route to self-knowledge. Our emotional responses, character traits, values, and beliefs are disclosed in our actions and in our second-personal interactions with others, and it is through such interactions that we achieve some degree of self-understanding. To make sense of ourselves we therefore need to be responsive to the way that others see us and interpret our behavior. Our first-personal narratives must also be responsive to third-personal description. For example, a person who thinks of herself as generous is likely to be self-deluded if she does not exhibit generosity in her relationships with others or if an accurate third-personal description of her behavior and character would include terms such as "selfish" or "mean-spirited." However, Schechtman's articulation and reality constraints on coherent self-narratives do not give sufficient recognition to the oppressive nature of many of the social norms of personhood. For these norms are not just norms of personhood *simpliciter*, they are usually bound up with norms of gender, class, race, sexuality, ethnicity, culture, religion, and so on. Thus the norms for intelligible personhood, and the social institutions, practices, conventions, expectations, and attitudes that support those norms, may be quite different if one is a woman than if one is a man, or if one is black than if one is white. Constructing a self-narrative in which first-, second-, and third-person perspectives on one's identity cohere may therefore be extremely fraught in social contexts marked by such oppressions, or in contexts where others do not recognize and treat one as a person and do not make an effort to understand one's narrative.[22]

In summary, according to Schechtman's analysis what makes us persons, or the same persisting subjects over time, despite personal change, is our ability to organize our experiences into an integrated and dynamic narrative self-conception. It is these narrative capacities that enable us to unify different psychic elements, to incorporate remembered past actions and experiences into our present perspective, to anticipate future actions and experiences, and so to lead the life of a person. Further, it is these narrative capacities that give rise to the distinct phenomenology of subjectivity, to the qualitative distinctness that marks out for each of us, our memories, experiences, character traits, and so on, as "mine."[23] The importance of these capacities for personhood is most evident when they break down—for example, when dementia sufferers forget their past, no longer know who they are, and fail to recognize their loved ones; or when survivors of trauma feel emotionally dislocated and disconnected from others, lack a sense of having a future, and cannot incorporate their traumatic memories into their present perspective.

From the foregoing discussion it should be evident that I have considerable sympathy for Schechtman's account of narrative self-constitution. In the next

---

22. Thanks to Sue Campbell for stressing to me the importance of reciprocity in narrative self-constitution—that our ability to make ourselves intelligible to others depends in part on others' willingness to listen and to make the effort to understand.
23. Korsgaard (1989) highlights the connection between what she calls the "authorial" character of agency and the qualitative distinctiveness of subjectivity. Ricoeur's account of *ipse* identity also stresses the phenomenological distinctiveness, or "mineness," of one's memories, body, and subjectivity (Ricoeur 1992).

section, however, I argue that what is missing from this account is an adequate explanation of the role of embodiment in the process of self-constitution.

3. NARRATIVE INTEGRATION AND EMBODIMENT

Within the personal identity literature the body tends to be conceptualized in impersonal or third-personal terms, for example, as a human animal or organism by bodily continuity theorists or, by psychological continuity theorists, as an impersonal and replaceable container for psychological contents.[24] It is this impersonal conception of the body, I contend, that provides a foothold for the idea that we can make sense of science fiction thought experiments such as replication, fission, or body-swapping. In these thought experiments the body we imagine being replicated or swapped or providing the container into which one hemisphere of the brain and its psychological contents is transplanted, is not the first-personal lived body of our subjective experience, our own body, it is just *a* body.[25] That we can imagine still being ourselves even though inhabiting an impersonal body (which might be someone else's or a duplicate of our own) is not due entirely to the legacy of a certain kind of Cartesianism. I think we can also arrive at the impersonal body of the philosophical thought experiment by extrapolating from ordinary experiences. When a person dies, for example, or is in a persistent vegetative state, her body no longer expresses her subjectivity and so seems to become impersonal.[26] Thus, it seems natural to distinguish between the person and the human body or organism that may or may not outlive her, and from there we can move to the idea that the history of the person is distinct from the history of that body.

It is this thought that lies behind Schechtman's approach to the person-body relation.[27] Schechtman agrees with psychological continuity theorists, and with

---

24. An exception among theorists is Bernard Williams (1973b), whose argument for the bodily continuity thesis critically depends on re-presenting in the first person a scenario first considered in the third person. For an animalist approach to continuity, see Eric Olson (2003).

25. Ricoeur (1992) stresses this point in his critique of Parfit. See also Kim Atkins (2000).

26. However, although the bodies of the dead or those in a persistent vegetative state seem to be impersonal, in the sense that they no longer express the person's subjectivity, cultural norms about showing appropriate respect for the bodies of the dead suggest that we do not regard dead bodies as mere matter, but rather as representing, in some sense, the person they once embodied. Thanks to Diana Meyers for helping me clarify this issue.

27. As Schechtman notes, the psychological continuity thesis "trades on the intuition that a situation where a person's body continues to function but his psychological life comes to an end (as in, e.g., a case of irreversible coma or total possession) seems like a failure to survive" (Schechtman 2005, 2).

Locke, that personal identity is distinct from human identity, and she does not rule out the conceptual possibility that a person could act and have experiences in more than one human body. What would be required to make sense of this possibility would be an intelligible and coherent narrative of the person's experiences. Schechtman points to the thought experiments in the literature as examples of such narratives. Although these violate the reality constraint, they nevertheless tell a coherent story as to how reality might be different given certain technological possibilities. However, she argues that what distinguishes the narrative constitution view from psychological continuity theories is that, whereas the latter regard the connection between a particular person and a particular human body as entirely contingent, in the narrative constitution view, there is a deep conceptual connection between them. Schechtman's explanation of the source of this conceptual connection is revealing. She argues that it is part of our culture's conception of a person that there is a one-to-one correspondence between a particular person and a particular human body. Further, the social institutions and interactions that sustain personhood as we know it are premised on a vast range of practices that require us to be able reliably and easily to identify and reidentify persons via their bodies. Therefore, "because the reidentification of human bodies plays such an important role in our social interactions, the narrative self-constitution view demands that it plays a central role in the constitution of persons and personal identity, even though this view does not simply *identify* persons with human beings" (Schechtman 1996, 134).

Schechtman is undoubtedly correct that our ability to identify and reidentify persons by identifying and reidentifying their bodies is central to our social institutions, interactions, and practices. However, this explanation of the significance of the body for personal identity is distinctly odd, because it is entirely third-personal, as are many of her examples involving the body—the adoptee who wants to know whether this woman is the one who gave birth to him, the bartender who wants to know if the person ordering the drink is really the twenty-one-year-old on the identification card, and so on (Schechtman 1996, 67–69).[28] While these questions are indeed important,

---

28. A notable exception is the example involving a character in the movie *Now, Voyager*, played by Bette Davis. As Schechtman tells the story, the character has been transformed by miraculous medical treatment from a "stocky, unattractive and highly neurotic spinster aunt of a wealthy New England family into a delightful, slim and attractive woman." On showing a photograph of her family to a man with whom she is becoming intimate, he asks her "Who is the fat lady with the heavy brows and all the hair?" to which she replies, "I'm the fat lady with the heavy brow and all the hair" (Schechtman 1996, 112–13).

our practical interests in the connections between embodiment and personal identity extend well beyond questions of third-person reidentification; indeed, I would say that they lie at the heart of many of our first-personal subjective concerns about identity. What Schechtman's approach to the body fails to explain then is the first-personal significance of one's own body for one's identity. The narrative self-constitution view has the conceptual resources to provide such an explanation. However, Schechtman fails to develop this aspect of her view because her solution to the stand off between bodily and psychological continuity theorists reproduces their problematic assumptions both about the body as mere organism and about our subjectivity, as entirely psychological. The following passage highlights these assumptions most clearly:

> Our concept of persons has a dual nature. On the one hand, persons are objects in the world, whereas on the other they are subjects, with agency, autonomy, and inner lives. When we think of persons as objects, we are interested in reidentifying them and find ourselves pulled toward the view that persons are to be identified with their bodies. It is when we consider persons as subjects, however, that . . . we find ourselves pulled toward the view that persons are to be identified with their psyches. (Schectman 1996, 68)

In what follows I want to explain why this dualism is mistaken. I shall argue that subjectivity is not merely psychological; it is also embodied. It is with our bodies that we perceive, act, experience, and engage with the world and with others. If narrative is the "lens through which we filter our experience and plan for actions" (Schectman 1996, 113) and develop an integrated conception of ourselves as persisting, temporally extended subjects, then a condition of possibility of this narrative is that we have an integrated, if not necessarily explicit, conception of ourselves as embodied agents. I call this conception a person's bodily perspective. My claim is not that a person is simply identical with her body, or with a particular human organism. It is rather that personhood is constituted in relation to an ongoing but changing bodily perspective that, along with character, provides a principle of stability and permanence that gives rise to a sense of ourselves as persisting subjects. The centrality of embodiment to a person's self-narrative is most evident when physical trauma, disability, or bodily processes such as pregnancy or aging bring about significant bodily changes that disrupt this narrative. However, such cases simply bring to the fore what is usually taken for granted as one of the background conditions for the ongoing unity and intelligibility of our lives.

To explain the notion of a bodily perspective I want to begin by counterposing the passage from Schechtman just quoted with a passage from Merleau-Ponty. He writes: "experience of one's own body runs counter to the reflective procedure which detaches subject and object from each other, and which gives us only the thought about the body, or the body as an idea, and not the experience of the body, or the body in reality" (Merleau-Ponty 1962, 231). Our subjective or lived experience of the body is that the body is what he variously describes as our "point of view" on the world, our "anchorage in the world," a "mediator of the world," the "vehicle of our being in the world," and our "means of communication" with the world and with others. What these metaphors highlight is that we experience our bodies not as objects in the world, but as the perspective from which we perceive the world and as our mode of engagement with it. Merleau-Ponty emphasizes that both perception and our engagement with the world are structured by our practical aims, that is, by our projects and intentions, which arise in response to the particular environment or situation in which we are immersed, and which open up specific possibilities for action. These aims foreground certain objects or features of the world as having practical significance while others recede into the background. For example, in getting up from my desk to make myself a cup of tea my attention is focused on certain features of the world—the kettle, the teapot, the cup, the milk in the fridge—that are necessary for realizing my intentions. In performing the actions involved in making a cup of tea I not only undertake certain bodily movements, but I also negotiate my way through my environment—walking down the stairs, going through the doorway, moving around the kitchen benches, turning on the tap to fill up the kettle, reaching for the tea, and so on. In doing so I am not consciously aware of what my body is doing, of the movements I am making and of the way I am moving through the environment, but I undertake the actions involved seamlessly and effortlessly.[29]

Shaun Gallagher uses the term "body schema" to refer to the non-conscious, non-intentional, sub-personal processes that direct this kind of bodily activity and follows Merleau-Ponty in arguing that the body schema is "the anterior condition of possibility of perception" (Gallagher 1995, 232). The body schema

---

29. Of course this kind of pre-reflective practical engagement with the world can be disrupted—I can trip going down the stairs, knock over the milk, forget what I was doing if I am interrupted by a phone call, and so on. As I discuss later, illness or disability can also make everyday activities like making tea far from effortless.

organizes the perceptual world, so that "every figure stands out against the double horizon of external and bodily space," for example, both next to the teapot and an arm's reach away (Merleau-Ponty 1962, 115). The body schema also gives rise simultaneously to a pre-reflective, proprioceptive awareness both of specific parts of one's body, such as the position of one's fingers on the keyboard, and of one's body as a whole. Gallagher distinguishes the body schema, thus understood, from the body image, which includes perceptual awareness of one's body (as when one becomes aware of tiredness in the legs when climbing the stairs), as well as mental representations of one's body, beliefs about it, and emotional attitudes toward it. The body image need not be present to consciousness, but in the body image the body is included within the subject's intentional arc, and the body image is bound up with a first-personal sense of one's body as one's own (Gallagher 2001).

Merleau-Ponty suggests that the development of the body schema gives rise to the development of a rudimentary sense of self. As he famously states, "Consciousness is in the first place not a matter of 'I think' but of 'I can'" (Merleau-Ponty 1962, 159). Perhaps when we imagine ourselves surviving a body transplant and simply carrying on our lives in someone else's body it is from the rudimentary self of the body schema that our imagination extrapolates. Nevertheless, in his view the body schema and the body image are developmentally interrelated, and both body schema and body image are dynamically constituted through a two-way interaction between the body and the world. The development of motor coordination, for example, requires not only neurological development but also bodily engagement with the environment, which discloses, and gives rise to reflective awareness of, both the limits and the capacities of one's body. Thus an infant can only start to develop an organized body schema and a more complex sense of self once it has some awareness of its own body.

In our lived bodily experience the body schema and body image are integrated, although the body schema and body image can come apart: for example, in delusions or psycho-physical conditions such as anorexia nervosa, gender dysphoria, and body dysmorphic disorder. It is this integrated experience of one's body that I call a person's bodily perspective. One's bodily perspective is both ongoing and changing, and thus, it involves what Merleau-Ponty calls sedimentation and spontaneity. A person's bodily perspective involves sedimentation in the sense that it is constituted on the basis of bodily habits—for example, of posture, movement, gesture—bodily capacities and bodily knowledge that are developed over time both in response to one's environment and in the pursuit of one's aims. This sedimentation is what enables newly learned movements or newly developed capacities—driving, typing, rowing—to become routine and habitual. Spontaneity is the general power of using sedimented habits, capacities, and knowledge to engage with a new situation. Merleau-Ponty gives the example of an organist who, within an hour of rehearsing at a new organ, has assimilated its feel and can perform (Merleau-Ponty 1962, 167–68). Sedimentation and spontaneity are thus not opposed but mutually enabling. They highlight what Merleau-Ponty calls the temporal structure of the body, the way in which present actions are made possible by the accumulated habits and capacities of past actions and open up new possibilities for action in the future. The body image also contributes to this temporal structure, as a system of ongoing, but also changing, mental representations of one's body, beliefs about it, and emotional attitudes toward it. For example, a thin young man's representation of himself as puny and scrawny may change over time into a representation of himself as lean, wiry, and fit as he develops into a cross-country runner.

I am suggesting that the "lens through which we filter our experience and plan for actions" incorporates this ongoing yet changing bodily perspective, which is central to a person's sense of herself as a temporally extended narrative self. However, the temporal structure of the body, and hence one's bodily perspective, reflects not only what the body can do, but also what kind of body one has and what happens to it. And with respect to what kind of body one has and much of what happens to it, one is passive, at least to a significant degree. For example, we have no control over our genetic characteristics or our primary and many of our secondary sexual characteristics, and only limited control over bodily capacities and biological functions, such as those involved in growth, metabolic functioning, digestion, and so on. Furthermore, the body as biological organism seems in some sense to have a life of its own and a distinct temporality from the temporality of subjectivity—cells replicate and die, fingernails and hair grow, hormonal cycles ebb and flow, and so on.[30] In fact, one's subjectivity seems as much constrained by one's lived embodiment as expressed through it. This passivity seems to tell against my claim that one's bodily perspective is central to one's narrative self-conception.

To respond to this objection, my claim is that subjectivity is actively constituted against the background of, and in relation to, the life of the body, which provides the implicit frame of reference for one's sense of self. Although

---

30. Thanks to Cynthia Townley for suggesting this point.

we may be constrained by and passive with respect to certain aspects of our bodily lives, these aspects of our embodiment nevertheless shape our identities and are incorporated into our self-conceptions. The notion of a bodily perspective aims to highlight the dialectical relationship between body and subjectivity, as well as the role of the lived body in the process of narrative self-constitution. In other words, making sense of oneself involves making sense of one's embodied subjectivity.

Crucially, embodied subjectivity is social from the outset. One's bodily perspective, and hence one's subjectivity, is primordially mediated by, and responsive to, one's relationships with other people, one's social situation, and social and cultural representations and practices, including those related to gender, ethnicity, sexuality and disability. To use Iris Young's metaphor, in learning to throw like a girl one not only develops, or fails to develop, certain bodily capacities, one also incorporates social and cultural meanings related to gender into one's bodily perspective and one's narrative self-conception (Young 1990).[31]

The centrality of a person's bodily perspective to her narrative self-conception, and the extent to which it is usually taken for granted as one of the background conditions for the ongoing unity and intelligibility of our lives, is made particularly clear by cases of disruption to one's bodily perspective brought about by dramatic or gradual bodily change. Those who have undergone such change often characterize the process of responding to it as a process of altering or reconstructing one's sense of self. Kay Toombs, for example, describes the lived experience of loss of mobility brought about by multiple sclerosis, which alters the "I can" of consciousness in so many respects (Toombs 2001). She describes how her subjective sense of space and time have altered as she has become dependent on a wheelchair, so that "near" and "far" take on different meanings; the environment becomes a series of obstacles to be negotiated; routine activities such as taking a shower or eating soup become a series of complex and time-consuming problems to be solved. Similarly, she describes how her sense of her own capacities and of the possibilities opened up by the future are dramatically altered, so that in thinking of goals and projects the assumption "I can do it again" is always in question. These disruptions to her sense of space, time, the future, and her

---

31. For related discussions of the way in which social and cultural representations (sometimes referred to as the social imaginary) of gender and sexuality are incorporated into women's individual experiences and body images see, for example, Sandra Bartky (1990); Moira Gatens (1996); Kathleen Lennon (2004); Catriona Mackenzie (2001); Diana Meyers (2002); and Gail Weiss (1999).

own capacities have also disrupted her sense of self. Toombs writes: "When I see myself on a home video, I experience a sense of puzzlement. I catch myself wondering not so much whether the body projected on the screen is my body, but, rather if the person in the video is really *me*. However, if I see old pictures of myself when I was walking, or leaning on a cane, I find it hard to remember how it was to be that person, or even *who* I was when I moved like that" (Toombs 2001, 254). These changes to the sense of self are not just the result of changes in bodily intentionality, but also of other people's responses and their emotional impact. Thus Toombs makes vivid the way other people's responses—of infantilizing her, staring at her, speaking about her in the third person even in her presence, invading her bodily space by pushing her wheelchair uninvited, and so on—give rise to a sense of shame that becomes "an integral element of disordered bodily style" (Toombs 2001, 256).

Toombs's account of the responses of others to her disability might explain why Schechtman wants to distinguish the history of a person from the history of her body. For these responses reduce the person to the current state of her body, and it is against this kind of reduction that we would all want to insist: "I am not just this body with a gradually degenerating central nervous system; I am also a person with my own inner mental life of thoughts and feelings." However, what motivates this insistence is the idea that our bodies are not just objects in the world; they are lived bodies—the vehicles of our agency, the expressions of our personhood. What Toombs's description of the lived experience of disability illuminates and makes explicit is the way in which we constitute ourselves as persons in relation to the dynamic interaction of our lived bodies and the social and natural worlds.

4. NARRATIVE INTEGRATION AND ALIENATED EMBODIMENT

I have argued that to be a person is to constitute oneself as a temporally extended persisting subject by organizing one's remembered past, experiences, emotions, character traits, and so on, into a narrative self-conception. Simultaneously, to be a person is to be constituted in one's ongoing second- and third-person interactions with others. Further, I have argued that who we are as narrative subjects cannot be understood if we think of our bodies in third-personal terms as objects in the world. Thus, to be a person is to be a temporally extended embodied subject whose identity is constituted in and through one's lived bodily engagement with the world and with others.

In response to the account of embodiment developed here, it might be objected that I have assumed that we experience our embodiment as more integrated with our subjectivity than it often is. Common experience, however, seems to suggest otherwise. Many women for example, experience extreme dissatisfaction with their bodies or with specific bodily attributes and feel that only by drastically altering their bodies will they be able to be, or to become, themselves. The increasing popularity of various forms of cosmetic surgery seems to attest to this gap between the body and subjectivity. The experience of serious illness, or of the deterioration of bodily capacities that can accompany aging, for example, is sometimes experienced and described as being let down by one's body, or feeling that one's body no longer expresses who one is. In more extreme cases, such as gender dysphoria, anorexia nervosa, or body dysmorphic disorder, not only are there conflicts within a person's bodily perspective—for example, between the body schema and the body image—but a person may feel thoroughly alienated from her body, or parts of it. People who experience gender dysphoria, for example, often describe themselves as being in the "wrong body" and in some cases can experience feelings of revulsion or disgust toward their bodies.[32] From the perspective of the theorist of personal identity, psycho-physical conditions of this kind can seem just as strange as the science fiction thought experiments of the philosophical literature, and may seem to pose an even more serious challenge to my claims about the constitutive role of embodiment in identity.[33]

I want to make three points in response to this objection. First, although I have argued that our embodiment is the taken-for-granted background condition of our subjectivity, my argument does not rely on the assumption that we always experience our bodies and our subjectivity as seamlessly integrated. Rather, I have argued that our identities are actively constituted in relation to an ongoing yet changing bodily perspective. This is compatible with the idea that a person's bodily perspective may be internally integrated to varying degrees and with the idea that a person may identify with, or feel alienated from, her

---

32. Both the DSM-IV and the ICD-10 (International Classification of Diseases—10), include as the two main components of gender identity disorder, both of which must be present for a diagnosis, strong and persistent cross-gender identification (sometimes expressed as the belief that one was born into the wrong sex, or has the wrong body) and persistent discomfort and distress regarding one's assigned sex. The diagnostic criteria in children of both sexes include an expressed desire to be, or a belief that one is, of the opposite sex, and persistent repudiation of male/female anatomical structures which may extend to disgust with one's own genitals, and the desire to alter primary and secondary sexual characteristics.

33. Thanks to Steve Matthews for pressing me on this issue.

bodily perspective, to varying degrees. My argument does assume, however, that because embodiment is the taken-for-granted background condition of our subjectivity, experiencing one's bodily perspective as internally conflicted, or feeling quite alienated from one's bodily perspective, such as feeling that one is in the "wrong body," is likely to be highly distressing. The distress experienced by people with gender dysphoria, for example, attests to this.

Second, such experiences of alienation do not undermine my claims about the constitutive role of embodiment in identity, but rather highlight the complex interplay among the biological, psychological, and social, and among the first-, second-, and third-personal, dimensions of identity.[34] Making sense of who we are, and making sense of our lived embodiment, involves constructing an identity that is shaped by, and responsive to, biological realities, the social and cultural imaginary, and one's individual psychic history, which includes one's relationships with others. In the case of women's dissatisfaction with their bodies or with specific bodily attributes, experiences of alienation from one's bodily perspective are clearly bound up with oppressive social and cultural practices, representations of gender and sexuality, and ideals of beauty. Given this fact, that some women might experience difficulty integrating their subjectivity with their lived embodiment and feel that their bodies do not express who they really are is hardly surprising.[35] In the case of illness, aging, or disability, as Toombs shows, alienation may arise from physical changes to one's body, from the changed character of one's interactions with others, from social and cultural meanings and representations, and from difficulties integrating these changes with one's former life. In the case of psycho-physical conditions such as gender dysphoria, multiple factors—biological, social, interpersonal, personal—may give rise to a sense of alienation and distress, and finding ways of achieving a more integrated sense of self seems to be of paramount concern. Whether this is best achieved through identification

---

34. For an interesting and insightful discussion of the interplay between first-, second-, and third-person perspectives that uses a narrative approach to identity to discuss a recent legal case involving a thirteen-year-old girl with gender dysphoria, see Kim Atkins (2005).

35. It is interesting that the evidence concerning whether cosmetic surgery leads to improved psychosocial outcomes is mixed. A recent review of the literature, which noted that many studies of patient outcomes have methodological limitations (such as lacking control groups, small sample sizes, or potentially biased assessments), suggests that in addition to the nature of the surgery performed (whether extensive—e.g., rhinoplasty—as opposed to "restorative"—e.g., face-lift, botox injection), age, gender, and patient expectations all have an impact on psychosocial outcomes following surgery. Being male, young, suffering from depression, anxiety, or a personality disorder seem to be factors associated with poor psychosocial outcomes. Notably, an estimated 6–15 percent of cosmetic patients appear to suffer from body dysmorphic disorder. See Castle, Honigman, and Philips (2002).

with transgender identity, through hormone therapy, or through hormone therapy followed by gender reassignment surgery, depends on the person and his or her situation.

Third, experiences of distress and alienation make evident the extent to which identity is bound up with agency and capacities for self-constitution. Our identities are not simply byproducts of biological, social, and psychic forces. They are constructed through an active and ongoing process of self-constitution, as Schechtman argues. One can succeed in this process, or fail, to varying degrees and at different points in one's life. The process, however, is likely to be significantly more fraught in social and cultural environments in which individuals' lives and possibilities are curtailed by poverty, neglect, or abuse. In such circumstances, developing the skills and capacities necessary for making a life, and for making sense of one's life, can be extremely difficult.[36] The process may also be made significantly more fraught by illness (including mental illness), trauma, and disability, which can be experienced as an unmaking or undoing of the self, as in the story of March, discussed earlier. However, as Susan Brison has argued, a person can only remake herself in the wake of such experiences if she can find a way to achieve some kind of narrative integration between her past, present, and future selves (Brison 2002).

In conclusion, I have argued that narrative self-constitution is an embodied process because our subjectivities and our narrative self-conceptions are actively constituted in relation to our lived bodily experience. The process of integrating ourselves as persons over time involves not only making sense of our pasts and possible futures, our emotions, character traits, and relations with others, but also making sense of our bodily lives. I have argued that this involves a complex and dynamic process of developing an integrated bodily perspective and that this perspective functions as a background condition for the ongoing unity and intelligibility of our lives. The importance of the bodily perspective to a person's narrative self-conception is brought into focus by experiences of bodily change, both dramatic and gradual, which can radically disrupt a person's sense of self and by the distress that often accompanies

---

36. Hilde Lindemann Nelson (2001) illuminates both the complexities of identity formation and deformation in such contexts, and the role of narrative in reconstituting the self. Feminist relational theories of autonomy have also highlighted the importance of social and relational factors in the development of the skills and competences necessary for successful self-constitution, as well as the way in which oppressive social environments can impede the development of these skills and competences. See, for example, Meyers (1989); Mackenzie and Stoljar (2000); and Friedman (2003).

experiences of bodily alienation. Such experiences highlight the way our identities are constituted in and through our lived bodily engagement with the world and with others.

REFERENCES

Atkins, Kim. 2000. Personal Identity and the Importance of One's Own Body: A Response to Derek Parfit. *International Journal of Philosophical Studies* 8(3): 329–49.
———. 2005. Re Alex: Narrative Identity and the Case of Gender Dysphoria. *Griffith Law Review* 14(1): 1–16.
Bartky, Sandra. 1990. *Femininity and Domination: Studies in the Phenomenology of Oppression.* New York: Routledge.
Brison, Susan. 1997. Outliving Oneself: Trauma, Memory, and Personal Identity. In *Feminists Rethink the Self,* ed. Diana Meyers, 12–39. Boulder, Colo.: Westview.
———. 2002. *Aftermath: Violence and the Remaking of the Self.* Princeton: Princeton University Press.
Brooks, Geraldine. 2005. *March.* New York: Viking Penguin.
Castle, David, Roberta J. Honigman, and Katharine A. Philips. 2002. Does Cosmetic Surgery Improve Psychosocial Wellbeing? *Medical Journal of Australia* 176(12): 601–4.
Christman, John. 2004. Narrative Unity as a Condition of Personhood. *Metaphilosophy* 35(5): 695–713.
De Sousa, Ronald. 1987. *The Rationality of Emotions.* Cambridge: MIT Press.
Frankfurt, Harry. 1988. *The Importance of What We Care About.* New York: Cambridge University Press.
———. 1999. *Necessity, Volition, and Love.* New York: Cambridge University Press.
Friedman, Marilyn. 2003. *Gender, Autonomy, Politics.* New York: Oxford University Press.
Gallagher, Shaun. 1995. Body Schema and Intentionality. In *The Body and the Self,* ed. Jose Luis Bermudez, Anthony Marcel, and Naomi Eilan, 245–66. Cambridge: MIT Press.
———. 2001. Dimensions of Embodiment: Body Image and Body Schema in Medical Contexts. In *Handbook of Phenomenology and Medicine,* ed. S. Kay Toombs, 147–75. Dordrecht: Kluwer.
Gatens, Moira. 1996. *Imaginary Bodies.* London: Routledge.
Gendler, Tamar Szabo. 1999. Exceptional Persons: On the Limits of Imaginary Cases. In *Models of the Self,* ed. Shaun Gallagher and Jonathon Shear, 447–66. Thorverton, U.K.: Imprint Academic.
Goldie, Peter. 2003. One's Remembered Past: Narrative Thinking, Emotion, and the External Perspective. *Philosophical Papers* 32(3): 301–19.
Johnson, Mark. 1997. Human Concerns Without Superlative Selves. In *Reading Parfit,* ed. J. Dancy, 149–79. Oxford: Blackwell.
Korsgaard, Christine. 1989. Personal Identity and the Unity of Agency: A Kantian Response to Parfit. *Philosophy and Public Affairs* 18(2): 109–23.
———. 1996. *The Sources of Normativity.* Cambridge: Cambridge University Press.

———. 2002. *Self-Constitution: Action, Identity, and Integrity*. John Locke Lectures. University of Oxford. Available at http://www.people.fas.harvard.edu/ korsgaar/#Locke%20Lectures (accessed May 2005).
Lennon, Kathleen. 2004. Imaginary Bodies and Worlds. *Inquiry* 47:107–22.
Lindemann Nelson, Hilde. 2001. *Damaged Identities, Narrative Repair*. Ithaca: Cornell University Press.
Mackenzie, Catriona. 2001. On Bodily Autonomy. In *Handbook of Phenomenology and Medicine*, ed. S. Kay Toombs, 417–39. Dordrecht: Kluwer.
Mackenzie, Catriona, and Natalie Stoljar, eds. 2000. *Relational Autonomy: Feminist Perspectives on Autonomy, Agency, and the Social Self*. New York: Oxford University Press.
Merleau-Ponty, Maurice. 1962. *The Phenomenology of Perception*. Trans. Colin Smith. London: Routledge and Kegan Paul.
Meyers, Diana. 1989. *Self, Society, and Personal Choice*. New York: Columbia University Press.
———. 2002. *Gender in the Mirror: Cultural Imagery and Women's Agency*. New York: Oxford University Press.
Olson, Eric. 2003. An Argument for Animalism. In *Personal Identity*, ed. Raymond Martin and John Baressi, 318–34. Oxford: Blackwell.
Parfit, Derek. 1984. *Reasons and Persons*. Oxford: Clarendon Press.
Ricoeur, Paul. 1992. *Oneself as Another*. Trans. K. Blamey. Chicago: University of Chicago Press.
Schechtman, Marya. 1994. The Truth About Memory. *Philosophical Psychology* 7(1): 3–18.
———. 1996. *The Constitution of Selves*. Ithaca: Cornell University Press.
———. 2001. Empathic Access: The Missing Ingredient in Personal Survival. *Philosophical Explorations* 4(2): 95–111.
———. 2005. Experience, Agency, and Personal Identity. *Social Philosophy and Policy* 22(2): 1–24.
———. 2007. Stories, Lives, and Basic Survival: A Refinement and Defense of the Narrative View. In *Narrative and Understanding Persons*, ed. Dan Hutto, 155–78. Cambridge: Cambridge University Press.
Shoemaker, Sydney. 1970. Persons and Their Pasts. *American Philosophical Quarterly* 7:269–85.
Strawson, Galen. 1999. The Self. In *Models of the Self*, ed. Shaun Gallagher and Jonathon Shear, 1–24. Thorverton, U.K.: Imprint Academic.
———. 2004. Against Narrativity. *Ratio* 17:428–52.
Toombs, S. Kay. 2001. Reflections on Bodily Change: The Lived Experience of Disability. In *Handbook of Phenomenology and Medicine*, ed. S. Kay Toombs, 247–62. Dordrecht: Kluwer.
Velleman, David 1996. Self to Self. *Philosophical Review* 105(1): 39–76.
Vice, Samantha. 2003. Literature and the Narrative Self. *Philosophy* 78:93–108.
Weiss, Gail. 1999. *Body Images: Embodiment as Intercorporeality*. New York: Routledge.
Wilkes, Kathleen. 1988. *Real People: Personal Identity Without Thought Experiments*. Oxford: Clarendon Press.
———. 1999. GNOTHE SEAUTON (Know Thyself). In *Models of the Self*, ed. Shaun Gallagher and Jonathon Shear, 25–38. Thorverton, U.K.: Imprint Academic.

Williams, Bernard. 1973a. Imagination and the Self. In *Problems of the Self*, 26–45. Cambridge: Cambridge University Press.
———. 1973b. The Self and the Future. In *Problems of the Self*, 46–63. Cambridge: Cambridge University Press.
Wollheim, Richard. 1984. *The Thread of Life*. Cambridge: Cambridge University Press.
Young, Iris Marion. 1990. Throwing Like a Girl. In *Throwing Like a Girl and Other Essays in Feminist Philosophy and Social Theory*, 141–59. Bloomington: Indiana University Press.

SIX

BODILY LIMITS TO AUTONOMY:

EMOTION, ATTITUDE, AND SELF-DEFENSE

Sylvia Burrow

Many of us took pride in never feeling violent, never hitting. We had not thought deeply about our relationships to inflicting physical pain. Some of us expressed terror and awe when confronted with physical strength on the part of others. For us, the healing process included the need to learn how to use physical force constructively, to remove the terror—the dread.
—bell hooks, *Talking Back: Thinking Feminist, Thinking Black*

1. INTRODUCTION

Feminist theories of autonomy acknowledge the complexities of cultivating and expressing autonomy under oppressive social structures. A prominent concern of these theories is that unreflectively endorsing oppressive social norms, beliefs, and values undercuts autonomy. Less attention has been paid to constraints on women's autonomy that are encoded in the body, what I will refer to as *bodily encoded* limits to autonomy. For instance, some physically restrictive postures and movements exemplify or express a femininity of compliance or passivity. Such bodily encoded limits to autonomy are not only worrisome in themselves, they are troubling in light of the prevalence of violence against women. Attitudes of compliance and passivity lessen the likelihood of active prevention or resistance against personal violence (Bart 1985). Moreover, often

I extend my appreciation to audience members at the Athens Institute for Education and Research International Conference on Philosophy and the Canadian Society for Women in Philosophy Conference at Dalhousie University, and to Michael Manson, Robin Dillon, Carolyn MacLeod, Letitia Meynell, Susan Sherwin, and Sue Campbell for their helpful comments and suggestions.

after experiencing personal violence, a sense of physical powerlessness, low self-esteem, self-blame, or shame further restrict agency (Penn and Nardos 2003).

Susan Brison (1999) has suggested self-defense training as a concrete means of developing autonomy in the aftermath of violence. However, she warns that self-defense is not a panacea. Quoting C. H. Sparks and Bat-Ami Bar On (1985), she asserts: "self-defense tactics are 'stopgap measures which fail to link an attack against one victim with attacks on others.' And . . . 'knowledge that one can fight if attacked is also a very different kind of security from enjoying a certainty that one will not be attacked at all'" (Brison 1999, 220–21). Is self-defense simply a stopgap measure? What kind of security might it offer? And how might it promote autonomy? Although Brison's account helps to motivate these questions, it insufficiently explores the potential self-defense training offers in answer to them.

If self-defense training were simply a stopgap measure, then it would function as a temporary solution for the problem of violence against women. But I hold out for a view of self-defense training as much more than a stopgap, for two reasons. First, self-defense training is valuable for women because it provides a security that one can avoid or counter personal violence directed toward oneself. Second, self-defense training is a source of self-confidence. For women living within a social network working to undermine their self-trust and self-esteem, it is important to cultivate self-confidence, particularly since elements of that network involve threatening displays of aggression or superiority. Self-defense training in my account is not simply a route to recovery in the wake of personal violence. Instead, and primarily, it is the development of skills aimed at preventing personal violence. My aim is to show that the development of self-defense skills functions as a means of overcoming bodily encoded limits to autonomy. Through this discussion, I hope to broaden our understanding of the embodied nature of autonomy by illuminating the connection between bodily training and responses such as self-confidence, self-trust, and self-esteem.

2. RESTRICTED SITE: THE BODY

Traditionally, autonomy theorists have upheld the view that autonomous action proceeds from beliefs, values, or desires that are "wholeheartedly endorsed" or otherwise reflective of one's "true self" or "real self."[1] Such theories lack reflective

---

1. Following Frankfurt's (1971) view or its Kantian precursor. For an overview see Wolf (1993).

attention to the self's historical and social context because they consider individuals to be independent and self-defining. Persons are autonomous if their actions proceed from wholeheartedly endorsed values; otherwise, they are not. In contrast, feminist autonomy theorists tend to view the self as inherently relational. This relational self is connected to other selves socially and historically and develops autonomy in and through relationships of dependence and interdependence.[2] Autonomy becomes a complex matter for the feminist autonomy theorist, who recognizes that it is not unusual for persons to act on the basis of internalized social norms and values not endorsed as "one's own," which may constrain autonomy to different degrees. Diana Meyers's (1987; 1989; 2004a) account of autonomy is notably instructive here.

Meyers's account widens the idea of autonomy beyond its traditional boundaries through conceiving of autonomy on a continuum. Autonomy progresses through the development of autonomy competencies: coordinated skills of introspection, imagination, reasoning, and volition (1987, 627; 2004a, 10). To the degree that one exercises autonomy competencies, one is autonomous. So, even persons lacking self-determination in many aspects of their lives may not thereby lack autonomy, not if they act autonomously within certain pockets of their lives. For instance, a woman who has not reflected upon her traditional feminine roles may exercise autonomy in deciding to be a stay-at-home mother, even if she lacks the wider autonomy we would attribute to her were she to have reflectively chosen her life plan.

Meyers argues that autonomous selves are relational selves who learn to become autonomous through concrete interactions with others, emphasizing that selves are socially constituted, embodied beings situated within historical and social frameworks (1989, 189–202). Nevertheless, earlier formations of her theory privilege psychological competencies—those cognitive and imaginative skills permitting critical reflection on one's beliefs, values, or preferences—suggesting that autonomy proceeds to a degree correlative to one's ongoing process of critical self-reflection. But, as Meyers recognizes in her later work (2004a; 2005), if the relational self must be understood as an embodied self to form and maintain its relationships and learn skills from others, then it matters to the development of autonomy that the self is embodied. We might wonder if the body matters even more directly to the development of autonomy. Is there some sense in which we can describe autonomy as itself *embodied*?

2. See, for instance, Code (1991), Whitbeck (1983) and Baier (1985).

One way to recognize the embodied nature of autonomy is to acknowledge the body as a site for suffering *constraints* on autonomy. Before turning to Meyers's later work, let me expand on how oppressive social norms and ideals of femininity can restrict autonomy through the body. First, a prominent element of traditional Western feminine ideals is the expectation that women and girls should take up as little physical space as possible (Frye 1983). Elbows are tucked in, ankles or knees are crossed or firmly pressed together, arms and hands are often folded together. Women are encouraged to view the body as, in Iris Marion Young's (2005) words, a "fragile encumbrance." Feminine socialization trains women to view the body as an object of appreciation rather than an instrument one might *use* to effect action in the world (34). Limited physicality undermines autonomy by reducing or removing the possibility of certain forms of self-expression. One's body represents to others how one values oneself; thus restrictions of bodily expression may undermine self-appreciation. Wilting, passive physical postures and movements represent a devaluing of oneself as unworthy of equal status and standing before others (Bartky 1990). As Marilyn Frye perceptively notes, feminine ideals are reflected in "a network of behaviors through which we constantly announce to others our membership in a lower caste and our unwillingness and/or inability to defend our bodily or moral integrity. It is degrading and a pattern of degradation" (1983, 16). Persons limiting their physical presence in and movement through the world in degrading ways thus appear to undermine the very possibility of their own self-appreciation.

Second, endorsing feminine ideals can limit one's capacity to act by literally weakening the body. Naomi Wolf's (1991) account of the Beauty Myth shows how girls and women often suffer depleted bodily energy through trying to achieve ideals of Western feminine beauty. Perceived body image is a common barometer of self-esteem and self-worth for women and girls (Castillo 1996). Thus it is no surprise that empirical studies have shown correlations between eating disorders and low self-esteem and dissatisfaction with bodily appearance (Button et al. 1997). In addition, those attempting to achieve an ideal of thinness often experience a lack of energy directly related to dieting or exercising excessively. Passivity, lack of energy, and low self-esteem work together to limit the freedom and vitality of one's bodily expression. Such limits suggest a familiar theme: that to be feminine is to be acquiescent. The acquiescent possess a reduced ability to act and thus a diminished resistance to socially and politically oppressive forces. Hence, I doubt Wolf is exaggerating matters in asserting that the Beauty Myth "is not an obsession about beauty, it is an obsession about female obedience" (1991, 187).

Third, a culture of violence against women and girls creates an environment that entrenches female passivity. Learning that one's responses for coping with or preventing personal violence are generally ineffective, persons can become passive and accepting of abuse; doing nothing becomes a defensive response. Lacking the motivation to prevent or resist harm to oneself is associated with feelings of helplessness, depression, and low self-esteem (Penn and Nardos 2003, 148–50). Furthermore, the threat of personal violence may be internalized in conjunction with imperatives of femininity such that women become unaware of the ways in which their own actions support a culture of female passivity and oppression. So in sum, women's bodies are a common site of bodily encoded constraints that limit autonomy.

In her more recent work, Meyers argues that emancipating women from oppressive ideals encoded in the body cannot occur unless women treat their bodies as repositories of meaning, learning to understand which meanings deposited in the body are pernicious so as to purge the body of them (2004a, 89). Through personal transformation of the body, such as changing beauty rituals, altering bodily looks, or using the body in new ways through dance or self-defense, women can reconfigure their "psycho-corporeal identity" (85). Since the body is an important site of agency and identity, "psycho-corporeal identity" is tightly tied to "psycho-corporeal agency" for Meyers. While I do not aim to provide a comprehensive account here, I endorse the view that physiological and psychological capacities each enable autonomous action, often in ways affecting one another. Consider, for example, Susan Brison's (1999) view that personal transformation in the aftermath of trauma needs to involve changing more than cognitive beliefs. Responses such as fearfulness, helplessness, anxiety, depression, tendency to self-blame, or an inability to get angry can each restrict action in the face of dangerous settings or situations. Physically retraining one's responses so that one can get angry or act defiantly to protect oneself can thus be an important step in the recovery of diminished or lost autonomy.

While I agree that personal transformation may prove to be an important source of expanding women's autonomy, a deeper explanation of how bodily encoded limits to autonomy could be addressed through such practices is needed. In what follows, I plan to construct an account of how training the body through self-defense practice might overcome bodily restrictions to autonomy. Although Meyers (2004a) appeals to Brison in endorsing self-defense as a route to personal transformation, neither offers much of an explanation as to how it might expand autonomy. I hope to show that self-defense training provides a means of developing those emotional and attitudinal responses essential to women's development of autonomy under threat of personal violence.

3. SELF-DEFENSE AND AUTONOMY COMPETENCIES

Persons who are oppressed face systematic limitations, barriers, and harms (Frye 1983). Women are oppressed by virtue of belonging to a worldwide group of persons who are routinely targeted by personal violence.[3] Violence and the threat of violence are among the most severe modes of oppression that affect women as a group. This particular form of oppression is inextricably tied to other systems of domination. Those who resist oppression and resolve to act despite or because of oppression risk severe reprisals. In the case of threat of personal violence, resisting oppressive practices can be prohibitively intimidating. Nevertheless, resistance is essential to autonomous action in oppressive contexts. To possess autonomy more fully over one's life, Meyers asserts that persons must "be *ready to resist* the unwarranted demands of other individuals along with conformist societal pressures, and ... *be resolved* to carry out their own plans" (1987, 627; emphasis mine). The following analysis of the skills acquired through self-defense training reveals that it develops the critical autonomy competencies of resistance and resolve; thus self-defense is one concrete means for fostering autonomy under threat of personal violence.

Personal violence encompasses many forms, including physical, emotional, sexual, and financial abuse.[4] The immediate aim of self-defense is to prevent physical or sexual harms to the self, so in speaking of self-defense as a response to personal violence I will refer to this narrower domain of harm. Oppressed persons who are attuned to a heightened threat of personal violence, as women are, have an awareness of the frequency with which others' intimidating or threatening postures, words, or actions may turn into assaults against their bodies. Accordingly, women often have a set of techniques aimed at avoiding or withstanding assault. We see women engage in evasive actions as part of a daily routine. Such actions include: strategically parking cars or planning walking and bus routes; arranging companions for traveling; attending to type and style of clothing and shoes; and purchasing security alarms or systems, guns, pepper

---

3. Amnesty International (2006) has accrued data from over fifty independent world surveys on violence against women indicating that, on average, *one in three* women worldwide will experience personal violence in her lifetime.

4. I appeal here to the classification of personal violence outlined in VAWD (2004).

spray, whistles, or guard dogs. These preparations aim to prevent harm to the self, but they do not constitute self-defense as I discuss it in this paper. Guns, tasers, pepper spray, or guard dogs may be *used* in self-defense, but their use does not cultivate what I shall call "the skills of self-defense." The skills of self-defense are cultivated through the development of coordinated sets of cognitive and physiological skills permitting one to defend oneself against harm.[5] Self-defense training is the endeavor to acquire and improve such skills.

Self-defense training cultivates interdependent skills acquired through repeated training over time.[6] These skills divide into two sorts. Most obviously, a repertoire of *physical* abilities and techniques is needed to prevent personal violence. Learning blocks, escape moves, strikes, kicks, punches, grappling, locks, and throws all count as the sorts of physical skills one might learn in self-defense training. Additionally, an importantly related set of *reactive* skills is acquired during self-defense training, those attitudes and emotional dispositions suited to successfully executing physical self-defense techniques. Physical and psychological competencies work together in producing accurately placed, well-timed responses reliant upon appropriate motivation. We might envision the complementary nature of both sorts of competencies through picturing a traditional martial arts class, which at its best trains students in physical techniques practiced with respect, confidence, pride without arrogance, tranquility of mind, and resolution of purpose. Self-defense classes abstracted from their martial art background including such elements of training will also qualify as developing self-defense skills.[7]

Self-defense training furthers the exercise and development of the capacities of resistance and resolve. It does so through developing a confidence in one's ability to protect and defend oneself that is rooted in the body in two sorts of ways, each correlating to the set of self-defense skills outlined above. First, confidence in the physical skills needed to defend oneself is gained through the process of learning to defend oneself, plus the subsequent testing and retesting of those skills. This self-confidence is borne out of bodily experience. Either

---

5. Of course, some of these actions might be most effective if one becomes skilled in doing them, and one might become effectively skilled in several of these sorts of actions. But skills such as setting an alarm, training a guard dog, or planning a walking route need not be skills that are developed in coordination with one another.

6. For the purposes of this paper I assume that traditional martial arts training is empty-hand training, which trains the practitioner in self-defense through using the body alone.

7. Taking a few classes in self-defense will not produce a person skilled in self-defense, but neither need one train for years in order to be skilled. One may be said to possess this skill when one is judged by senior experts as capable of defending oneself in training exercises and tests.

one can escape a tight grip on one's wrist or one cannot; repeated success entails self-confidence in that technique. Success in many different sorts of techniques and responses will generate a broader sense of self-confidence in one's self-defense skills on the whole. Second, training in self-defense develops confidence in one's emotional and cognitive reactions to threats of personal violence. Physical training succeeds well or poorly according to the emotional and cognitive responses of the practitioner. The body concretely reflects those responses. Those who become frightened or startled, or who fail to move due to hesitation or uncertainty, lose the timing essential to successfully executing self-defense techniques. Attackers will not wait while one overcomes one's initial responses or contemplates what to do.

It is thus essential to self-defense training that emotional and attitudinal competencies are trained in conjunction with physical competencies. These components of self-defense training are distinct, but they are developed concomitantly—indeed, it is typically the aim of this training to develop such physiological and psychological elements together. Through self-defense training one develops confidence not only that one can execute specific physical techniques but that one will also possess the motivational wherewithal to successfully perform those techniques, even under pressing circumstances. The self-confidence produced through self-defense training is a significant source of the resolve to act to defend oneself and of the motivation to resist threats to the self. Since both resistance and resolve are key autonomy competencies, the self-confidence produced through self-defense training promotes autonomy.

4. SELF-DEFENSE AND SELF-APPRECIATION

A number of feminist theorists have recently offered analyses of the importance of positive self-regarding attitudes to women's agency. The discussion above has shown that self-defense training fosters self-confidence. I shall now expand my analysis to consider the contribution of this training and the self-confidence it furthers to other attitudes of self-appreciation, the cultivation of which support the flourishing of autonomy. I aim to show how my account is able to both accommodate and enrich recent feminist reflection on the nature and importance of self-regard. Autonomy is a function not only of the capacity to choose freely and to act on those choices, it is also a function of the ability to do so as a person situated within concrete relational contexts, contexts that may undermine or enhance choice and action. Hence, my account more widely shows how self-defense training improves the prospect for autonomy, understood both in its traditional and relational senses.

In an importantly generative work on the concept of self-trust, Trudy Govier draws parallels between self-trust and the trust we have in others. One trusts oneself if one can expect behavior that is not harmful to oneself, that proceeds from favorable motives, and that reflects one's sense of what it means to be a good person. Self-trust involves one's willingness to rely or depend upon oneself, to regard oneself as well-intentioned and competent to make and act on judgments or decisions. Moreover, one regards oneself in this sort of positive light even in the face of others' superficial evidence or criticism (Govier 1993, 105–6). Indeed, self-trust seems to reveal itself just at those times others challenge or question us. "And, that is often: other people, the social world, and the physical world challenge us in many ways, and we have to act. We have to make judgments about what is going on, make decisions and implement them, and do this ourselves. If we are insecure in our sense of our own values, motives, and capacities, we cannot think and act effectively" (106). With Govier's description of self-trust in mind, we can understand how the self-confidence I have discussed is integral to self-trust: to doubt oneself is to question one's competence. Self-doubt, whether through doubting one's capacities or one's resolution to act, entails that one does not trust oneself to act.

Carolyn McLeod (2002) and Karen Jones (1996) argue that self-trust is an attitude toward one's motives for action; recognizing the risk of self-sabotage, self-trusting people are nevertheless optimistic about their own motives. This point is worth expanding. Self-trust varies in degree according to context: we may be confident that we are competent in certain areas, but doubt our competence in others. The self-confidence produced through self-defense training produces self-trust—one trusts that one's emotional, attitudinal, and physical responses will come together to enable one to defend oneself when required. This self-confidence arguably supports an optimism, not just about one's motives or ability to act, but about how one will act if challenged by others. Thus we can see close links between self-trust and self-confidence and how self-defense training fosters both. Since both Jones and McLeod are concerned to *contrast* self-trust to self-confidence, each misses this importance of self-confidence to self-trust.

Govier's account provides further links between self-trust and self-esteem. She draws a picture of the self-esteem essential to self-trust as consisting of basic self-acceptance, a noncomparative, internally held view that one is fundamentally a worthy and adequate person (Govier 1993, 113). Autonomous persons have the sort of basal self-esteem that affords them a resiliency of the self against the claims of others, a resiliency that is evident in those who trust themselves. Similarly, Govier explains that self-esteem is essential to the autonomy that is often revealed in one's self-trust: "Should one be in a context in which others ignore or insult one, treat one as inadequate, incompetent, or unworthy, strong trust in oneself will be a major source for resistance and emergence. We allude to such self-trust when we speak of 'inner strength' and 'inner emergence'" (114). This inner strength seems to be present in those possessing autonomy competencies of resistance and resolve; indeed, the willingness to resist and the resolve to act may just *be* this inner strength. Through cultivating self-trust, self-defense training fosters the self-esteem and self-respect essential to the autonomy competencies of resistance and resolve. Resiliency on Govier's account appears to be a resiliency of the self to psychological threats such as insults or offences to one's standing in the moral community. But, as we saw earlier, autonomy may be undermined in concrete, bodily encoded ways associated with oppressive ideals of femininity. Women thus need to develop their capacities to resist and resolve to act both despite and *because of* these bodily encoded limits to autonomy.

Finally, Govier's view that self-esteem is required for autonomy can be paralleled to Paul Benson's view that self-worth is integral to autonomy. Autonomous persons regard themselves not only as able to respond to the various expectations others may have of them, but *worthy* of responding to others' expectations. Benson argues that lack of self-worth is evidenced when we do not regard ourselves as competent to answer for our conduct in light of others' expectations and demands (Benson 1994, 660). We should be careful, however, to distinguish a felt competence to answer to others from a felt obligation to do so. Self-worth includes considering oneself worthy to respond to inappropriate expectations as one deems fit. So, for example, a person confronting another with an aggressive expectation of sexual compliance deserves a rejection of that expectation. This rejection evidences self-worth, particularly if it stands alone without justification or explanation. Such rejections demonstrate trust that one's responses are appropriate.

Often women face inappropriate expectations that effectively undermine their autonomy—ideals and expectations such as passivity, servility, or docility endorsed by traditional standards of femininity like those captured in the Beauty Myth. These expectations inappropriately foster the oppression of women, particularly through encouraging women to submit to personal violence rather than to act against it.⁸ Self-defense training provides a concrete way of overcoming bodily encoded limits to freedom associated with those ideals. When women act against these ideals through self-defense training they enhance their autonomy by fostering their abilities, physical and emotional, to reject certain expectations as inappropriate and so assert their self-worth.

Bodily intactness and wholeness, what we might call *bodily integrity,* is an essential component of protecting and defending self-worth.⁹ Those who live under oppression are familiar with the ease with which an individual may override another's bodily integrity through acts of personal violence aimed at dominating the other. Cultivating the ability to protect oneself indicates one's resolve to uphold one's commitments in the face of the threat of personal violence that accompanies women's oppression. *Personal* violence against women is not, however, simply a *personal* matter; it is deeply woven into systems of oppression operating in society. Self-defense training is not a means of changing those oppressive systems but of changing women's possibility for autonomy as persons living under those systems. Until those systems are eliminated, self-defense training provides a concrete means of protecting and fostering women's autonomy under threat of personal violence.

Self-defense training is, of course, not the only means of increasing resistance and resolve in contexts of oppression. Physical strength or athletic training provide sources of physically countering or resisting others, while intellectual skills such as reasoning, argumentation, and persuasion provide other sources of resistance and resolve.¹⁰ So too, emotions such as courage, trust, or anger may each supply key bases for the resistance and resolve essential to autonomy.¹¹ Yet self-defense training differs from these other avenues of autonomy development. Self-defense training introduces an important element in virtue of learning to defend one's self from possible harm. This training implicitly develops the attitude that what one is defending is *worth* defending. Thus, undertaking this training expresses one's value of oneself, seen in its development of self-worth, self-trust, self-esteem, and self-respect.

---

8. Another way is through encouraging women not to see personal violence as personal violence but to redescribe it in seemingly innocuous ways: sexual assaults can be said to be "sexual advances," for instance.

9. I say more about the relation of self-defense to the notion of integrity in my paper "Protecting One's Commitments: Emotion, Integrity, and Self-Defence" (in progress).

10. Thanks to Carolyn McLeod for pointing out the relevance of these skills.

11. Sometimes resistance and resolve are required to develop those emotional skills. Learning to trust one's emotional responses or recovering one's ability to become angry may call for one to resist others' interpretations of one's emotions or to resolve to separate oneself from dominant groups (Burrow 2005).

5. AUTONOMY UNDER THREAT OF PERSONAL VIOLENCE

In this section, I consider four different responses to my view that self-defense skills provide an important resource for furthering autonomy for women as a group under threat of personal violence. First, one might object to the whole idea of learning self-defense with the claim that it takes less time and effort to learn how to use a gun, which is perhaps an even better form of defending oneself. Aside from legal or moral considerations against gun ownership, I see two practical reasons to reject that view of self-defense. The first is that the attacker may use that weapon against the defender. The second reason is that if the weapon is taken away, and if it is the only way one has to defend oneself, the defender is left without any defense. Of course, one could learn supporting skills of self-defense training to prevent both of the above possibilities of harm. But given the potential for further harm by carrying a weapon, it is in one's best interest to learn traditional self-defense instead.[12]

Second, self-defense training might only seem to work as a means of enhancing autonomy for those with the ability to undertake that training. A corollary of considering autonomy as a function of both bodily and psychological competencies is that it may appear to advantage those with developed abilities in both areas and thus support an implicit ableism. However, this response fails to appreciate the fact that the skills of self-defense are inherently adaptive to one's constitution as a part of being effective responses. Effective self-defense training develops an awareness of one's own best proficiencies. Some persons best defend themselves with their feet, others with their elbows, legs, knees, or hands, while others simply evade attacks. Those who are incapable of moving their bodies either directly or indirectly will be unable to develop physical skills of self-defense, just as those who are incapable of fairly complex cognition and judgment will be unable to develop the attitudinal and emotional skills required to react in a controlled and deliberate manner. Thus, while some might excel at developing an array of varying self-defense skills, others may possess little or no ability to do so.

The implication that those who are unable to acquire self-defense skills thereby necessarily possess a weakened autonomy is indeed ableist, but it is not entailed by my argument. I have not argued that *only* the skill of self-defense furthers autonomy. I have aimed to establish the narrower claim that acquiring

---

12. Martial arts training may, of course, include weapons training. However, martial arts weapons training only introduces the same two vulnerabilities outlined above if the practitioner does not also possess the ability to defend herself with empty hands.

self-defense skills is a valuable means of increasing one's degree of autonomy. Disability activists concerned about the implications of viewing self-defense as a means to autonomy would do well to consider the distressingly high rates at which women with disabilities experience personal violence. In Canada, 39 percent of women reported that they were sexually assaulted at least once in their lives, while 83 percent of women with disabilities made a similar report (AVAW 2002; VAWD 2004). Self-defense training for women with disabilities, far from undermining their autonomy, has the potential of benefitting those who need it the most.

Third, promoting self-defense skills as a means of furthering women's autonomy may seem elitist.[13] While many martial arts and self-defense groups are nonprofit organizations, some do operate for profit. The worry is that training might be available only for the privileged few who can afford the time and money to engage in regular self-defense training. To prevent such inequality, self-defense training could be offered as part of a regular school curriculum. I am not the first to consider such an idea. As early as 1904, Tsuyoshi Chitose (2000) introduced martial arts training as part of the school curriculum in Japan with the aim of instilling attitudes of respect between persons in general and with a focus on practical self-defense for girls. In contemporary societies, teaching self-defense to girls in school will need careful consideration of the political structure of its implementation. As a rule, the threat of violence against girls and women varies depending on factors such as race, ability, sexual orientation, age, and cultural, educational, and economic status (Savary 1994; McIvor and Nahanee 1998; Jiwani 2000). If teaching self-defense does not address the needs of women and girls facing intersecting systems of oppression that support a culture of violence, then it will not meet the needs of all equally well. Relatedly, like teachers in general, instructors of self-defense must be aware of teaching practices that implicitly endorse biases, because children, in particular, may easily internalize oppressive norms and values. How self-defense will be taught thus requires careful attention to ensure that limitations to autonomy are not implicitly endorsed as part of the training.

If teaching self-defense to girls and young women were systematic, then it would not be merely a personal solution but instead would constitute a political move challenging oppressive patriarchal systems.[14] So, widespread self-defense

13. Thanks to Susan Sherwin for stimulating exchanges concerning this worry.
14. My suggestion that self-defense classes can be offered in the public school system to obviate equality imbalances has since been suggested to me by audience members at Dalhousie University and also appears in Meyers (2004a).

training promises to weaken the social structures supporting violence against women. Of course, overturning the valorization of aggressive male stereotypes and the glamorization of male dominance over women might also undermine the prevalence of violence toward women. But until that happens, girls could be raised to subvert the system in one concretely attainable way, through learning self-defense. Some might object here that introducing self-defense training in schools could increase school violence, already a serious problem.

This concern about school violence is a special case of a more general concern, which brings us to the fourth response. It might seem that self-defense encourages aggression in the individual, which has negative implications for the self and for society in general. It is a common feature of self-defense training that students are encouraged to get angry, to yell, and to attack other persons. So we might think that encouraging a system of self-defense broadly promotes aggressive attitudes, thereby supporting a culture of violence or aggression.[15] While self-defense training may *begin* with emotions and attitudes such as anger and aggression, this is not the aim or ideal of traditional self-defense training. Initially, becoming angry or aggressive is a key point of training, particularly for women who have internalized feminine ideals of passivity and acquiescence. Getting angry, yelling, grabbing physical space around oneself, or otherwise being physically assertive are all instances of engagement with the world that girls and women have been socialized to avoid. Their bodies are unaccustomed to such actions. It is difficult to disrupt typical patterns of behavior, but in the case of self-defense training it is a requirement.[16] Women who are adept at commanding their bodies to act in physically assertive ways and who have also developed the self-confidence to avoid conflict have attained a skill that is both central to self-defense training and inherently paradoxical. The end of self-defense training is paradoxical, for it aims to produce skilled persons capable of self-defense so that they have no need of using self-defense: its ideal is the path of nonviolence. While bell hooks (1989) is right to say that learning to use

---

15. Angry or aggressive attitudes can actually undermine the execution of self-defense techniques because strong emotional responses such as these are likely to impede the judgment and flexibility of responses required for effective self-defense. Here the aim is not to produce passionless persons, but to cultivate an ability to calm oneself in pressing moments of danger so as to allow self-defense techniques to be the most effective at the time they are needed the most.

16. Initially overcoming restrictive bodily behaviors must be within the command of students of self-defense if they are to progress. Imaginative practices of envisioning dangerous or discomforting situations aids this endeavor, because imagining one's best responses in such situations increases one's actual ability to react appropriately in self-defense. Such effects of imaginative training on physical performance are commonly understood as key elements of athletic training, both by sport psychologists and athletes. For an overview of the literature, see Grouios (1992).

physical force is a way to remove the terror and dread of violence, it is also a greater source of pride that one is capable of using physical force but does *not* feel a need or desire to use it.

6. SECURITY AND SUBVERSIVENESS

I have aimed to show how the emotional, attitudinal, and physical competencies developed through self-defense training foster autonomy through promoting two required autonomy competencies, resistance and resolve. Self-defense training provides a concrete avenue for women to lift bodily encoded limits to autonomy: it frees women from typically encoded restrictions in posture, movement, or reactions; and it encourages women to claim their rightful physical presence and to defend it as reasonable. The degree to which one is confident in one's ability to defend oneself is closely related to increased autonomy. One cannot freely choose to draw boundaries on one's interactions with others if one does not consider it safe to leave, to disagree, or to otherwise reject others' demands of oneself. Learning self-defense supplies a certain degree of self-confidence, confidence in one's competency to protect oneself against personal violence in threatening situations. Self-defense training is, in effect, a socially subversive act. Being able to take a stand before others while living under social pressure to be passive and accepting—to possess self-confidence rather than to be dispirited or dissuaded by the possibility of personal violence—serves to exemplify how autonomy may thrive in spite of oppressive circumstances.

Self-defense training is not a panacea for the problem of violence against women and girls. It may ultimately do nothing to prevent the prevalence of attempted personal violence. But neither is it just a stopgap measure until the culture of violence against women is overthrown. Self-defense training provides a theoretically and practically significant opportunity for developing women's autonomy. Feminist theories of autonomy have shown us that autonomy is best understood in terms of degrees, proceeding according to the sorts of psychological competencies one possesses. My account shows how bodily and psychological competencies may work *together* to promote autonomy. Self-defense training produces self-confidence that fosters self-trust that both one's psychological and bodily competencies will come together to act as needed. Self-trust here widens one's possibilities for action in virtue of promoting associated attitudes of self-worth, self-esteem, and self-respect that are essential to autonomy. The interrelationship between psychological capacities and bodily capacities is essential to recognize in a relational account of autonomy because its aim is to show that autonomy is not merely a function of one's capacity to choose, it is also a function of one's ability to form and exercise choices within contexts that often constrain choice and action. A culture of violence against women introduces constraints to autonomy that self-defense training is well suited to overcome through developing closely linked bodily and psychological capacities significant to the formation and exercise of choice.

REFERENCES

Amnesty International. 2006. *Amnesty International Report 2006: The State of the World's Human Rights.* London: Amnesty International Publications.
AVAW. 2002. *Assessing Violence Against Women: A Statistical Profile.* Federal-Provincial-Territorial Ministers Responsible for the Status of Women. http://www.swc-cfc.gc.ca/pubs/0662331664/200212_0662331664_e.pdf (accessed October 28, 2008).
Baier, Annette. 1985. Cartesian Persons. In *Postures of the Mind: Essays on Mind and Morals,* 74–92. Minneapolis: University of Minnesota Press.
Bart, Pauline. 1985. *Stopping Rape: Successful Survival Strategies.* New York: Pergamon Press.
Bartky, Sandra Lee. 1990. *Femininity and Domination.* New York: Routledge.
Benson, Paul. 1994. Free Agency and Self-Worth. *Journal of Philosophy* 91(12): 650–68.
Brison, Susan. 1999. The Uses of Narrative in the Aftermath of Violence. In *On Feminist Ethics and Politics,* ed. C. Card, 200–225. Lawrence: University Press of Kansas.
Burrow, Sylvia. 2005. The Political Structure of Emotion: From Dismissal to Dialogue. *Hypatia: A Journal of Feminist Philosophy* 20(4): 27–43.
Button, E. J., E. J. S. Sonuga-Barke, J. Davies, and M. Thompson. 1996. A Prospective Study of Self-Esteem in the Prediction of Eating Problems in Adolescent Schoolgirls. *British Journal of Clinical Psychology* 35:193–203.
Castillo, Richard. 1996. Culture and Clinical Reality. In *Culture and Mental Illness: A Client-Centered Approach,* 25–38. Pacific Grove, Calif.: Brooks/Cole.
Chitose, Tsuyoshi. 2000. *Kempo Karate-do: Universal Art of Self-Defense.* Trans. C. Johnston. Toronto: Shindokan International.
Code, Lorraine. 1991. *What Can She Know?* Ithaca: Cornell University Press.
Frankfurt, Harry. 1971. Freedom of the Will and the Concept of a Person. *Journal of Philosophy* 68(1): 5–20.
Frye, Marilyn. 1983. *The Politics of Reality: Essays in Feminist Theory.* Trumansburg, N.Y.: Crossing Press.
Govier, Trudy. 1993. Self-Trust, Autonomy, and Self-Esteem. *Hypatia: A Journal of Feminist Philosophy* 8(1): 99–120.
Grouios, George. 1992. Mental Practice: A Review. *Journal of Sport Behavior* 15(1): 42–59.
hooks, bell. 1989. *Talking Back: Thinking Feminist, Thinking Black.* Toronto: Between the Lines.

Jiwani, Yasmin. 2000. The 1999 General Social Survey on Spousal Violence: An Analysis. *Canadian Woman Studies* 20(3): 38.
Jones, Karen. 1996. Trust as an Affective Attitude. *Ethics* 107:4–25.
McIvor, S. D., and F. T. Nahanee. 1998. Aboriginal Women: Invisible Victims of Violence. In *Unsettling Truths: Battered Women, Policy, Politics, and Contemporary Research in Canada*, ed. Kevin D. Bonnycastle and George S. Rigakos, 63–69. Vancouver: Collective Press.
McLeod, Carolyn. 2002. *Self-Trust and Reproductive Autonomy*. Cambridge: MIT Press.
Meyers, Diana. 1987. Personal Autonomy and the Paradox of Feminine Socialization. *Journal of Philosophy* 84(11): 619–28.
———. 1989. *Self, Society, and Personal Choice*. New York: Columbia University Press.
———. 2004a. *Being Yourself: Essays on Identity, Action, and Social Life*. Lanham, Md.: Rowman and Littlefield.
———. 2004b. Feminist Perspectives on the Self. *The Stanford Encyclopedia of Philosophy*, ed. Edward N. Zalta. http://plato.stanford.edu/entries/feminism-self/ (accessed February 2004).
———. 2005. Decentralizing Autonomy: Five Faces of Selfhood. In *Autonomy and the Challenges to Liberalism: New Essays*, ed. John Christman and Joel Anderson, 27–55. Cambridge: Cambridge University Press.
Penn, M., and R. Nardos. 2003. *Overcoming Violence Against Women and Girls*. Lanham, Md.: Rowman and Littlefield.
Savary, R. 1994. When Racism Meets Sexism: Violence Against Immigrant and Visible Minority Women. *Vis-à-vis: A National Newsletter on Family Violence*, 12(1): 1–13.
Sparks, C. H., and Bat-Ami Bar On. 1985. A Social Change Approach to the Prevention of Sexual Violence Against Women. *Work in Progress*. Ser. 83-08. Wellesley, Mass.: Wellesley College, Stone Center for Developmental Services and Studies.
VAWD. 2004. Violence Against Women with Disabilities. *National Clearinghouse on Family Violence*, Government of Canada. http://www.phac-aspc.gc.ca/ncfv-cnivf/familyviolence/pdfs/2005femdisabl_e.pdf (accessed October 28, 2008).
Whitbeck, Caroline. 1983. Feminist Ontology: A Different Reality. In *Beyond Domination*, ed. Carol Gould, 64–88. Totowa, N.J.: Rowman and Allenheld.
Wolf, Naomi. 1991. *The Beauty Myth*. New York: Random House.
Wolf, Susan. 1993. The Real Self View. In *Perspectives on Moral Responsibility*, ed. J. Fischer and M. Ravizza, 151–69. Ithaca: Cornell University Press.
Young, Iris Marion. 2005. *On Female Body Experience: Throwing Like a Girl and Other Essays*. Bloomington: Indiana University Press.

PART TWO

EMBODIED RELATIONS, POLITICAL CONTEXTS

SEVEN

RELATIONAL EXISTENCE AND TERMINATION OF LIVES:
WHEN EMBODIMENT PRECLUDES AGENCY

Susan Sherwin

1. INTRODUCTION

Efforts to reach consensus regarding morally acceptable policies governing the deliberate termination of human lives are at a stalemate in North America. The law clearly permits competent agents to refuse life-sustaining treatment—even to commit suicide if they choose (provided they can do so without the assistance of others). Matters are far less settled, however, when dealing with humans who cannot choose either life or death because their state of embodiment is so restricted that agency (understood as the ability to engage in purposeful action) is not possible. I have in mind specifically cases where the human brain is either insufficiently formed or so severely damaged that neocortical function is absent, precluding agency on the part of the beings in question. Humans in this category include fetuses (broadly construed to include embryos and pre-embryos) and patients such as Theresa (Terri) Schiavo who have been diagnosed as being in irreversible coma or persistent vegetative state (PVS).[1]

There are some areas of agreement regarding the status of humans in these categories. Virtually all parties agree that the embodied state of humans in these categories prohibits (or at least severely restricts) their capacity for intentional actions (agency);[2] all also agree that the absence of neocortical function

---

1. For an overview of the medical and judicial details of Terri Schiavo's case, see Gostin (2005) or Wolfson (2005).

2. There are, of course, many different interpretations of agency. For the purpose of this argument, I am going with the common-sense view that agency involves deliberate action. This view

---

I am grateful to members of the Dalhousie University philosophy department who heard an early version of this essay and provided helpful feedback. I am especially indebted to Françoise Baylis and Richmond Campbell, who took the time to provide very detailed suggestions on the essay.

renders these beings unusually dependent on others for their continued existence and, therefore, uniquely vulnerable. There is serious disagreement, however, concerning the appropriateness of different policy options aimed at ensuring their continued biological life. No one seriously proposes mandatory termination (though some authors object to the costs of maintaining the lives of those in PVS). The debate, of course, is whether the state should require maintenance of the lives of these beings or permit intentional termination by others. Intense political battles rage over the policy decision as to who, if anyone, has the right to initiate the termination of the life of a human who is incapable of agency.

I shall argue that the highly charged political debates regarding proper public policy concerning the question of termination of the lives of fetuses and PVS patients rest on a problematic understanding of personhood. I seek to reframe the moral conversation by being more attentive to relational dimensions of key terms. I shall propose approaching the policy questions through reflection on the social and moral significance of the particular sorts of needs and constraints generated by the embodied status of the humans in question. I will argue for two points. First, I urge participants in the debates to rethink their starting point(s) on these matters; specifically, I propose a shift in their understanding of the nature of personhood, moving from a traditional abstract conception to one that explicitly embraces the embodied, relational reality of persons. Secondly, I explore the question of what obligations moral agents have toward fetuses and PVS patients. Before building my argument for these claims, I look briefly at how and why the major debates have become stalled. This is followed by an explanation of my alternative proposals for relational personhood and relational morality; these proposals form the basis for a relational approach to policy regarding termination of life for humans incapable of agency.

2. THE CURRENT DEBATES

Although I focus on the similarities between the debates regarding public policies in the realm of abortion and termination of the lives of PVS patients, it is important to acknowledge that there are some important differences in the embodied status of these two spheres. In particular, in the abortion debate,

---

figures largely in discussions in law, political theory, action theory, moral theory, and metaphysics. My own view is spelled out more fully in Sherwin (1998).

while fetuses currently lack agency, in most cases those that survive will develop sufficiently to acquire it and to become full members of the community. Because of its future prospects, it is widely presumed that the fetus "wants" to be born—to live. (The purported desire is metaphorical, since it is commonly recognized that fetuses lack sufficient cognitive capacity and experience to actually form abstract desires.) In the case of PVS patients, there is no reasonable hope of regaining agency, and it is common (though by no means universal) to believe that the quality of these patients' lives has deteriorated so badly that if they could form preferences, they would choose death over continued existence in their current state. Indeed, the purported desire commonly attributed to them is the desire to die. Hence, where the abortion debate focuses on whether fetuses have a right to life, many ask whether PVS patients have a right to die. But we cannot lose sight of the fact that both kinds of beings involve bodies with insufficient neocortical capacity to permit agency, and there are no existing actual preferences for us to respect.

Another important difference between the two kinds of cases is that with fetuses, there is always a single individual (the pregnant woman) who has the unique ability to maintain the life in question and who is, therefore, the direct target of restrictive policies about abortion. For each PVS patient, in contrast, many people could, in theory, be responsible for maintaining or terminating that life. Hence, policies prohibiting his or her termination do not necessarily entail obligations on any specific individual.

Despite the very significant differences involving the moral and policy decisions with respect to terminating the lives of fetuses and of PVS patients, there is an important similarity between the most common arguments in these two domains. In each case, most people begin by assuming that what is centrally at issue is the morality of one human deliberately ending the life of another. Whether the discussion is focused on abortion or termination of biological life for those in irreversible coma, the public debate (like the debate within much of the bioethics literature) moves quickly to discussion of what sort of moral status to attach to human lives of either sort—that is, whether or not such beings should be treated as persons with a right to life that would prohibit deliberately killing them.

In the case of abortion, conservatives generally bring forward images of near full-term fetuses and stress the similarities between third trimester fetuses and newborns, demanding that we consider all abortions as a form of "baby-killing." When debating the morality of ending life-prolonging treatments for PVS patients, they offer up cases of people miraculously recovering from many years of coma in order to dissuade us from "writing-off" anyone for whom treatment may seem futile.[3]

Liberals counter with descriptions of microscopic early embryos and remind us of the enormous dissimilarities between these clusters of cells and a full-term human infant.[4] In response to the reported stories of miraculous recovery of someone declared to be permanently comatose, they remind us of the much more common experience of heartache borne by people who try to act responsibly toward a beloved family member or friend in the gray zone of perpetual unconsciousness for years on end.

Moderates, being moderates, resist universal solutions and remind us of the broad spectrum of human capacity that develops over the course of gestation; they ask us to take a developmental approach to moral status rather than a stark all or nothing position. In dealing with patients who have permanently lost consciousness, they remind us that most were formerly competent persons and they may have indicated their wishes should they undergo total loss of neocortical function. Moderates urge us to respond in accordance with any available evidence regarding that individual's own prior preferences in an effort to respect their earlier history and attachments.[5]

I find it striking that despite the profound differences among these three positions, there is quite a lot of agreement as well. Conservatives share with liberals and moderates an assumption that what is needed to resolve these contentious issues once and for all is a clear understanding of the moral criteria that determine the presence (or absence) of personhood. Once we can establish these criteria, they all believe, we can agree on appropriate measures by which to judge whether or not a being satisfies the definition of personhood; at that point, presumably, science will be able to devise a reliable test that can be applied to the hard cases before us. All sides seem to believe that if we could just demonstrate that the fetus—or the PVS patient—is actually a person (or not), then we will know whether or not it is morally legitimate to terminate that being's life.[6]

---

3. Important conservative voices include Pope John Paul II (1995), John Noonan (1970), Baruch Brody (1974), and Donald Marquis (1989).

4. Important voices in the liberal camp include Michael Tooley (1983) and Mary Anne Warren (1973). Although conservatives tend to use third-trimester images, the vast majority of abortions are performed in the first trimester, and third-trimester abortions are extremely rare and normally only done for medical reasons.

5. Sumner (1981) has offered a particularly clear and influential version of the moderate position on abortion; see also McMahan (2002).

6. See Conee (1999) for a technical discussion of various attempts to resolve the abortion dilemma by settling the metaphysical question of whether or not a fetus is a person. (Conee argues that such attempts are all misguided and doomed to fail.)

And so the controversy continues. Conservatives support humanness as a necessary and sufficient condition for personhood and worry that any effort to draw a line among biological humans risks getting it seriously wrong and violating a strong moral and/or religious injunction against killing (or at least against killing "the innocent"). They believe that this equation is either simply obvious or a matter of faith; either way, it should need no further support.

Liberals and moderates, in contrast, fear that biological criteria are morally arbitrary and lead us to unjustified prejudice in favor of our own species and against all others (a position they dub "speciesism"). They seek a morally relevant set of criteria that can be defended according to an underlying moral theory. They generally specify consciousness as at least a necessary condition on the grounds that morality is chiefly concerned with some combination of avoiding hurting others, helping people to satisfy their preferences, respecting desires, meeting needs, and promoting well-being. Thus, they argue, morality must be concerned with beings that can experience hurt, have preferences, desires or needs, or have a meaningful state of well-being; all of these conditions require consciousness. For them, the question is one of logic and abstract reasoning.

The major assumption on all sides is that there is a single true answer to the question of what criteria constitute personhood, and it is the job of responsible moral agents to use their reason—or faith—to discover what that answer is and then to struggle to persuade others of the moral legitimacy of their position (and the illegitimacy of all alternatives).

As I have argued elsewhere (Sherwin 1992), each of the major positions outlined makes the same mistake in attempting to address the question of personhood. Each pursues the question in an abstract, a priori fashion—that is, in trying to imagine what it is to be a person in terms of the self-contained bodily or psychological characteristics that constitute necessary and sufficient conditions of personhood. Each assumes that whether or not an entity is a person is purely a feature of that being's biology or psychology, that it is a question about the genetic makeup of the organism or about its cognitive capacities. I contend, however, that persons are not freestanding entities. They are essentially social beings who do not, and cannot, exist in isolation. Hence, we cannot determine if a being is a person simply by looking at their biological or psychological characteristics. We need a theory of personhood that acknowledges that the embodied nature of a human being is always situated in a specific social, historical context; persons are embedded within the social environments that constitute and sustain them. In the next section I shall outline a more contextual approach to the concept of personhood.

First though, I want to note that conservatives, liberals, and moderates make a second mistake in their implicit assumption that we can develop policies regarding practices that involve deliberate termination of the lives of humans who lack agency in isolation from a larger set of moral and social conditions. In the final sections of this paper I shall explain how a relational approach to morality requires us to think not only of the claims of the beings in question but to think broadly about the meaning of assigning a right to life to humans in these (and other) circumstances. I shall then propose and defend a relational understanding of personhood and morality and show the relevance of this approach to the question of setting policy in the area of termination of such human lives.

3. RELATIONAL PERSONHOOD

Given the intractable and bitter debate over the question of whether or not fetuses are persons, it seems clear that we will not be able to reach consensus on a single set of necessary and sufficient scientifically measurable conditions for being a person. This is because personhood is not simply a descriptive label but is, primarily, a moral category—that is, its application confers significant moral status on its bearers. What has been less clear in the debate so far is that it is also a social category. Personhood is an interactive status that requires social connections with other persons. No one is a person on his or her own. All are, in a fundamental sense, relational beings in that they do not even come into existence apart from the relations that help to form them. While the physical conditions of embodiment may significantly affect the types of relationships one can participate in, they do not, in themselves, determine personhood.

We need, therefore, a theory of personhood that makes this social feature explicit. The familiar accounts we have discussed all treat persons as self-contained units. While the leading theories make room for persons to engage in social and political relationships, they treat these as a contingent (non-essential) matter of their existence once their personhood is established. Individuals are portrayed as acquiring their personhood status in a way that makes their existence as persons metaphysically prior to all social relationships and to society as a whole. Each of the traditional accounts assumes that a human simply possesses or develops the requisite biological or psychological characteristics, and, once the presence of these characteristics can be established, he or she is undoubtedly a person.

In contrast, I claim that we need an account of personhood that recognizes persons as beings with certain types of bodies and biological capacities that allow certain forms of social interaction. That is, persons are embodied beings that are formed—in essential respects—through their social relations. One's status as a person is inseparable from one's interconnectedness with other persons. While that interconnectedness is mediated through the body, it involves more than simple possession of a certain type of body. As several feminists have argued, it is the social fabric that makes personhood possible (see, e.g., Baier 1985; Code 1987; Koggel 1998). The social connections are also what make persons especially valuable.

As Annette Baier (1985) argued, we can only become persons by being treated as such by other persons, and, therefore, are always "second persons," created through social processes; we must learn from other persons how to be persons ourselves. The practices of nurturing, education, and socialization that are essential to creation of persons are mediated through the bodies of both parties. Humans who somehow survive without receiving adequate amounts of these caring practices are damaged as persons; they lack important capacities that the rest of us rely on in our interactions with them. In particular, they may lack capacities that make them effective moral and political agents, and this gap may have serious consequences for themselves and for others in their communities. The consequences of allowing humans to grow up without such socialization can be very serious for all.

It is important to be explicit about the fact that persons are moral subjects—they are our fellow citizens in the moral community; specifically, they are the sorts of beings who are moral agents, or at least can be moral agents if all goes moderately well in their lives. Creatures of other species may have particular moral traits: many species display courage, altruism, loyalty, and honesty. Individual humans may form intense bonds of affection, even love, for particular members of other species. They may also invest significant labor in training and socializing particular animals to thrive within their communities. (Here, I speak with the authority of a new puppy owner—a very labor-intensive job.) Members of other species are limited, however, in the range of moral actions they can undertake; as a result, there are definite limits to the sorts of behaviors for which we hold them morally responsible. Persons, in contrast, when developed and engaged in actions within our communities, are expected to comply with prevailing moral rules.[7]

---

7. For an extensive discussion of the moral significance of relational status of persons, see Koggel (1998).

Like liberals and moderates, I believe that the concept of personhood differs in important respects from the biological concept of being a member of the species homo sapiens. It requires something more. I differ from them, however, in my belief that the "something more" cannot be found wholly within the entity as a freestanding unit. It is not simply a particular kind of capacity that is needed, but rather a set of relations within a social structure of other persons.

At the same time, I share with conservatives a belief that biology is significant, although not for the same reasons as they adopt. I do not believe that persons have a special status because we have been created in God's image, but rather that biology has "built us" in ways that make us particularly inclined to treat other members of our species as members of our moral community, that is, to be inclined to treat them as moral persons. So, I imagine, we are biologically disposed to regard other humans as persons like ourselves; commonalities in our embodied nature are very significant in framing the social practices that generate persons.

Unfortunately, this biological (or God-given) propensity is not entirely reliable in its execution. It is all too clear that some cultures have managed to restrict the category of persons to humans that are very like their own most privileged members with regard to race, religion, language, ethnicity, able-bodied status, gender, age, tribe, or kinship group. Moreover, some human cultures are far more generous than ours: some socialize their members to be quite inclusive in their approach to personhood such that they readily welcome members of other species into the moral community. It seems that nature (or God) has not created us to have a single approach to this complex question. Nonetheless, despite the many differences as to who or what is included in the moral community, it seems that all cultures ascribe a special status to those granted the honorific moral label of "person" (or some linguistic equivalent). And, all cultures socialize their members to be cooperative, rule-governed members of their own communities; that is, all engage in the work required to create persons according to their understanding of the meaning of the term.

Let us, then, restart the debates regarding termination of life for fetuses and PVS patients by reflecting on the social (relational) nature of personhood and keeping in mind that societies create persons from the biological base of human existence through collective social practices. To identify someone as a person is to recognize her place within a moral community and to appreciate her relational connections to other members of that community who have been integral in generating that status for and with her. It is also to place moral demands on others in their relations with those designated as persons.

This move should make clear why it is so difficult to resolve the question of how to assign the label of "person": ascribing personhood involves more than determining the physical or psychological characteristics of the being in question; it also requires determining the moral understandings of the community in which that being resides. Hence, determining the personhood of fetuses and PVS patients is particularly challenging: these humans are not able to participate as moral agents (or even moral subjects, really) in our community even though they (may) meet the biological criteria of basic eligibility (species membership). Their particular forms of biological embodiment make agency impossible, particularly the aspects of agency that represent social interaction with other persons. And yet their forms of embodiment necessitate some particularly intimate types of relations with specific persons, since others must provide the necessities of their continued bodily lives. Fetuses exist within the bodies of women and are dependent on those women for nurturance; PVS patients can survive only as long as others tend to their bodily needs for nutrition, hydration, and hygiene. But these are not *social* relationships, since the limited neocortical function of the beings in question prevents any degree of reciprocal interaction.

This is not to say that these beings are wholly lacking in social status. Fetuses are often welcomed and considered family members from the earliest awareness of their existence. Patients with PVS have been full persons and have usually formed important relationships that survive their current limitations. Family members and close friends may still feel love and loyalty to them. In both cases, however, the relationships are not, at present, fully social because of the inability of one party to actively participate in an interactive way.

Clearly, these types of beings share some characteristics with prototypical persons—citizens like ourselves who are considered fully responsible moral agents: their human bodies have many of the same sorts of basic needs (nutrition, hydration, hygiene, sleep, warmth) that human persons have. Yet, they also differ in important respects: they can take no part in providing for their own needs, not even forming desires around them. They are, then, borderline cases and it is a matter of significant moral deliberation how we should respond to them. Deciding on who shall be treated as a moral subject (as a person) requires reflection on what kind of moral community we inhabit (or wish to participate in).[8]

---

8. It is important to note, here, that not all decisions about personhood are equally open to debate. Early European settlers in North America who treated aboriginals as nonpersons made a serious moral error, for aboriginal humans were clearly agents who were capable of entering

In order to decide what sorts of attitudes we should take, and what sorts of policies we should develop regarding termination of life for fetuses and PVS patients, we need now to reflect on the nature of moral theorizing. We can begin by acknowledging that morality is, first and foremost, an activity that is carried out by humans in conversation with other humans. In other words, personhood is not the only relational concept at work here. Morality itself is also a relational category, in the sense that it, too, cannot exist within a solitary individual in isolation from all others. No one can become moral on his or her own. Each of us needs others to provide us with the conceptual framework of morality—the language of rights, duties, virtues, and responsibilities—and with training in the behaviors that constitute morality. No one can act in accordance with any moral principle without learning the meaning of that principle and receiving training and opportunity to practice the requisite skills. (Even those who believe that morality is conveyed directly from God must acknowledge the importance of training people to understand and appreciate the meaning of the commandments they are to live by.) That training and interpretation are part of the relational work of morality as a social practice. It is this relational nature of morality that leads me to the next part of the paper where I will explore how a relational understanding of morality can guide our deliberations about end of life decision-making for fetuses and persons in irreversible coma.

4. RELATIONAL MORALITY

In explaining a relational approach to morality and its role in this debate, I will rely on work done by feminist theorists, especially as represented in two important books: Joan Tronto's *Moral Boundaries: A Political Argument for an Ethic of Care* (1993) and Margaret Urban Walker's *Moral Understandings: A Feminist Study in Ethics* (1998). In both books, the authors argue persuasively that ethics is inherently a social and political activity; they also argue that questions regarding the responsibility for attending to the human needs among us should be placed at the center of our moral thinking. I want to build on these two important points, so I shall first sketch out key elements of the argument in each book.

---

into moral community with the settlers. They had the social experience of interacting with other persons and the moral sensibilities to engage in cross-cultural moral conversations. Fetuses and PVS patients are much more difficult cases since their lack of the capacity for agency means that they cannot participate in any form of active social relationships with other persons.

I begin with Tronto's discussion of the role of care in ethics. Tronto defines caring "as a species activity that includes everything that we do to maintain, continue, and repair our 'world' so that we can live in it as well as possible" (Tronto 1993, 103). She identifies four distinct, but interconnected, phases of caring; with each phase, there is an associated element that must be present if caring is to be done well.

1. *Caring about* is the recognition that specific care is necessary through noting the existence of a need and a judgment that this need should be met. This phase requires a capacity for attentiveness to the needs of others; ignorance of needs is a moral failing.
2. *Taking care of* is assuming some responsibility for the identified need and determining how to respond to it; it requires the ability to assume and assign responsibility.
3. *Care giving* is the direct meeting of the identified needs and often requires physical work; it demands a level of competence in the delivery of specific care services. Of course, incompetence is not an automatic excuse from the responsibilities of care giving, but it may be an indication of the need to develop the necessary skills.
4. *Care receiving* is the mode by which the object of care is expected to respond to the care given; such responses are necessary to determine whether we have accurately identified and attended to the needs of the care receiver. Here, the focus switches from the abilities of the care provider to the capacities of the one cared for who must possess a degree of responsiveness so that we can evaluate the effectiveness of caring from her or his perspective and not simply from our own assumptions.

All four phases of care are necessary if we are to care for the needs of ourselves and others; to care well we need to maintain the corresponding elements and strive to integrate the various aspects of caring. In most cases, the work of caring is complex and requires the engagement of multiple actors and the support of the surrounding society. Good caring requires coordination across the various levels, determining who does what for whom. Clearly, care must often extend far beyond personal responsibilities and private actions. We need to situate discussions of care responsibilities within a social and political, as well as a private, context.

When we do look at the broader social and political context for care we notice that it is extraordinarily unjust. First, most societies are very uneven in terms of whose needs are attended to. This is clearly true in affluent Western nations. Some needs are so routinely attended to that we barely perceive them as needs at all. For example, our common needs for safe drinking water and food supplies are, for the most part, well addressed within modern societies (in the absence of natural disasters or severe tax cuts, at least). All Western nations provide universal education at least through high school for those without significant levels of mental or physical impairment and the necessary elements for safe and effective health care (e.g., trained professionals, certified hospitals, medical research). For those who have relatively secure levels of income, and are reasonably healthy and able bodied, many of our basic needs are so easily met that it is possible to overlook the fact that the state must provide the basic structures that allow us to satisfy them.

Of course, for those without sufficient income, or for those with serious health or impairment issues, the story is often different. The state frequently fails to meet their distinctive needs, or if it does the quality of service is so low that it is questionable whether or not to consider this level as constituting appropriate caring. Be it access to a healthy diet, a safe place to live, transportation, adequate education, or health care, those with special needs or low income are often represented as being very demanding in wanting special services to meet their needs for things the middle class takes for granted. Insofar as our public agencies pay any attention at all to the poor, they provide for some of their needs in a grudging and incomplete way. In other words, our social and political structures are far more attentive to the needs of the privileged than to those of the disadvantaged.

Justice enters into caring at the other levels as well. The first three phases of caring involve the taking up of responsibilities by care providers, but the work and nature of their various responsibilities are unjustly distributed. By and large, the tasks of caring about (determining which needs shall be addressed) and those of taking care of (determining how to respond to identified needs) are managerial tasks. They belong to people with power and authority in society; the jobs involved are relatively well rewarded in terms of both status and income. The actual labor of caring, that is, care giving, especially for those who are dependent on others for assistance with bodily needs, is very heavily concentrated among the ranks of the disadvantaged in society. In North America, it is women, immigrants, and people of color who do most of the actual hands-on physical care giving, though in most cases they have relatively little authority in determining how the work should be carried out (i.e., taking care of). While the work of those doing care giving for those requiring personal assistance is essential to integrated caring, it has far less social prestige, and it is rewarded at much lower rates (if it is rewarded at all) than the managerial tasks of caring about and taking care of. The skills involved in care giving usually go unrecognized, and the importance of this work is frequently overlooked. In many cases, it is assumed that caregivers will provide care simply out of a sense of personal concern, a sense of identity, or instinct (e.g., mothering); often, no social resources are provided to assist with such labor.

Tronto's analysis reveals a particular difficulty when reflecting on the moral responsibilities associated with the care of humans whose embodied status involves significant needs for care but precludes agency (i.e., fetuses and PVS patients). Such beings are unable to be responsive care receivers who can help us to determine the value to them of the care they receive (the fourth element). We cannot achieve fully integrated care for those who cannot respond to the care provided.

Tronto argues for the importance of moving considerations about care into the mainstream of our ethical and political theories so that we can adopt fairer and more adequate approaches to caring. Justice requires that the burdens of providing care be more equitably distributed and rewarded and also that we ensure a fairer distribution of care receiving. Although Tronto is very persuasive in her claim that care is a political and moral ideal that can only be ethically deployed in a social context of justice, she is vague on the details of how, in practice, we can ensure that these decisions are made more fairly.

Hence, I find her work to be nicely complemented by that of Margaret Walker, who argues that we should move away from the standard model of morality as an exercise in pure reason in favor of a relational, social understanding of morality. Walker describes traditional approaches to morality as falling under a "theoretical-judicial" model; in this model, morality is conceived of "as a compact, propositionally codifiable, impersonally action-guiding code within an agent . . . [which] shrinks morality 'proper' down to a kind of purified core of purely moral knowledge" (Walker 1998, 8–9). Traditional conceptions of morality, like traditional views of personhood, treat morality as a matter of abstract reasoning and neglect the fact that these are phenomena that are deeply social in our knowledge and experience of them.

Walker provides a relational alternative model for morality, which she refers to as an "expressive-collaborative" model. It encourages us to view morality "as a socially embodied medium of mutual understanding and negotiation between people over their responsibility for things open to human care and response" (Walker 1998, 9). Through practices of communication and negotiation, people learn to understand themselves and others as bearers of particular identities and as actors in various relationships. They learn "to express their understandings through practices of responsibility in which they assign, accept, or deflect responsibilities for different things. . . . In other words, morality consists in a family of practices that show what is valued by making people accountable to each other for it" (Walker 1998, 9–10). Walker stresses the fact that morality is essentially and fundamentally interpersonal; it is a set of practices that occur between or among people.

Walker highlights two important features of morality: the first is its fundamental relational character—it is a collaborative practice, through and through. Thus, to investigate difficult questions in morality, we need to look beyond personal reason or private faith, and engage in conversation and negotiation with others who share our moral community. Secondly, Walker joins Tronto in stressing the fact that morality is principally concerned with determining how to assign and accept (or deflect) responsibilities for what we value. Its focus is about determining who is responsible for what within our world and for making us accountable to one another for fulfilling our responsibilities. In her words, morality is a set of "practices of responsibility that implement commonly shared understandings about who gets to do what to whom and who is supposed to do what for whom" (Walker 1998, 16).

The pressing question is how we are to determine fair mechanisms for engaging in these practices of assigning responsibility for care. As Tronto has reminded us, our own North American society has not been very successful at producing a just distribution of caring labor. Walker is well aware of this problem and most of her book is spent exploring some of the conditions that distort the distribution of responsibilities within a society, with particular attention to the effects of systematic patterns of oppression. A common obstacle is the practice of excluding important segments of society from conversations about who and what is to be cared for. According to Walker, morality is about engaging with integrity in a process that genuinely seeks to find fair solutions to the questions of how we determine responsibilities for caring for what we find valuable. At a minimum, it is essential to engage all parties to caring practices in the negotiations about assigning of responsibilities. One set of people cannot simply take it upon themselves to determine that there is a need to be met (caring about, in Tronto's language), decide that someone else should do that caring work (taking care of), and exclude both the caregivers and the care receivers from the conversation. Determining responsibilities requires the active engagement of all those who are made responsible for something in the negotiations that represent societal moral deliberations.

5. A RELATIONAL APPROACH TO POLICY REGARDING TERMINATION OF LIFE FOR FETUSES AND PVS PATIENTS

I am finally ready to explain my proposal regarding a morally appropriate approach to setting policy dealing with the deliberate termination of life for fetuses and PVS patients. The first step is to acknowledge that there exists a significant diversity of views regarding the moral status of these types of humans. The moral question of whether such humans should be treated as persons with a right to life that would prohibit deliberate efforts to terminate their lives remains unresolved and it is likely to continue to be contested even within a relational framework. It is not the only moral question before us, however. There is a related—though distinct—question as to what our public policy should be regarding efforts to maintain or terminate the lives of these types of humans. For both questions, we need to engage in conversation with our fellow members of the moral community, even though these conversations are unlikely to achieve consensus. We can, with difficulty, continue to tolerate disagreements on the first question. In contrast, we must determine a way of moving forward on the public policy question; hence, it is the more urgent of the two. To address it, we need to engage in the kinds of deliberative societal discussions that Tronto and Walker propose.

In order to determine what policy to adopt regarding abortion and possible termination for some PVS patients, we must first acknowledge that the beings in question have the same bodily life-support needs as all other humans, though they are utterly dependent on others for the care required to maintain their lives. Hence, our discussions must address how we, as a society, plan to provide the needed care for the very dependent human beings in question. The relational theories we have examined make clear that we can only approach this question through serious public conversations.[9] Because these types of humans lack all capacity for moral conversation or deliberation, they cannot themselves be party to these conversations, but all others who are capable of moral reflection and communication and who are likely to be affected by the

---

9. Lindemann (2005) refers to the practice necessary if we decide to treat such marginal humans as persons as *holding* them in personhood.

outcome of the discussions must be included in our working out of moral responsibilities. If we determine that the lives of fetuses and PVS patients are to be preserved, someone must assume the responsibility for meeting the physical needs of each one; this responsibility cannot simply be assigned without the active involvement of those who will be expected to take up key aspects of that responsibility.

To be sure, there are often ready volunteers for this care-giving work. Many people feel strongly connected to particular humans in these conditions. Many pregnant women experience pregnancy as a relational state with the fetus and they interpret fetal movements as clear signs of care receiving (e.g., "the baby likes it when I dance" or "the baby hates it when I eat spicy food"). Family members may feel attached to a PVS patient and be quite willing to provide the care giving needed to sustain that patient's life. In such cases, there is no plausible case for requiring the persons who choose to provide for the needs of the humans in question to agree to termination. When the caregiver is also the one who decides if and how care is to be given, there is no place for a social policy that would prevent such activity, although there may well be need for economic and social policies that will facilitate the necessary practices.

The difficulty at the heart of current controversies about allowing individuals to terminate the lives of fetuses or of family members in PVS is different, however. It concerns the fact that not all of those called upon to be caregivers agree that sustaining the life in question is appropriate. The willingness of some individuals to be caregivers for their own fetuses or loved ones in PVS cannot serve as a basis for compelling others to assume a comparable relationship to their fetuses or family members. Without reciprocity in a relationship, there is room for the person whose own embodied state does constitute her as a moral agent to determine what relational status she assigns to the human who is dependent on her for its ongoing needs (Sherwin 1992).

From Tronto and Walker, we can see that in the case of abortion, it is absolutely essential to engage the cooperation of the pregnant woman in each case, since it is only through her nurturance and protection that the fetus has a chance of survival. Others, no matter how keen to protect the life of a particular fetus, or of all fetuses, are simply not in a position to maintain these lives without the cooperation of the women contemplating termination. Those who are eager to influence women's deliberations would do well to try to determine each woman's reasons for considering termination and see if there is some way they can be of assistance. (For example, if she believes she cannot afford to raise a[nother] child, they can try to ensure financial support or social services that would relieve the economic pressures facing her; if she will be penalized at her job or her educational institution for carrying the pregnancy to term, they might seek to change punitive policies that treat pregnancy as a form of work avoidance.)

Similarly, as a minimum condition for developing policies that would enhance families' ability to choose to maintain the lives of loved ones in irreversible coma we should ensure that families are not being expected to assume an unbearable financial or emotional burden for continued support. Our decision, as a society, should not be whether or not to insist on keeping humans in these dire straits biologically alive as long as possible; rather, it should be about how we are going to ensure a fair distribution of the burdens of providing the significant care their continued existence involves.

But before we get too busy trying to negotiate the care of these humans at the margins of personhood, we need to set the rest of our moral house in order. We need to talk very seriously about how we are to share the responsibilities for meeting the needs of the people among us whose embodied status does permit them to exercise agency and who are, unquestionably, moral persons. We really do need to do a better job of providing for the needs of those who can be effective care receivers and who are now telling us, in very clear terms, that society is not adequately responding to their needs. At present, in virtually all developed nations, we are failing to care properly for very large sections of our population, especially those who occupy the socioeconomic category of "the poor." In most communities there are inadequate facilities for meeting the basic needs of many persons for shelter, nutrition, safety, education, and health and health care.

In other words, the question of whether or not a human's embodied status is compatible with agency makes a significant moral difference in the social policies we should put in place regarding attending to their bodily needs. Any conversation about treating fetuses and PVS patients (i.e., humans incapable of agency) as persons with a right to life must be situated within a moral framework that takes seriously the need to engage in what Walker referred to as "practices of responsibility that implement commonly shared understandings about . . . who is supposed to do what for whom" (Walker 1998, 16). We cannot insist that others undertake the burdens of keeping alive those who lack all agency (fetuses and humans in PVS) before we establish just practices of caring for all humans who have, at least, the capacity to be active care receivers. There are, simply, no grounds for privileging the needs of the not yet born and the no longer conscious over those who are, without question, fellow members of our moral community. Surely, each moral community needs to find ways of meeting the needs of all persons within their midst before it requires anyone to tend to the bodily needs of those wholly lacking in the criteria for agency.

REFERENCES

Baier, Annette. 1985. *Postures of the Mind: Essays on Mind and Morals*. Minneapolis: University of Minnesota Press.
Brody, Baruch. 1974. On the Humanity of the Fetus. In *Abortion: Pro and Con*, ed. Robert L. Perkins, 35–46. Cambridge, Mass.: Schenkman.
Code, Lorraine. 1987. Second Persons. In *Science, Morality and Feminist Theory*, ed. Marsha Hanen and Kai Nielsen, 357–82. Calgary: University of Calgary Press.
Conee, Earl. 1999. Metaphysics and the Morality of Abortion. *Mind: A Quarterly Review of Philosophy* 108(432): 619–46.
Gostin, Lawrence O. 2005. Ethics, the Constitution, and the Dying Process: The Case of Theresa Marie Schiavo. *Journal of the American Medical Association* 293(19): 2403–7.
John Paul II. 1995. The Unspeakable Crime of Abortion. March 25. *Evangelium Vitae*. Città del Vaticano: Libreria Editrice Vaticana.
Koggel, Christine M. 1998. *Perspectives on Equality: Constructing a Relational Theory*. Lanham, Md.: Rowman and Littlefield.
Lindemann, Hilde. 2005. On the Mend: Alzheimer's and Family Caregiving. *The Journal of Clinical Ethics* 16(4): 314–20.
Marquis, Donald B. 1989. Why Abortion Is Immoral. *Journal of Philosophy* 86(4): 183–202.
McMahan, Jeff. 2002. *The Ethics of Killing: Problems at the Margins of Life*. Oxford: Oxford University Press.
Noonan, John T., Jr. 1970. An Almost Absolute Value in History. In *The Morality of Abortion: Legal and Historical Perspectives*, ed. John T. Noonan Jr., 51–59. Cambridge: Harvard University Press.
Sherwin, Susan. 1992. *No Longer Patient: Feminist Ethics and Health Care*. Philadelphia: Temple University Press.
———. 1998. A Relational Approach to Autonomy in Health Care. In *The Politics of Women's Health: Exploring Agency and Autonomy*, ed. Feminist Health Care Ethics Research Network, coord. Susan Sherwin, 19–47. Philadelphia: Temple University Press.
Sumner, L. W. 1981. *Abortion and Moral Theory*. Princeton: Princeton University Press.
Tooley, Michael. 1983. *Abortion and Infanticide*. New York: Oxford University Press.
Tronto, Joan. 1993. *Moral Boundaries: A Political Argument for an Ethic of Care*. New York: Routledge.

Walker, Margaret Urban. 1998. *Moral Understandings: A Feminist Study in Ethics.* New York: Routledge.
Warren, Mary Anne. 1973. On the Moral and Legal Status of Abortion. *The Monist* 57(1): 43–61.
Wolfson, Jay. 2005. Erring on the Side of Theresa Schiavo: Reflections of the Special Guardian ad Litem. *Hastings Center Report* 35(3): 16–19.

EIGHT

A BODY NO LONGER OF ONE'S OWN

Monique Lanoix

1. INTRODUCTION

Many of the significant changes that are taking place in the area of health care services in North America are attributable, at least in part, to the growing numbers of seniors. It is anticipated that there will be increased health care costs and a greater demand for care giving, specifically, for care activities that are directed at helping individuals who need assistance to accomplish the activities of daily living (ADLs). Media reporting is directed at this particular demographic shift, though other populations are certainly implicated in the need for ADLs. As medical advances become more sophisticated, individuals who earlier would have died because of grave congenital problems or severe injuries are increasingly able to survive.[1] These individuals may often have ADL care needs even though they are not frail elders.

The care practices that support ADLs include, but are not limited to, activities relating to personal hygiene, household chores, and the preparation of meals. Although they are obviously crucial for the health of the care receiver, these practices are not considered medical and indeed can be performed by a friend or family member. Significantly, however, paid workers increasingly

---

1. The American war in Iraq illustrates this: the conflict has had unprecedented consequences in terms of long-term injuries and disabilities among the soldiers and the civilian population (Glasser 2005).

I thank the editors for their patience and suggestions; Letitia Meynell was most generous with her time, and her comments were of invaluable help in revising the manuscript. A version of this paper was presented at the Canadian Society for Bioethics, and I benefited from their questions and contributions. This research was funded by a fellowship in the Strategic Training Grant in Ethics of Health Care Research and Policy from the Canadian Institutes of Health Research.

perform this type of care labor. The shift of care labor from the private to the public realm is often thought to have predominantly economic consequences; however, it also has an important bearing on how care giving is conceptualized, on how it is practiced, and on how individuals requiring assistance are portrayed in contemporary western societies.

For the above reasons, the spotlight on the needs of an aging population presents a timely opportunity for a critical analysis of care giving and the roles played by subjects in the care relation. By examining the paid care-giving practices that are specifically aimed at helping adult individuals carry out the ADLs, I hope to elucidate the effects of an institutional or public framework on the activities of care.[2] Sociological studies have examined the implications of such waged labor, and feminist analyses of care have argued for policies that are attentive to the realities of care giving, both paid and unpaid.[3] Nevertheless, further theoretical work on the consequences of care giving's entrance into the market is called for, especially since this labor is in greater demand.[4]

In this paper, I explore the effects of ADL care-giving practices on the person requiring assistance. Although my title implies ownership, it is rather meant to stress how a person's relationship to her own body can be undone to the point where she might feel it is no longer her body. My concern is for the consequences of the objectification of the body for the person requiring assistance; specifically, I explore how institutionalized practices of care can affect the agency of the care receiver. Even though I use the accepted terms "care receiver" and "caregiver," I fully recognize that they can imply a dichotomization of the care relationship as taking place between a person who is passive and one who is active. While I make use of these terms, my goal is to draw attention to the problematic assumptions that are embedded in this binary and their perpetuation through institutionalized practices of care.

In the second section of the paper, I analyze how the practices of care are shaped by the contexts in which they arise. Because care is often needed as the

---

2. A note of caution here: it may seem that there is an easy division between paid and unpaid care labor. However, this is becoming less and less the case, especially for adults needing care. Increasingly there are tax breaks as well as allowances to pay informal caregivers. Here, I want to focus on paid services that are regulated by an autonomous body.

3. For example, see the writings of Clare Ungerson (1990; 2006), Sheila Neysmith (1991) as well as Jane Aronson (1999, 2000) on care labor. The writings of Joan Tronto (1993; 2001), Selma Sevenhuijsen (1997), Eva Feder Kittay (2001; 2002), Martha Fineman (2004), and Margaret Urban Walker (1998) on care, public policies, and care ethics have done much to clarify many conceptual issues pertaining to care giving.

4. The number of personal care workers tripled in the United States from 1989 to 2004 (Kaye, Chapman, Newcomer, and Harrington 2005).

result of a medical condition, the practices of care are embedded from the start in a medical discourse and are inappropriately structured on analogy with acute care procedures. The entry of care labor into the market further affects how care labor is provided, and I make the case that, as commodities, the activities of care alienate the caregiver from the care receiver, affecting, in turn, the care receiver's sense of embodiment and also her agency.

In the third section, I examine how the care receiver is posited as a consumer of care. Consumer discourses characterize care services as commodities that can be bought by economic agents. However, the organization of care services also relies on the construal of the care receiver as someone who needs to be managed, a passive object upon which care is practiced. Thus, two competing discourses arise: the care receiver as an autonomous purchaser and the care receiver as a helpless person with a defective body that requires management. The person requiring assistance is caught at the intersection of these two discourses, and I shall argue that her agency, which may have been at risk because of her increased frailty, is further compromised. The binary of passive care receiver and active caregiver that is assumed and reified through the current institutionalized practices of care is shown to be inadequate, and I make the case for reconceiving the care relationship in institutionalized settings where care giving practices that assist with ADLs are controlled by third parties.

2. INSTITUTIONAL PRACTICES OF CARE

Historically, care, especially in the sense of taking care of, has been assumed to be a natural practice akin to instinct—one that does not require any truly volitional act or deliberative ethical reflection on the part of the caregiver. However, as Joan Tronto and others have made clear, care is a multifaceted concept encompassing complex sets of volitional and ethically inflected practices.[5] The subsequent development of care theory and the increasing visibility of and demands for home and institutional care have brought forward new analyses and a more sophisticated understanding of care.

Selma Sevenhuijsen (1997), for example, has examined health care policies using an ethics of care framework; her attention is directed at health care reforms that can meet the needs of all citizens, from home care to acute care services. Eva Kittay (2001) also frames the right to care under an ethics of care/social justice

---

5. See for example, Joan Tronto (1993; 2001) and the writers cited in note 3.

model. These writings have been crucial for a more adequate comprehension of the impact a right to care might have on social policies and of the complexities of care as an activity. Of particular relevance to my discussion is Kittay's (2002) examination of the abuse of individuals with mental retardation at the hands of paid caregivers. Kittay makes the case that situations of abuse will not be readily eliminated if care work is not socially valued. She proposes that care workers be provided with appropriate training, compensation, and a voice in the care they provide so that they can accomplish their care-giving activities well (2002, 295). To build on this work, more analyses are needed of the effects of the market on care activities.

I proceed in the spirit of Kittay's work. Hence, my focus is specifically on the practices of care that are regulated by a third party. This third party is either an agency that profits from care-giving labor, a nonprofit institution, or a governmental body where care labor is structured as an ancillary health care service.[6] I call such activities institutional practices of care, whether they are performed in an institutional setting or in a home setting. These practices represent the ways in which care enters the public realm; it is important, then, to examine how the discourse shapes the manner in which the person requiring assistance is perceived and, in turn, how her body becomes inscribed by the practices of care. It is only through drawing attention to these patterns that the binaries implicit in the regulated relation of care can be countered and the relation transformed.

2.1. *The Context*

Shifts in social and familial organization have meant that for adults in need of assistance, care is increasingly likely to be taken out of the private realm. One of the consequences of this shift is that care needs are being assessed by public agencies and that care labor is performed by paid caregivers.[7] The currency of familial ties of interdependence is left behind, and care practices are adapted to the types of transactions that are prevalent in the public sphere.

Feminist theorists writing on this subject have tended to emphasize the continuities between care in the public and private realms. Thus Kari Waerness

---

6. This third party regulation also affects the agency of the caregiver; however, it will not be the subject of the present analysis.

7. These public bodies can be governmental, not for profit, or for profit. The care workers can be government employees or private workers. In Canada, the way care is managed varies widely according to province or territory.

(1984) suggests that there is no distinction between care work that is done in these contexts. She argues that care work, and she uses the term "work" to emphasize her point, is work regardless of whether it is paid or not. Her point is well taken; however, when care giving is paid and regulated by a third party, it is subject to regulations and institutional structures not present in unpaid care giving. In order to understand the effects of such regulations, I examine first, the context in which the practices of care arise; second, the implication of structuring the practices of care as services to be rendered by a paid worker; and, third, the power differentials embedded in care giving when it is tied to the care receiver's well being or even to her survival.[8]

As the name implies, ADLs involve the daily activities that allow the individual to survive and even thrive; help with bathing and eating and, for those who remain at home, help with daily chores are the most common such activities. The institutional practices of care are ongoing practices; unlike some medical interventions, ongoing care generally will not return a person to her normal, self-sufficient state.[9]

While the institutional practices of care are not medical practices per se, they originate in a medical environment and are, consequently, embedded in a medical discourse.[10] They may be needed for a short term after a person has undergone surgery, or for longer periods as in cases of chronic, debilitating illness, long-term impairment, or aging. Typically, a doctor refers the person needing care to appropriate health care practitioners, such as a physiotherapist or an occupational therapist. These professionals then assess the functionality of the person needing care as well as her ability for self-care. The team, in conjunction with a social worker, determine the extent of the help required and refer the individual to either a care agency or an institution, such as a nursing home. The person needing care can assent to or decline the services proposed; however, it can be seen that already she is entangled in web of professional assessments and prescriptions. The ADLs, activities that had been of a private

---

8. I want to acknowledge the fact that the precariousness of employment will affect the caregiver and may disempower her, but I cannot engage this issue here.

9. This is a loaded term, and the ideology of functional self-sufficiency will be put into question later, but I want to draw attention to the fact that acute care is often perceived as involving a one-time procedure. There is a pervasive understanding of acute care as being short term and restorative as opposed to ongoing care, which is assistive; this illustrates the cure versus care dichotomy.

10. There has been controversy over whether such activities are medically necessary; see Forrow, Daniels, and Sabin (1991). I do not want to engage this point here; but for my purposes, it is important to note that such care practices are not included in the Canada Health Act. In this sense they are not medically necessary.

and personal nature, have now become the subject of expert discourses and professional involvement.

From their inception, these practices of care are tinted by an aura of medical practice that is in turn constrained by economic institutions. In *No Place Like Home?* Jennifer Parks demonstrates how home care, within the American context, is organized according to a model of acute care. She explains that this framework "has been the preferred model for organizing home care services because it avoids the messy, complex, and expensive chronic care demands that a chronic care model would have to address" (Parks 2003, 49). In the Canadian context, ongoing care is not part of the Canada Health Act; it need not be covered by universal Medicare and can fall under a scheme of private insurance.[11] Although there are differences in the Canadian and American models of health care services, ongoing care is treated in a similar manner, and in both countries it is subsumed under an acute care model.[12] If care is seen as an acute intervention, it will be reimbursed for only a limited period of time under a scheme of private insurance. This framing is obviously advantageous from the perspective of insurance companies or health management organizations. However, there is good reason to expect that individuals with chronic complaints requiring assistance with ADLs will be poorly served by the acute care model, as it simply misdescribes their situation.

2.2. The Structure of Care Labor

When the person needing care has seen the appropriate health care professionals and has agreed to the proposed care plan, an individual from either a public or private agency will then organize and structure the required practices of care. These practices may be daily services, such as meals, or weekly ones, such as help with a bath. If the person is in a care facility, then a care plan will involve help with some or all of the ADLs. When the care receiver is at home, the caregiver is hired by the agency to perform the required labor.[13]

---

11. In the Canadian context, provisions for care may be available as social services; this varies according to provinces and territories. In the United States as well, persons who qualify for Medicaid may be provided with some services.

12. The Romanow report (2002) acknowledged a need for subsidizing the care needed after hospital discharge. The greater demand for home care is forcing governments to examine social programs for persons requiring assistance and/or tax incentives for informal caregivers.

13. As noted earlier, I focus exclusively on caregivers who are hired by a third party, but I want to bring attention to Clare Ungerson's work (2006) on the various involvements of caregivers depending on the type of remuneration they get for their labor.

When care labor becomes a service to be rendered for wages, it becomes a market commodity and falls under a contractual model of exchange of service for remuneration. For-profit agencies strive to give the best care for the least amount of money.[14] Public institutions and not-for profit organizations may not have the same strict economic constraints, but they also subject care practices to efficiency considerations and manage care work using the same framework as for-profit organizations. In order to maximize efficiency, care work is broken down into discreet actions where each action is expected to be performed within a set amount of time. By drawing attention to the fact that "small time allotments [are] given to aids to help clients out of bed, bathe, perform toiletries, dress, and eat breakfast" (Parks 2003, 45), Parks makes the case that home care is organized around a mechanical model of care.

In the case of facility-based care, the need to judge efficient performance means that attention must be paid to the physical tasks of care (see, e.g., Foner 1994). In her study of hospice care, Nicky James (1992) found that the physical labor of care is not only given emphasis but is *the framework* under which care labor is organized. Her findings are corroborated by the fact that formal caregivers, whether they work in a home or facility setting, are trained primarily in the mechanical tasks of care giving, such as how to lift a frail individual. They are given little training in the psychological aspects of aging or even in aging processes in general (*Les Dernières Violences* 2005).

Care activities are given time allotments according to the time it takes to perform mechanical tasks such as lifting, bathing, or feeding. Other activities that are constitutive of the relational aspects of care giving, such as talking to the care receiver when it is not directly tied to a particular care activity, are not factored in. This structure means that not only is the physical component of the work primary, but that other needs cannot be addressed within the framework since no time is scheduled for them. A care receiver's need to talk or to defer a bath to a later time, for example, cannot be accommodated easily within a framework that constructs help with bathing solely as the physical activity of washing. Thus, care giving falls under an imperative of schedules; as Robin Fiore discusses in "Caring for Ourselves," third-party regulation implies that the "delivery of care is regimented rather than individualized" (2000, 254).

This manner of structuring care obscures the emotional labor involved in care and effectively diminishes the opportunity for the agents in the care relation

---

14. In Canada, there is a trend to hire private agencies to do care work. This has been documented in Stinson, Pollak, and Cohen (2005).

Alienation / Alienated bodies

to establish a sustainable rapport.[15] Care activities are further constrained by the inflexibility of having to negotiate many individuals' needs within a set order. Whether in home care or a facility, the caregiver is typically responsible for various care receivers during the day. Time-tabling puts an imperative on the care worker to accomplish each task within a set schedule. It may be argued that this reduction is what happens when certain activities that are crucial to the care receiver must be accomplished, and that ultimately this situation is not as damaging to the care receiver as not accomplishing the activity at all—not giving a bath, for example. However, the practice of care itself is diminished when it is defined as an essentially physical task to be accomplished in a set amount of time regardless of the relational rapport needed for the activities of care to take place in a dignified way. Although the care receiver has a cleaner body, if she has not had the opportunity to relate to the caregiver and vice versa, her sense of self and dignity may be damaged.

The mechanical nature of the practices of care as well as the small time allotments put the care receiver in the role of a passive entity simply waiting to have her bodily needs attended to. Her body is managed by a schedule, and she may not feel part of this scheduling process, as, in fact, her role is quite minimal. Jane Aronson (1999; 2000) has shown that the image of the care receiver as that of an individual who needs to be managed is prevalent for older people in need of care. The above analysis shows how the institutionalization of care supports this image.

Bodies having to fit into organizational structured time schedule

2.3. Alienability of Care

The activities of care, constructed as a series of mechanical gestures, resemble assembly line work. The caregiver is not in a relationship with the care receiver; rather, it is as if the caregiver were laboring on an object. This objectification of the care receiver is further exacerbated by the deep economic structure of institutionalized care labor, which alienates the activities of care from the caregiver and alienates her from the care receiver. This alienation, in turn, affects the care receiver.

Alienation is not usually employed within the context of care giving, because care activities are personal services and, for Marx, would be a type of unproductive

---

15. The point of James's (1992) article is to put forward the importance of emotional labor in nursing. Other nursing theorists have examined emotional labor in nursing, for example, Staden (1998).

labor.¹⁶ However, as I will show, Marx's concept of alienation provides a useful lens for understanding how the deep economic structure of labor constrains care practices. As well, alienation is better suited to understanding embodied experience within a determinate framework than reading Marx may suggest: within patriarchy, for example, women may often feel alienated from their bodies. Iris Marion Young makes use of this concept in her critical analysis of pregnant embodiment. As she explains: "[a]lienation here means the objectification or appropriation by one subject of another subject's body, action, or product of action" (Young 1990, 168). The person objectified may fail to recognize her body, action, or experience as fully her own. In technologically advanced societies where pregnancy is medicalized, Young argues "that a woman's experience in pregnancy and birthing is often alienated because her condition tends to be defined as a disorder, because medical instruments objectify internal processes in such a way that they devalue a woman's experience of those processes, and because the social relations and instrumentation of the medical setting reduce her control over her experience" (168). I examine first how alienation affects the care worker. Then, in the spirit of Young's application of alienation to women's experience of embodiment, I discuss the impact of the caregiver's alienation as it is lived by the care receiver.

Marx wrote about the various ways in which the worker becomes alienated by the capitalist forces of production. Of relevance is the alienability of the laborer's product from the laborer herself. Because those owning the means of production control the object produced by the laborer, "the worker relates to the product of his labor as to an alien object" (Marx 1977, 78). Underlying the concept of alienation is the idea that the laborer's labor power is her own; it is part of her being. For Marx, labor has more than just economic dimensions; labor, in the sense of creation, is an intrinsic part of what makes the laborer human. By losing control over the product of her labor, the worker is alienated from her product and, hence, from her humanity.

While physically it appears the caregiver has extensive and immediate control over the product of her labor—the well-being of the care receiver is in her hands at least for a limited time—as a laborer she is alienated from the services she provides. Since the agency purchases, defines, assesses, and reaps the financial benefits (if there are any) of the caregiver's labor, the latter has little control over the scheduling of her activities or the manner in which

---

16. From Marx's writings, it can be argued that productive labor can create surplus value; this implies that care activities can be analyzed as surplus creating labor. I discuss this point more fully in Lanoix (2007).

these are to be performed. The emphasis on the physical activities of care transforms care labor into a series of actions that are directed at a passive other. Thus they become easily characterized as instrumental actions only.[17] Their instrumentality effectively obscures or erases the relational aspects of care labor, because no time will be allotted for communication to take place except within the circumscribed context of the physical acts of care. However, caregivers often say that it is the relational aspect of their work that makes it important to them (see Zeytinoglu and Denton 2006).

There are many layers of alienation that affect the caregiver. As a laborer, the caregiver is alienated from her labor. She lacks control over the performance of her work, as it is difficult for her to perform the activities of care if she does not have the time to relate to the care receiver and to care adequately. Not only do economic imperatives cause the caregiver to distance herself from her labor, they encourage her to treat the care receiver as a passive object of care. Structured as mechanical gestures, her labor becomes dehumanizing both for herself and the care receiver. Therefore, the caregiver becomes alienated from her labor and ultimately from the care receiver because of the manner in which her labor is structured by a third party. This alienation, in turn, may affect how the care receiver relates to her embodied self within the relation of care.

I want to explore this last point through the case of bathing.[18] Personal care such as bathing is intimate care; for most people, it means taking care of one's body. Bathing may be done quickly in a utilitarian manner or as a relaxing exercise, combining cleansing with pampering. In either case, there is, ideally, a sense of owning the experience of bathing. The bather decides when to best fit it in with other activities and how to accomplish the task. The bather is both the object and the subject of her care.

Bathing also has elements of touching. One surveys one's own body when bathing; it draws attention to one's embodiment. When a person takes care of herself there is a way in which bathing becomes self-nurture through the manner in which she relates to herself. Moreover, by caring for herself in a way that attends to her own embodiment, the activity often reinforces a sense of self-integration.

---

17. In Lanoix (2007) I argue that the activities of care are characterized as instrumental actions by formal agencies when they should be structured as communicative actions.

18. The case of bathing is examined by Julia Twigg (2000). She argues that although community care focuses on policies and regulations, it is about the care and management of the body. In order to make her point she considers the experiences of bathing from the perspectives of caregivers and care receivers.

In the case of help with bathing, the care receiver is entrusting herself to the caregiver, and a rapport may be established between them. Surrendering to another can be pleasurable, and a positive sense of one's own embodiment is not necessarily absent when the care receiver is bathed by another. Insofar as the other is caring for one as one would care for oneself, the person assisted may feel nurtured by the bath and may even continue to experience a sense of self-integration. Bathing is intimate care, and the care receiver's body is revealed in all its vulnerability. Because the care receiver is exposing herself so completely, she expects at least some attentiveness on the part of the caregiver, and this attentiveness may contribute to a respectful, nurturing, and satisfying experience.

If time is apportioned only according to the physical dimensions of care labor, however, the activity of bathing a person becomes the actions of washing her body. The emphasis on the mechanical gestures of washing will not be conducive to encouraging the caregiver to be involved with the care receiver. The caregiver may wish to do a good job, but what counts as doing so is determined in large part by the agency employing her. Making sure the care receiver has a proper bath does not require any relationship with her; it only requires that the end result be a clean body. In these circumstances the care receiver may perceive a lack of consideration on the part of the caregiver or feel that she has disappeared as a person for the caregiver.

The objectification of the care receiver may, in turn, affect how she relates to herself as she is being cared for. The bather is no longer the subject of her bath: she has become a passive body that needs to be washed. The embodied experience of nurture and self-integration that occurs when one cares for one's own body or when one is being cared for in a supportive manner will be unavailable to her, and she may experience an alienating and unpleasantly dualistic perspective on her own apparently troublesome embodiment. The loss of control over the care that is given to her may cause the care receiver to feel that she has been reduced to a faulty body while, at the same time, making her feel estranged from her own body. The care receiver's sense of self-worth, which may already be precarious, will be further damaged through the encounter.

The care receiver only has a limited input into the care she receives. She can agree or disagree with the proposed care plan, but if she disagrees, alternative options are limited. In addition, she has little control over the manner in which the care is given to her. Her agency is already quite limited in her interactions with the organizations responsible for facilitating the care she receives, and it may be even further constrained by the manner in which care is delivered. If the care activities make her feel like a burdensome individual, this objectification further diminishes her agency and can also obscure her vulnerability.[19]

2.4. *Power Imbalances*

The vulnerability inherent in accepting help from another person directs us to the power dynamics inherent in the practices of care. As Kari Waerness explains in "Caring as Women's Work in the Welfare State," there are three types of care services: personal services, care-giving work, and spontaneous care. Personal services can be services such as house cleaning that an individual decides to purchase because she does not have the time to perform them herself. However, personal services become care-giving work when the person requiring these services cannot perform them. Waerness recognizes that the same activity can be both care-giving work and personal service depending on the context (1984, 70). Finally, an example of spontaneous care is the help provided to a stranger encountered on a busy street experiencing difficulty with her parcels. Of relevance to my discussion are care-giving work and personal service; in these cases, power relationships become complicated by the vulnerabilities of the caregiver and the care receiver.

When an individual decides to purchase personal services, the buyer's sense of empowerment is not diminished because she has the option of performing these chores herself. In fact, as Clare Ungerson explains, "[p]ersonal service care is characterized by an unequal relationship between carer and cared for where the cared for person is of superior social status to the carer" (1990, 14).[20] The person doing this type of care work can become subservient to the one contracting for it. The object of care still remains the care receiver's well-being, but the care receiver, the subject of care, is the one in control.

When a care receiver requires care because she is incapable of performing the ADLs without assistance, this personal service becomes care giving, and the power may shift. In addition to her increased vulnerability, the care receiver is in danger of becoming solely an object of care and no longer the subject of her care. If she is at home, she may retain a certain sense of self, but she may be

---

19. In the novel *Slow Man*, J. M. Coetzee explores the care-giving relationship through the standpoint of man who has lost a leg in a road accident. Coetzee highlights the complex facets of care giving and the emotional expectations, whether or not appropriate, that such a relationship can elicit. This illustrates that care giving often involves intimacy, and boundaries may be hard to set in such instances.

20. Ungerson (1990) suggests that Waerness's (1984) understating of personal service care work can be extended to include paid caregivers.

dismayed at the seemingly incessant stream of workers that come through her home. If she is in an institution, she may feel even more powerless.

As a service that needs to be delivered in a fast and efficient manner, the practices of care cannot take into account the power imbalances that may be felt by the care receiver.[21] The caregiver simply does not have the time to attend to all these elements nor, in many cases, does she have the training to do so. The discourse of care as a commodity obscures the power imbalance inherent in practices of care commodified. This inattention to power further contributes to pressing the care receiver into a passive role.

3. THE CARE RECEIVER

3.1. *The Care Receiver as Consumer*

The media portrays home care as empowering for care receivers, emphasizing the sense of well-being associated with residing in one's own home. However, underlying the discourse of home care is an economic incentive—institutionalization is more costly.[22] Because the public discourse offers a narrative of self-sufficiency coupled with an understanding of autonomy as having a right to choose, the independence that is lost through impairment is transferred into buying power. Not only can the lack of certain kinds of dependence be staved off if the individual is allowed to purchase care, she can still be seen as autonomous as the shift from autonomy as self-reliant individual to buyer of services preserves an ideal of autonomy. All the agency of the care receiver is directed at her purchasing power.[23]

If the consumer model of care is prevalent for home care, it is also present for facility-based care. In the case of institutional care, the person in need of care is frequently cast as someone who chooses to enter a particular establishment. This characterization is certainly true for many entering facilities such as retirement communities. Nevertheless, the discourse of consumer choice is still present for facilities that cater to less autonomous individuals. Whether the

---

21. It needs to be acknowledged that caregivers are often in precarious positions, especially when they are not unionized. I have examined this is in Lanoix (2006).

22. This is the type of argument put forward to encourage public funding of home care.

23. If care services are public, then the person requiring care will not be purchasing these services but will have an entitlement to them. Nevertheless, care is seen as something that is consumed as noted above (Aronson 1999).

institution was a freely chosen option or a necessity for lack of resources at home is irrelevant: the notion of choice dominates.[24]

The practices of care are always inscribed within the greater social system that frames their availability. As Sheila Neysmith remarks, "[t]he language of 'consumer' and 'provider' blurs the fact that health and social service professionals determine the organization of services as well as the consumer/client decisions on the use of those services" (1991, 79). As seen in the previous section, because care is enshrined within a medicalized discourse, the regulatory bodies in charge of administering care will be the principal agents deciding what type of care the person requiring assistance should receive. The care receiver, as a layperson without any access to the proper technical knowledge, does not have the required epistemic authority to make demands, and it may be difficult for her to voice her decisions about the type of care she needs.[25] This situation of epistemic powerlessness serves to position her as a passive consumer of care, in contrast to the discourse of choice and agency that prevails.

By becoming a consumer of care services, the care receiver is put into a tenuous relationship to her body. She now requires that her body be cared for by someone else, a stranger.[26] Although the message is that care can help her stay independent, the care receiver is confronted with this other message—one informing her that her body has become a troublesome appendage that requires maintenance from someone else. Still, the primary message behind the consumption of care is that one can live or even live well in spite of one's own body. Thus the defective body can be overcome and a fuller life resumed, or, in the case of home care, life in an institution can be postponed if the proper care services can be found.

Behind this model of care is the hegemonic ideal of the independent individual who is self-sufficient for all her needs.[27] Under a discourse of

---

24. Even if retirement homes can be advertised as attractive environments, long-term care institutions do not have such a cachet. Nevertheless, in a competitive market, long-term care facilities will display themselves as ideal environments providing "total care" and will promote themselves to family members. This is the case in the United States, for example.

25. Robin Fiore discusses the right to refusal of treatment as pathologized "as irrational self-endangerment" in the case of adults needing care (2000, 246).

26. This will have implications for the relationship that the caregiver can establish with the care receiver. Tracy X. Karner (1998) makes the point that the care receiver can build some intimacy by incorporating the care workers as a type of kin.

27. Disability activists and theorists have highlighted the artificial boundaries between those who are deemed self-sufficient and those who are not. These boundaries are not objective but are socially constructed. Susan Wendell (1996) makes this point, and Lennard Davis (2002) also argues that dependency is a universal norm and not the special case of disabled individuals. It is worth

independence, all the relational activities of individuals involved in the care receiver's life are obscured, including the informal care of family members or friends that often supplements paid care giving.²⁸

3.2. The Care Receiver as Needing Management

As care practices are needed predominantly by older individuals, the discourse that frames the care practices are shaped in part by ageist assumptions.²⁹ In a society that rewards youth and the appearance of self-sufficiency, the aging body is seen as defective, is more readily subjected to medical interventions, and is portrayed as shameful. The problematic relationship that western society cultivates with aging is revealed in that the institutional practices of care are not seen as an integral part of a normal process due to biological factors, but as a burden on society. Jane Aronson notes that "[t]ypically, elderly people are cast as consumers of services rather than as citizens with social entitlements" (1999, 53).

In "Restructuring Older Women's Needs" (2000), Aronson examines the ways in which care receivers are constructed as needing to be managed. She explains, "[w]ithin the imagery of 'being managed,' research and service practices cast elderly women in very confined ways—they appear as 'cases' to be counted and fitted into organizational forms or to be processed in efficient and standardized ways" (2000, 66). Although this study focused on older women, Aronson has previously shown that for older people in general, "[b]eing managed is the dominant, privileged imagery embodied in the practices of policymakers and health and social service organizations"(1999, 48). Her analyses are congruent with the previous discussion of the construction of the care receiver as passive, which results from the ways in which the practices of care arise and the ways in which they are structured.

Policies play a pivotal role in determining how certain types of bodies are viewed in the public realm. By examining Australian policies dealing with new reproductive technologies as well as cosmetic surgeries, Carol Lee Bacchi and Chris Beasly (2002) identify two ways in which problematic embodiment is constructed. While some citizens are seen as individuals who can control their own bodies,

---

noting that self-sufficiency is often problematically equated with autonomy. For critical discussions of autonomy from a relational perspective see the writings of Susan Sherwin (1998) and Catriona Mackenzie and Natalie Stoljar (2000).

28. This issue has been discussed extensively in the literature, as women are typically the informal caregivers. See Sheila M. Neysmith, ed. (1999).

29. For example, Susan Wendell (1996) argues that society is constructed for a young male body type. This affects not only the way buildings and streets and transportation are designed but the pace of life as well.

others are portrayed as being controlled by their bodies. Those who are controlled by their bodies are lesser citizens and deemed to be in need of some form of control. As Bacchi and Beasly write: "political subjects who evince forms of control over their bodies are constituted as full citizens, which at times is equated with a degree of distance from government surveillance. Political subjects who are deemed not to exercise this control, who are considered to be controlled by or subject to their bodies, do not measure up on the citizenship scale; hence, their activities can be regulated in ways deemed inappropriate for full citizens" (2002, 34).

Although the institutional practices of care may not be under the same type of government regulations, the way in which they are monitored and enacted does exemplify the type of control Bacchi and Beasly are talking about. Those who need care are deemed to have deviant bodies and, therefore, need to be under some form of control. This control further restricts the care receiver's agency.

4. CONCLUSION

The need for assistance in the performance of the acts of self-care is usually assessed by health care practitioners. Since the institutional practices of care originate within a medical discourse, they are easily characterized as acute care interventions. In addition, subsuming this type of care to an acute-care model is both ideologically and monetarily convenient. Framed as short-term interventions, regardless of the fact that they might be needed for long periods of time, attention is placed on the individual physical activities of care to the detriment of the relational activities the caregiver and care receiver must engage in to establish a sustainable rapport.

I have argued in this paper that the context in which care takes place, a medical environment coupled with care's entrance into the market, has fashioned the institutional practices of care into commodities. This commodification is not merely an expedient way of translating the activities of care to the public realm. Rather, it serves to enshrine the care receiver into a discourse of passivity as it makes her role in the care transaction that of a consumer whose care is both practiced on her and alienating for her. While the public discourse surrounding the institutional practices of care positions itself as promoting the autonomy of the care receiver, her autonomy is actually (usually) diminished by these practices.[30]

30. This is also the thrust of Robin Fiore's article (2000).

Such a framework distorts the care relationship and casts the person who requires assistance as a passive individual who does not contribute to the care relationship. The care relationship can thus be easily dichotomized as a relation between an active purveyor and a passive consumer. Even though the current practices of care put forward a supportive discourse toward those who require care, in effect they undermine the agency of those requiring care. They problematize frail bodies and objectify those who require assistance. They contribute to the vilification of dependency while masking an ageist and ableist discourse with one of consumerism.

If Aronson indicates in her studies of elders that the prevailing image of elders is that of needing to be managed, she also presents evidence that some elders are able to direct their care or even demand better care. These individuals achieve their small victories at great cost, however, as they may have to disengage from others by refusing offers of formal services (2000, 61) or risk being typecast as difficult and ungrateful individuals. In addition, such individuals are more the exception than the rule; as Aronson states, "managing in the face of disability, or illness or old age, is in contrast to being managed a fairly private and muted narrative" (1999, 54). The few individuals who are able to make claims and to retain a sense of agency remain marginalized. Their struggles for agency tend to be reduced and reread as personal tensions between care workers and care receivers or "as private sorrow rather than also the unfair manifestation of politically determined divisions of resources, entitlement, value, and work" (2000, 62).

If the relational aspects of the practices of care go unrecognized by regulatory bodies that typify care as a commodity, they are more fully confronted by people from other types of organizations who understand care practices differently. For example, Pamela Cushing and Tanya Lewis (2002) have studied the relationships of caregivers and care receivers in L'Arche homes, where mutuality is emphasized.[31] In her own "Negotiating Power Inequities in Caregiving Relationships," Cushing calls attention to the power imbalances between the individuals in the care relationship but maintains that they do not preclude enriching the relationship on both sides (2003, 83).

I acknowledge that L'Arche communities are founded on a particular philosophical perspective that may not be applied generally to all paid care

---

31. L'Arche homes are small group homes for persons with developmental disabilities. Based on the philosophical perspective of Jean Vanier, that all human beings possess intrinsic value, L'Arche homes strive to foster community through caring relationships. See http://www.larche.ca/en/resources/welcome (accessed October 28, 2008).

work, but it is nonetheless important to recognize the beneficial elements that the model provides. In this instance, care is not a practice directed at an inert other; it is understood as a practice that enables both the care receiver and the caregiver. Rather than privileging the physical activities of care, it pays attention to the relationship of care itself. By emphasizing the uniqueness and value of the care receiver, L'Arche homes create a space in the care relation for the care receiver. Because the care relation is seen as ongoing, consideration is given to the quality of the relationship.[32]

This alternative model of care puts the care relation in a different perspective; the care relation is no longer one that is primarily unidirectional, but one where exchange is encouraged. L'Arche communities make it easier to recognize the ethical and emotional components inherent in the intimate practices of care. Their understanding of care puts into practice Tronto's fourth phase of caring, care receiving, where the input of the care receiver is as important as the activities of care themselves (1993, 107–8). Although Tronto sees this phase as one that will be indicative of the adequacy of care giving, it is also a way of understanding the care relation as one that is dialogic.

The practices of self-care characteristic of ADLs are distinctive activities because they involve an individual's well-being and intimate personal needs. In many cases, the individual is in the unique role of being both the object and the subject of the activities of care. Hence, the practices of care are a way of relating to oneself. In this sense, they are functional activities yet remain intimate, a reminder of one's embodied reality. Performed with the assistance of another individual, self-care can become an unpleasant and alienating activity instead of one that is nurturing. It is essential that those involved in organizing the practices of care become acutely aware of this risk. As Martha Holstein reminds us, "one task, as we think about the mutualities that inhere in care giving and care receiving is to imagine situations that have the opportunity to be exemplary" (2000, 240).

REFERENCES

Aronson, Jane. 1999. Conflicting Images of Older People Receiving Care. In *Critical Issues for Future Social Work Practice with Aging Persons,* ed. Sheila M. Neysmith, 47–69. New York: Columbia University Press.

32. Parks (2003) makes the case that a chronic model of care would be better suited for home care.

———. 2000. Restructuring Older Women's Needs: Care Receiving as a Site of Struggle and Resistance. In *Restructuring Caring Labour*, ed. Sheila M. Neysmith, 52–72. Oxford: Oxford University Press.

Bacchi, Carol Lee, and Chris Beasley. 2002. Citizen Bodies: Is Embodied Citizenship a Contradiction in Terms? *Critical Social Policy* 22(2): 324–52.

Cushing, Pamela. 2003. Negotiating Power Inequities in Caregiving Relationships. *Journal on Developmental Disabilities* 10(1): 83–91.

Cushing, Pamela, and Tanya Lewis. 2002. Negotiating Mutuality and Agency in Care-Giving Relationships with Women with Intellectual Disabilities. *Hypatia: A Journal of Feminist Philosophy* 17(3): 173–93.

Davis, Lennard J. 2002. *Bending over Backwards: Disability, Dismodernism, and Other Difficult Positions*. New York: New York University Press.

Les Dernières Violences. 2005. Produced by Lise Payette for Telefilm Canada. Broadcast on Radio Canada, *Zone Libre*, September 10, 2006.

Fineman, Martha. 2004. *The Autonomy Myth: A Theory of Dependency*. New York: New Press.

Fiore, Robin. 2000. Caring for Ourselves: Peer Care in Autonomous Aging. In *Mother Time: Women, Aging, and Ethics*, ed. Margaret Urban Walker, 245–60. Lanham, Md.: Rowman and Littlefield.

Foner, Nancy. 1994. *The Caregiving Dilemma: Work in the American Nursing Home*. Berkeley and Los Angeles: University of California Press.

Forrow, Lachlan, Norman Daniels, and James Sabin. 1991. When Is Home Care Medically Necessary? *Hastings Center Report*, July–August, 36–38.

Glasser, Ronald J. 2005. A War of Disabilities: Iraq's Hidden Costs Are Coming Home. *Harper's*, July, 59–62.

Holstein, Martha. 2000. Home Care, Women, and Aging: A Case Study of Injustice. In *Mother Time: Women, Aging, and Ethics*, ed. Margaret Urban Walker, 227–44. Lanham, Md.: Rowman and Littlefield.

James, Nicky. 1992. Care = Organization + Physical Labour + Emotional Labour. *Sociology of Health and Illness* 14(4): 488–509.

Karner, Tracy X. 1998. Professional Caring: Homecare Workers as Fictive Kin. *Journal of Aging Studies* 12:69–83.

Kaye, H. Stephen, Susan Chapman, Robert J. Newcomer, and Charlene Harrington. 2005. Personal Assistance Workforce: Trends in Supply and Demands. *Health Affairs* 25(4): 1113–20.

Kittay, Eva Feder. 2001. A Feminist Public Ethic of Care Meets the New Communitarian Family Policy. *Ethics* 111(3): 523–47.

———. 2002. Caring for the Vulnerable by Caring for the Caregiver: The Case of Mental Retardation. In *Medicine and Social Justice: Essays on the Distribution of Health Care*, ed. Rosamond Rhodes, Margaret P. Battin, and Anita Silvers, 290–300. Oxford: Oxford University Press.

Lanoix, Monique. 2006. Care Labour and Mistrust. Paper presented at the annual meeting of the Canadian Society for Women in Philosophy, Trent University, Peterborough, October.

———. 2007. Caring for Money. Paper presented at the annual meeting of the Canadian Society for Women in Philosophy, University of Alberta, Edmonton, October.

Mackenzie, Catriona, and Natalie Stoljar, eds. 2000. *Relational Autonomy: Feminist Perspectives on Autonomy, Agency, and the Social Self*. Oxford: Oxford University Press.
Marx, Karl. 1977. *Selected Writings*. Ed. D. McLellan. Oxford: Oxford University Press.
Neysmith, Sheila M. 1991. From Community Care to a Social Model of Care. In *Women's Caring: Feminist Perspectives on Social Welfare*, ed. Carol T. Baines, Patricia M. Evans, and Sheila M. Neysmith, 272–99. Toronto: McClelland and Stewart.
Parks, Jennifer A. 2003. *No Place Like Home?* Bloomington: Indiana University Press.
Romanow, Roy J. 2002. *Building on Values: The Future of Health Care in Canada*. Commission on the Future of Health Care in Canada. http://www.hc-sc.gc.ca/english/care/romanow/hcc0086 (accessed March 13, 2008).
Sevenhuijsen, Selma. 1997. Feminist Ethics and Public Health Care Policies: A Case Study on the Netherlands. In *Feminist Ethics and Social Policy*, ed. P. DiQuinzio and I. M. Young, 49–76. Bloomington: Indiana University Press.
Sherwin, Susan. 1998. A Relational Approach to Autonomy in Health Care. In *The Politics of Women's Health: Exploring Agency and Autonomy*, ed. Feminist Health Care Ethics Research Network, coord. Susan Sherwin, 19–47. Philadelphia: Temple University Press.
Staden, Helene. 1998. Alertness to the Needs of Others: A Study of the Emotional Labour of Caring. *Journal of Advanced Nursing* 27:147–56.
Stinson, Jane, Nancy Pollack, and Marcy Cohen. 2005. *The Pains of Privatization*. Ottawa: Canadian Centre for Policy Alternatives.
Tronto, Joan. 1993. *Moral Boundaries: A Political Argument for an Ethic of Care*. New York: Routledge.
———. 2001. Who Cares? Public and Private Caring and the Rethinking of Citizenship. In *Women and Welfare: The Theory and Practice in the United States and Europe*, ed. N. J. Hirschman and Ulrike Liebert, 65–83. New Brunswick: Rutgers University Press.
Twigg, Julia. 2000. *Bathing: The Body and Community Care*. New York: Routledge.
Ungerson, Clare. 1990. The Language of Care: Crossing the Boundaries. In *Gender and Caring: Work and Welfare in Britain and Scandinavia*, ed. C. Ungerson, 8–33. New York: Harvester Wheatsheaf.
———. 2006. Care, Work, and Feeling. *Sociological Review* 54(1): 188–203.
Waerness, Kari. 1984. Caring as Women's Work in the Welfare State. In *Patriarchy in a Welfare Society*, ed. Harriet Holter, 67–87. Oslo: Universitetsforlaget.
Walker, Martha Urban. *Moral Understandings: A Feminist Study in Ethics*. New York: Routledge.
Wendell, Susan. 1996. *The Rejected Body: Feminist Philosophical Reflections on Disability*. New York: Routledge.
Young, Iris Marion. 1990. Pregnant Embodiment: Subjectivity and Alienation. In *Throwing Like a Girl and Other Essays in Feminist Philosophy and Social Theory*, 160–74. Bloomington: Indiana University Press.
Zeytinoglu, Isik U., and Margaret Denton. 2006. Satisfied Workers, Retained Workers: Effects of Work and Work Environment on Homecare Workers' Job Satisfaction, Stress, Physical Health, and Retention. Canadian Health Services Research Foundation. http://www.chsrf.ca/final_research/ogc/pdf/zeytinoglu_e.pdf (accessed March 13, 2008).

NINE

PREMATURE (M)OTHERING:
LEVINASIAN ETHICS AND THE POLITICS OF
FETAL ULTRASOUND IMAGING

Jacqueline M. Davies

1. INTRODUCTION

One of the most notable features of the work of Emmanuel Levinas is his philosophical reorientation toward the *maternal* face of ethics, a move comparable to the turn in feminist philosophy toward the ethics of care. Turning to Levinas, therefore, may nourish new developments in care theory. It may also provide another perspective from which to explore apparently conflicting intuitions about maternity, the ethical demands of pregnancy and motherhood, and the political rights of pregnant women. Changes in the social relations of reproduction as well as new developments in reproductive technology make the call for such an exploration all the more compelling. Prenatal ultrasound imaging, in particular, reframes the ethical relationship between a pregnant woman and the fetus she carries. One troubling consequence of this is the prima facie case that can be made in Levinasian terms from ultrasound images of fetuses to the enforcement of what Amy Mullin (2005) calls an ideology of sacrificial motherhood.

This prima facie case is made and used strategically by anti-abortion activists. Something like it also seems to underlie the medical and legal treatment of some pregnant women.[1] Some feminist critics, including Mullin, take the possibility of making such a case as evidence of Levinas's philosophical reproduction of well-worn patriarchal constructs, and thus as an argument against a Levinasian account of ethics. From a feminist perspective Mullin contests "Levinas's vision of ethics as about complete self-sacrifice" and questions "the appropriateness of

---

[1]. See Petchesky (1987) for an early feminist discussion of the role of ultrasound in anti-abortion politics.

this model of ethics and its application to pregnancy in a way that only reinforces the ideology of motherhood" (Mullin 2005, 77).

Whether arguing from a pro-natalist perspective that maternal sacrifice should be regarded as a feminine ideal or from a feminist perspective that it represents an intolerable restriction of women's ethical horizons, arguments from the fetal face to the ideology of sacrificial motherhood depend on, and regenerate, confusion of political identity with ethical relation. My objective is to highlight some of the errors and dangers of discursive misappropriation of Levinasian ethics. Such a mistaken deployment of Levinas depends, I argue, on an approach to pregnant embodiment in which ethical concerns are confused with, and perhaps subordinated to, political considerations. We need to differentiate the way a patriarchal ideology of sacrificial motherhood frames the message with which ultrasound is supposed to confront us from the call of a maternal voice of ethics to which Levinas's oeuvre is a response. The voice he hears calls us to attend to the ethical significance of discovering oneself as intimately bound to a vulnerable Other. A nuanced feminist understanding of Levinas's maternal ethics takes this difference seriously and can deepen our understanding of both ethics and maternity.

2. ULTRASOUND: THE IMAGE OF THE FETAL FACE AND THE CALL TO MATERNITY

According to Emmanuel Levinas it is the encounter with the face of the Other that constitutes the ethical moment.[2] In this moment the ethical subject discovers her- or himself as one who is *called* to respond to an Other. For Levinas ethics cannot be a question of the correct application of the correct principles by an autonomous ethical subject because the ethical subject itself has no prior existence. The ethical subject first comes into being *in* the encounter with the Other. Indeed, the ethical subject exists *only* in this relationship. For feminists the insistence on relationality is not a foreign approach. The relational quality of Levinas's ethics is reminiscent of the emphasis on situated knowing and webs of care in much feminist philosophy (e.g., Haraway 1988; Noddings 1984). In

---

2. The face (*le visage*) is the metaphor Levinas uses to speak of that presence that is necessarily encountered when you meet someone, that is, when you know someone by acquaintance. This contrasts with the category through which anyone met might be known (even through the elevated category of personhood). The face (*le visage*) should not be equated with the phenomenal surface (*la face*) that we would refer to as the empirical face. See Perpich (2005) for a critical discussion of some of the difficulties generated by the face as a rhetorical figure.

some cases the similarities are especially striking. Levinas's distinction between ethics and politics, for example, resonates with Carol Gilligan's distinction between care and justice (Taylor 2005).

There are shared trouble spots too. Among feminist care theorists the mother-child relationship is a privileged archetype in the psychology of moral development; for Levinas maternity is the paradigmatic site of ethics, at least metaphorically (Levinas 1981). Yet motherhood has long been a site of women's oppression, and images of the vulnerable faces of children have proven to be among the most powerful ideological tools with which to demand and justify maternal self-sacrifice (Rich 1986). Further, the equation of ethics and maternity risks recognizing women as ethical subjects only if and when they are mothers. Thus, even though feminists find it an ethically compelling site of human experience, as does Levinas, feminists are perhaps more conscious of compelling reasons to be wary of the appearance of maternity in ethical theory. Various feminist care theorists have, therefore, tried to disengage the concepts of care and relationality from motherhood and mothering. These contributions move us closer to an adequate appreciation of how socially fundamental care is and toward rethinking how the work that has traditionally been privatized, essentialized, and naturalized as mothering can be less oppressively, less exploitatively, and even more effectively accomplished.[3] To repeat Joan Tronto's emphatic observation: "care is not a parochial concern of women, a type of secondary moral question, or the work of the least well off in society. Care is a central concern of human life. It is time we began to change our political and social institutions to reflect this truth" (Tronto 1993, 180).

Despite the arguments for its universal significance, feminist models of care retain persistent traces of particularly maternal responsiveness and responsibility. From a Levinasian perspective they may be right to do so. However, in light of the power of patriarchal ideologies of sacrificial motherhood, even a trace association of feminist ethics with the maternal threatens to limit women's horizons, especially in the context of pregnancy. It also threatens the credibility of feminist theorists who simultaneously subscribe to care ethics and pro-choice politics (Wolfe-Devine 1997). These threats are further magnified by the way in which maternity is envisioned by new technology for fetal monitoring, especially ultrasound imaging. This method of revealing the fetal face presents it as a witness to a woman's maternal and moral status, bringing her experience of pregnant embodiment under a kind of scrutiny that

---

3. Mullin (2005) is an important recent example of this work.

alarms feminist observers. Mullin echoes Glenda Wall's concerns about "the recent 'remoralization of pregnancy' that has accompanied recent advances in the monitoring and visualizing of the fetus"(Mullin 2005, 99). I share these concerns. I hesitate though to use the term *re*-moralization in case it can be read to imply a restoration of an original or essential moral dimension. I would like to leave open here the question of whether embodied experience has essential moral meanings. The questions I regard as more urgent to address relate to which specific moral meanings are currently being invested in pregnancy and what relations they bear to the political contexts in which they are emerging.

In the sections that follow I indicate how the current (re)moralization of pregnancy coincides with the reinforcement of sacrificial maternal identity within a patriarchal political and cultural context. Later I shall contrast this context with the metaphorically maternal context out of which Levinasian ethics is born. It is my contention that ultrasound appears to reinforce and personalize an abstract discursive relation between mother and child within the dominant cultural paradigm of sacrificial maternity; it presents images of a woman and the fetus she carries as sentimental yet documentary-quality illustrations of that cultural story. Within this illustrated narrative a woman can only entertain the idea of aborting the fetus that has been shown to her on pain of grave violence to her own moral identity. By contrast, I argue, the maternal Levinasian construction of ethics leaves open the question of whether ultrasound technology can reveal a face at all, in the Levinasian sense. It therefore also leaves open the question of the kind of sense that a woman can make of her experience of pregnant embodiment. My discussion should be read as feminist reflection on pregnant embodiment responsive to the provocation of Levinasian ethics,[4] an exploration of how we might use his ethics to do so.

2.1. Focus on The Fetal Face: A Frame for (M)Other-hood

Arguing that the latest technological advances in ultrasound imaging provide morally salient information, pro-life activists have taken steps to ensure that more pregnant women get this information. In 2004 the American Christian organization Focus on the Family began a six-year project to bring ultrasound to "crisis pregnancy centers" (Rettig 2005). Organization members believe that

---

4. Other feminists who have found Levinas similarly provocative include Rosalyn Diprose (2002) and Lisa Guenther (2006).

ultrasound images have a powerful effect on the viewer. One FOTF spokesperson observed, "[It] really has an impact on the guy as well, because guys are so visual. And seeing something really always seems to impact a fellow even more than it does a girl; so they are also very [deeply affected] by this" (Rettig 2005). American politicians have been affected too, to the tune of $3 million contained in a bill to provide up to half the cost of ultrasound equipment. The money is destined for nonprofit crisis pregnancy centers, the vast majority of which oppose abortion (O'Keefe 2003).

Meanwhile, in the United Kingdom, politicians are being urged to limit legal access to abortion. Some argue that due to the knowledge provided by ultrasound imaging abortion should no longer be permitted after three months (Foxnews.com 2004; BBC News 2004b). Particularly influential in this debate has been a recent publication by Stuart Campbell of London's Create Health Clinic. Campbell's popular book, *Watch Me Grow* (2004), showcases his "pioneering" use of the 4-D scanner—an imaging device that produces detailed 3-D images in real time. A one-hour consultation with this new technology is available at the clinic for a fee of £275 (BBC News 2004a).

Exposure to images of this sort is not limited to those who can afford a private screening in London or who visit a well-equipped American crisis pregnancy center. Many have seen them in their own living rooms. On March 6, 2005, for example, The National Geographic Channel broadcast a two hour television special, *In the Womb*, using images produced by 4-D scanning as well as a "bumpcam" and a "fetoscope, specially fitted with a high definition mini-camera...inserted in the mother's stomach [sic]." According to one enthusiastic description the broadcast, "*In the Womb* sheds light on a delicate but dark place and takes viewers right into the fragile and mysterious world of pregnancy" (Illinois Federation 2005). *Knocked Up*, a tremendously popular and successful movie released in the summer of 2007, has reached a still wider audience. Ultrasound imaging is a key narrative device in this film. The meaningful passage of time is marked for the audience by regular ultrasound images of a developing fetus, whose steady growth is also expressed through the increasing musical complexity of its personal theme music.

Feminist pro-choice advocates do not regard the pointed use of ultrasound imaging as empowering for women, however. They describe it instead as a "weapon" deployed against women, often at taxpayers' expense (O'Keefe 2003). But proponents of the strategic use of ultrasound have a ready reply that, ironically, relies on feminist sounding rhetoric of empowerment: "Information is knowledge and knowledge is power and that's why this is a threat to [the pro-choice organization] Planned Parenthood" (O'Keefe 2003). This rhetoric and the strategy it supports cry out for deeper feminist analysis. What is the impact of ultrasound intervention on the processes that inform a pregnant woman's moral experiences and capacities? What kind of information does ultrasound supply? For whom is it empowering?

How might Levinas have answered these questions? The essential particularity of the relation between a fetus and the woman who carries it supplies a vivid though potentially misleading model of the Levinasian ethical relation—a relation he describes in terms of maternity (Brody 2001; Katz 2003; Taylor 2005; Guenther 2006; Bevis 2007). Prenatal "maternity" as it is constructed within the discourse connecting fetal ultrasound and pro-life politics does share at least one important characteristic with the definitive scene of Levinas's maternal ethics, namely that it is discovered, not chosen. One discovers, through ultrasound or more old-fashioned methods, that the relationship with the conceptus exists independently of one's determination to take responsibility for it or not. In Levinasian terms, it is one's encounter with the face of the Other that reveals that one is already ethically bound to him or her. The question remains as to whether the revelation enabled by ultrasound, or other diagnostic means, is relevantly similar to the Levinasian revelation.

Neither revelation is empowering in the sense in which feminist pro-choice discourse imagines empowerment (e.g., by acknowledging and sustaining a woman's right as an autonomous agent to make her own choices or by increasing the options she has). Levinasian ethical discourse emphasizes that the ethical moment precedes and is even antithetical to free choice. As Chloë Taylor (2005) notes, Levinas typically uses language expressive not only of the involuntariness of the passage into the ethical but also of the violation of autonomy that it involves. Levinas speaks of the ethical subject being *held hostage* by the face of the other (Levinas 1981, 127).

However, the use of ultrasound imaging by pro-life advocates to reveal a woman's maternal identity to her is disempowering in a *different* way. The pregnant woman is not held hostage by the *particular* Other whose face she encounters, as Levinas would have it. Rather she is held hostage to interpretive norms that compel her to have an ethical encounter with a fetus or at least to imagine or behave as if she has. This kind of hostage taking is a kind of substitute violation that obscures ethical relation in addition to violating a woman's autonomy.

The face encountered in Levinasian ethics is not a phenomenon, expressly not a representation or image of the essence of personhood. Having a face is not a sufficient precondition of being ethically encountered. But consciousness of being encountered in a face-to-face relation is necessary. The ultrasound image does not provide access to the subjective experience of those in a relationship (a pregnant woman and a fetus); no image could do this. Rather, it represents a relationship as it is conceived from an external, third-person perspective, a perspective occupied moreover by scientists and politically interested observers. The imagined moral content of the image is presented as objective scientific fact. Ultrasound technology, thus, seems to produce a vantage point from which to objectively visualize a woman's moral condition as well as her medical condition. Within patriarchal discourse, the normatively loaded image of maternal identity is inferred by the external observer from the *image* or other externally observable sign of the fetus, rather than from the unmediated experience of the pregnant woman. Thus, in cases where a woman has doubts about whether to continue a pregnancy, ultrasound technicians can present her with an image of her maternity whose authenticity she is afforded no authority to reject. If she considers abortion after being presented with this image, she can be represented as defective in her capacity for moral encounter with others rather than as having an alternative experience of the encounter she is supposed to be having (vis-à-vis the gestation of a fetus). As someone interviewed as an expert for Fox TV put it, "If she makes that choice [abortion] after having seen those pictures I perhaps feel she is not suited to be a mother" (Foxnews.com 2004).

Similarly, Marc T. Newman, president of MovieMinistry.com, sets aside his strong objections to *Knocked Up*'s representation of substance abuse, premarital sex, and bad language to give two thumbs up to the popular romantic comedy's pro-life message.

> No rationale is given in the film for [Alison's] decision to keep her baby, but certainly seeing the evidence of her child's beating heart must have played some role. Images of children *in utero* can help to overcome our culture's irrational idea that the physical fact and moral worth of the human person that is in a woman's womb from the moment of conception should be determined solely on the basis of whether or not she is happy about her pregnancy at the time. Sure, Alison cries at this first, conclusive evidence of her untimely pregnancy. But it is not long after that she commits to carry her baby. *Knocked Up* is an outstanding argument for the need for women to see what is going on inside their bodies when they are pregnant. If your local pro-life pregnancy counselling center is not equipped with an ultrasound machine and a licensed technician to run it—help them get both—quick! (Newman 2007)

The reviewer is clear about the powerful role played by the way that conception and pregnancy are represented. The film, he notes, shows "the development of an unborn child as an unbroken stream of events beginning with conception and continuing through birth" (Newman 2007). What the reviewer fails to notice is that we are not in fact looking at an unbroken series of events but rather a highly constructed montage of images. The sort of "argument" Newman sees presented in the film is the sort that led Plato to call for the banishment of the poets. This call resonates in Levinas's critique of idolatrous aesthetic diversion from the ethical. It reflects a similar concern with the power of images to mislead. A spectator to a relationship is not in a position to determine whether you are in a face-to-face relation with another or not. A viewer of an image of a relationship is even less well placed to do so.

2.2. *Envisioning the Normative Form of the Fetal Face*

In the work of a number of recent continental philosophers, including Levinas, vision is figured as a particularly suspect mode of perception (Jay 1993; Levin 1997; Grandy 2001; Taylor 2006). Feminist epistemologists and philosophers of science also note that vision, especially vision aided by scientific instrumentation, is a dominant trope in the "view from nowhere" approach to objectivity (Bordo 1987; Haraway 1988). In this view objectivity implies an epistemological distance analogous to the distance between a visual observer and the objects in his or her visual field. Such distance is taken to signify the absence of observer bias, interference, or manipulation in contrast, say, to the kind of knowledge one has when one is touched by or feels another. The apparently disembodied nature of the figuratively "visual" approach to the facts "out there" obscures its embodied and normative content. In light of this analysis, the dominant emphasis on visualization in pro-natalist deployment of ultrasound is worth noting.

Visual images, of course, do not reflect a view from nowhere. They are constructed within specific political and technological histories. They express, to use Donna Haraway's term, situated knowledge. Holding situated knowers accountable does not require that we strip away technology, to look at the world with the naked eye, nor that we privilege some other sense, nor even that we privilege a standpoint that we suppose to be epistemologically innocent.[5]

---

5. Haraway (1988) maps out a feminist position that is to be distinguished from a science and technology–hostile earth mother feminist romanticism. It is also distinct from the approach of various French feminists, especially Luce Irigaray, who take a tactile turn away from the phallogocentric visual economy (Grosz 1994, 104). Further, it is distinct from Sandra Harding's

Rather, accountability is to be pursued through attention to how a particular perspective is informed at its specific site of technological and political embodiment. And feminist epistemology demands in particular that women be accounted for. A good place to start in this context, then, is with the literal and discursive framing of prenatal ultrasound images that illumine the fetal face while obscuring the maternal context within which it appears.

Prenatal ultrasound functions as a technology that performs maternal sacrifice. Ultrasound images highlight the being *for* whom the pregnant woman exists; her identity is otherwise essentially disappeared (Stabile 1992). Of course, this way of framing pregnancy did not originate with ultrasound technology. It has a long history in the medical illustration of pregnant embodiment. One relative constant throughout this history is that the *woman's* face is not part of the picture (Kukla 2005).[6] Her body is transformed into a container, incubator, or cave. She does not even appear as a welcoming host who shelters and nourishes a vulnerable visitor; she *is* the shelter itself, the ground in which a human seed is nourished.

This perspective is represented in the well-known anti-abortion film *The Silent Scream* (1984), in which we hear a clear voice-over description of the fuzzy ultrasound images of a twelve-week abortion in progress. The viewer's attention is directed to the "child," "moving serenely" in its "sanctuary" prior to the introduction of a medical instrument in the uterus. This description is delivered with the sober neutrality of the evening news, and its authority is cemented by the revelation that the narrative perspective is in fact embodied by a medical doctor—the traditional expert in matters both scientific and moral. Dr. Bernard Nathanson, the film's director as well as narrator, explains the meaning of a dark and mysterious site in order to reveal and protect its inhabitants from the unenlightened. The enlightened viewer is encouraged to identify with the narrator, who functions as her or his ethical proxy.

If fetal monitoring technology did reveal the ethical interests or rights of the fetus, then third parties, as well the pregnant woman herself, would be ethically obliged to respond to it. But such a revelation posits a more normatively complicated picture than the scientific technology alone could possibly present. It requires the support of culturally generated discursive technologies that can

---

(1991) standpoint epistemology, which seems to suggest the possibility of an innocent perspective from which to examine the blind spots of dominant western epistemology and philosophy of science.

6. A truly remarkable exception to this pattern is the painting featured on the cover of Kukla's *Mass Hysteria* (2005).

normatively frame the visual images. The necessity of such support becomes more obvious on closer examination of some of the specific rights that some take to be revealed by fetal monitoring. These include a right to medical intervention, a right to an optimal gestational environment, and even a right *not* to be born.

The idea that a fetus has a right to life as soon as its presence is externally detectable (e.g., in the "quickening" phase) has a long and well known albeit controversial history. The belief that this right goes beyond the right not to be killed, but is a positive right to have life sustained, and sustained well, is expressed in the belief among medical personnel that a fetus (at least a fetus that a pregnant woman intends to carry to term) has independent status as a patient and a moral claim on their assistance, one that may even override the pregnant woman's treatment choices (Martin and Coleman 1995). Feminists have observed that the felt necessity among providers of expert assistance intended to optimize the fetus's gestational environment is sometimes used to justify the use of ultrasound to support efforts to educate, persuade, or coerce a pregnant woman to engage in certain behaviors and refrain from others (Mullin 2005, 103).

Compared to the right to life and a right to optimal gestational environment, the idea that a fetus might have an interest or right not to be born might seem odd. Yet that is precisely what is indicated in the rhetoric of "wrongful life suits." These legal actions are brought on behalf of severely disabled infants and children whose disability it is alleged should have been visible to ultrasound technicians or doctors who negligently failed to recognize not only the disability of the fetus but also the interest it had in not being born (Nelson and Robertson 2001). Though perhaps counterintuitive, what this presumed instance of identifying a fetal right or interest shares with the others is its illustration of the normative force of fetal imaging.

Though pregnant women are those whose character or behavior is most likely to come under scrutiny, the power of fetal imaging to regulate behavior can extend its sphere of influence beyond them. It can include anyone who it could be said should feel morally compelled to protect the unborn as well as those who are held legally accountable for not providing adequate prenatal care or advice. From the perspective of a scientific viewpoint that is taken to have revealed all of these rights and interests, women who resist recommendations as to how best to serve fetal interests are often regarded as noncompliant or not sufficiently "bonded" with the fetus. Sometimes in such cases, prenatal ultrasound imaging is used to "promote bonding" and "encourage compliance"

(Mitchell 2001; Mullin 2005). Maternal bonding is not directly visualized. It is inferred from the signs for which a woman's behavior is scrutinized. What counts as a sign of adequate bonding seems often to be measured by compliance with expert advice. This mode of determination implies a tacit comparison of a pregnant woman's apparent emotional or ethical response to the fetus and the felt emotional or ethical response of medical experts or other concerned outsiders. Although there is no evidence to think that it is more objective, the external response here is accorded more respect. It bears on its face the values associated with the objectivity of disinterested and distanced scientific observation.

The context of interventions motivated and informed by ultrasound imaging generates a picture of the good mother as one who either naturally embodies an ideal gestational environment, or who identifies with and acts according to the authorized external perspective on what it takes to support this environment. The embodied knowledge of the pregnant woman is easily erased in this picture. So long as she remains pregnant the scope of her agency is reduced to the role of guardian of the fetal habitat. In cases of "willful noncompliance" she appears and is often treated as behaving negligently or mutinously.[7] A woman who fails to adequately inhabit her prescribed role is disqualified as an agent altogether and reduced to the fetal habitat itself.

2.3. Looking to the Fetal Face to Mirror Maternal and Medical Identities

In ultrasound images a pregnant woman is envisioned as the ground against which the fetus is figured. She is thus disappeared from the image. Women are also often marginalized at the scene of ultrasound imaging itself. Their "presence [is] minimized, when all attention (doctor and expectant father's) [is] on the screen."[8] The pregnant woman becomes a site in which mysterious and fascinating human drama unfolds. She herself is a mere backdrop. Maternity is rendered as passivity—something that *happens* to a woman rather than something that she *does*. But one route back to agency in this scenario is to become a fellow spectator and co-participant in the hermeneutic production of (her) maternal identity.

---

7. This is comparable to a woman's historical status in rape law as guardian rather than owner of her sexuality—a legal tradition treating her not as victim but as witness, and often as a hostile witness, with weak credibility to boot (Brownmiller 1975).

8. Sandelowski (1994) cited in Morton (n.d.b).

It should not be surprising then that ultrasound imaging is used by many pregnant women and their partners to help them reconstruct their identities. For many prospective parents ultrasound has become a routine part of the experience of pregnancy. Its predominant function almost seems to have shifted from the medical monitoring of pregnancy to an opportunity to take the first baby pictures for the family album. It would be easy to be critical of what some call "Keepsake Ultrasounds," yet feminist researchers like Christine Morton argue that it is not a frivolous activity (Mitchell 2001; Rados 2004; Morton n.d.a; n.d.b). Morton's research focuses on the role of ultrasound in pregnant women's efforts to imagine pregnancy relationally, finding that it enables women to make an anticipated relationship appear more real to themselves. For many it supports efforts to cope with the changes the birth of a baby is expected to bring. For many it also provides a way of coming to terms with the experience of pregnancy itself.

Morton's research shows that it is not so easy to imagine that a pregnancy entails the existence of another person, even when that is what is desired. That is why signs of personhood are so anxiously sought. One particularly important sign is sex. Given that our conception of sex is so bound up with our conception of human personality, Morton explains, sexing the fetus helps to place it in the genre "person." Many respondents spoke of the usefulness of being able to plan for a boy or a girl, but Morton also found something more fundamental at stake. This is the sense that it is less disturbing to experience an unusual relation with another *person* than to feel inhabited by something that not only is not oneself but is of a more fundamentally unknown, indeterminate nature. Morton describes how personifying the fetus enabled a pregnant woman to better cope with the peculiar experience of "quickening":

> This is referred to as active movement, feeling the baby kick, and is often eagerly anticipated by the pregnant woman as a way of relating to the fetus and making the baby become more real. Sometimes, though . . . the feeling does not correspond to the image "baby." In the case of one woman I interviewed, the movements connoted some kind of furry, soft footed creature, like a rabbit or a mouse. This image was unsettling to her, and was one reason why she convinced her physician to do an extra, non-diagnostic ultrasound to determine fetal sex. In this way, she could think of "Jennifer" moving around inside her body, not a rodent. (Morton n.d.a)

Some researchers note that ultrasound technicians often passively resist and appear scornful of expectant parents' desires to know the sex of the fetus

(Mitchell 2001; Morton n.d.a). Yet they seem to share a desire to personify the fetus even if they regard other aspects of personhood as more salient, namely those that identify the fetus as a patient. Morton provides an example of a technician, Caroline, whose rhetoric is suggestive of a protective medical relationship with a young patient to whom she is "listening." "Caroline says, 'this is the top most part of the cervical spine, at the base of the baby's skull. Now I'm scanning the abdomen lengthwise, you can see the separation of the heart and stomach, here's the diaphragm . . . he's turning around there, OK? He's acting up, his hands are clasped, one over the other, he's got them in between his legs, he's saying no more pictures today'" (Morton, n.d.a). Stuart Campbell's concern about the impact of late abortion on medical personnel is also suggestive of a "doctor-patient" relational identity formation. He argues: "After 17 weeks the procedure is . . . extremely distressing for the doctors and nurses carrying out the procedure" (BBC News 2004b).

The approaches of prospective parents as well as medical personnel to ultrasound images often reflect a powerful need on the part of the viewer to orient her- or himself to a relationship with a person, and a need to overcome the practical and psychological difficulties of relating to the unknown. There is a need to understand what is happening. Though this is a reasonable impulse it is one that, from a Levinasian perspective, threatens ethical encounter rather than signifying it. The encounter with alterity, with infinitely uncategorizable otherness, lies at the heart of Levinasian ethics. For Levinas l'autrui/the Other cannot be known by assimilating it to the categories of my understanding.

For some prospective parents resistance to the categorization encouraged by sex identification helps them to leave a space open to enter relation with the Other whose arrival they anticipate. From a Levinasian perspective such resistance may be necessary in order to allow the ethical relation to occur, initiated as it must be by the call of the Other her- or himself. One woman in Morton's study mused along these lines: "I wonder if knowing the gender of the little wiggly would incline me towards making an identity for it and so we would miss those first few days of getting to know each other in the outside world" (Morton, n.d.a).

Resistance to premature identification may account for other strategies used by pregnant women to come to terms with pregnancy. These strategies emphasize women's experience of their own embodiment. Pregnant women (and their partners) come up with pet names that express their experience of the pregnancy. Names like "[d]umpling, cookie monster, boink, sidekick, spot, and smidgen," says Morton, have roots in food cravings, abdominal pressure sensations, and blurry ultrasound images. "These names," she observes, "highlight some of the ambiguity that women encounter as they experience the sensation of an 'other' inside them and the creative methods they employ to make sense of and in some way account for this 'othering' sensation" (Morton n.d.a). While these women experience an other of some sort, it is not quite wholly Other, and they are not quite yet mother to this Other.

The distinction between "other" and "Other" reflects a conventional solution to a difficulty in translating Levinas's crucial distinction between *l'autre* and *l'autrui*.[9] The term "other/*autre*" can refer to anything that can be subsumed under categories or "genres." Levinas argues that to understand something as belonging to some category or "genre" that distinguishes it from me is still to understand it on my terms and in this sense as a kind of projection of myself. The other is assimilated under the categories of my understanding. *L'autrui*/the Other, however, cannot be assimilated to the categories of the understanding. It cannot be known in that sense, though it can be encountered, but only as something utterly exterior to me. A pregnant woman can thus understand a fetus as an other, but it is a mistake to assume that in doing so she encounters an Other.

Women vary in their experiences of pregnancy, and any given woman's experience varies over time. The distinction between what is me and what is not me seems throughout the course of a pregnancy to be a relatively fluid matter. This fluidity may be experienced as everything from interesting and pleasurable to uncanny or threatening. One may try to orient oneself in this experience by trying to understand it, that is, by thinking of the other with whom one is related through the categories of one's own understanding. But this strategy both assimilates the other to one's own categories and then mistakes this conception of the other for an *encounter* with an *Other*. In an attempt to make sense of one's experience of pregnancy in terms of motherhood—a relationship with a dependent Other—prospective parents can prematurely generate that identity through their conceptions of an other person during pregnancy. Those conceptions are powerfully informed by the cultural matrix within which they are generated. As we have seen, many women and their partners seek reflections of themselves as mothers, or parents, in ultrasound images of the fetus, or in

---

9. The standard orthographic conventions to express the distinction between other and Other are explained by Levinas translator Alphonso Lingis: "With the author's permission we are translating '*autrui*' (the personal Other, the you) by 'Other,' and '*autre*' by 'other.' In doing so we regrettably sacrifice the possibility of reproducing the author's use of both capital or small letters with both these terms in the French text" (Levinas 1969, 24–25).

other signs of its presence (e.g., abdominal movements). Still, the experience of those who do not attempt this premature (m)Othering suggests that this experience is not an inevitable or necessary one. Waiting for an encounter is a possible alternative, and from a Levinasian perspective, perhaps one that is preferable to premature assumption of motherhood.

3. THE POLITICS OF PREGNANCY AND THE MATERNAL FACE OF ETHICS

Levinas has a special appeal for many feminists because he locates ethical authority in a relational matrix rather than in the realm of abstract impersonal universal imperatives. Nonetheless, relational ethics has been subject to serious feminist critique, given the inherent risk of legitimating abusive or exploitive relationships (e.g., Card 1990; Houston 1990). In response to this problem some feminists emphasize relational qualities like mutuality and reciprocity. But if this emphasis is necessary then feminist appeal to Levinas would be misplaced. Levinas is explicit in his critique of relational philosophers who emphasize mutuality and reciprocity, most notably Martin Buber (see Levinas 1993; 1996; Murray 2003; Atterton et al. 2004; Taylor 2005). In contrast to the mutuality and reciprocity of Buber's dialogical "I-and-Thou," Levinas's account of the dialogical ethical relation with the Other highlights its asymmetry. He argues that precisely this asymmetry is necessary to generate the moral authority of the Other. The height from which the Other addresses one is what entails an ethical ought. Simply having a dialogical attitude toward the world is not sufficient to situate one ethically.

But perhaps feminists need not insist on mutuality and reciprocity in relationships in order to sustain a critique of feminine self-sacrifice. Mullin, for example, "open[s] up space to challenge assumptions that self-sacrifice should be the norm without going to the opposite extreme of concluding that acts of unreciprocated care are unhealthy" (Mullin 2005, 188). It is easy to see the sense of this. As long as a woman is *free* to choose to undertake an action of unreciprocated care, no matter what the cost to her, her action can be understood as supporting rather than sacrificing her agency, and as such not a self-sacrificial action. This qualified acceptance of nonreciprocal relationships, however, is not available for a would-be Levinasian feminist. The nonreciprocal relationship that characterizes the ethical according to Levinas is not a relationship that one *chooses,* freely or otherwise. For Levinas one is made an ethical subject by being taken hostage by the Other.

For feminists concerned with the politics and ethics of pregnancy, talk of hostage taking inevitably evokes Judith Jarvis Thomson's (1971) famous violinist analogy. The success of her argument relies on the intuition that it would be wrong to force someone to remain a hostage even if doing so would save the life of a vulnerable and valuable person. Nonetheless, just as Mullin allows that unreciprocated acts of care need not be unhealthy, Thomson affirms the praiseworthiness of *choosing* to make life saving sacrifices. What these feminist philosophers address, and correctly in my view, are the *social and political* forces that put women into such potentially self-sacrificial situations, keep women in them, or make it difficult to escape them—forces that unacceptably restrict women's choices (cf. Sherwin 1991). What they do not address, however, is the meaning of being an *ethical* hostage, if such a thing is actually possible. A Levinasian perspective may prove useful in considering if and/or how pregnancy or maternity are, in ethical terms, properly understood through a hostage analogy. As Claire Elise Katz argues, "Levinas's use of the image of maternity not only teaches us a great deal about responsibility via the image of maternity; it also teaches us a great deal about maternity" (Katz 2003, 155). But learning from Levinas is not a simple task, "Levinas's project does offer something of use to feminists, but it will not offer it to us easily and it will not be found by applying a straightforward reading of his work motivated by a typical set of feminist concerns. Levinas's work may offer us the opportunity to see feminist concerns in a different light and to see a wider range of what those concerns might be" (Katz 2003, 155).

3.1. *Pregnancy and Maternity: Relationality Through a Levinasian Lens*

Questions about the justice or injustice of restrictions on choices that can legitimately be made by pregnant women are political rather than ethical questions. If every person is ethically held hostage by every Other, as Levinas's account of ethics suggests, then a politics that legitimates some of these demands while ignoring others is not ethical. How and if a choice could be politically justifiable are questions that would need to be answered in some other way. Still, insisting on the openness of the political questions as to whether or when one can refuse to sacrifice one's interests for the sake of another does not rule out the possibility that a Levinasian account of ethics is correct and characteristic of (pre- or postnatal) maternity.

It is crucially important at this point to distinguish between pregnancy and maternity. Maternity is for Levinas a metaphor for the ethical relation.

But, I shall argue, pregnancy is not necessarily a form of maternity in the sense in which he uses the term. The distinction I make between pregnancy and maternity is made in a Levinasian spirit. It depends on distinguishing between maternity as an ethical, dialogical relation and pregnancy as a relational phenomenon that is epistemologically only accessible from a third-person perspective. The pregnant woman can take up this third-person perspective on her pregnancy just as other people can (e.g., through data generated by ultrasound technology), although she also has unique access to some of the data that can be interpreted from this perspective (e.g., pressure felt on her internal organs).

To clarify the terminology of this distinction it is worth noting that though Levinas rejects the mutuality of Buber's dialogical relations, he shares with Buber the view that an ethical relation is a dialogical one, a relation between first and second persons—between an *I* and a *you*.[10] The third-person perspective is the I-it perspective. This, according to Buber, is the perspective that reigns over science and technology. Dealing with the world in this mode allows us to understand the *kinds* of beings with which we must deal. It is an impersonal mode, one of estrangement rather than communion. Like Buber, Levinas recognizes the threat this mode poses to the ethical but also, like Buber, its practical value. Levinas extends the domain of the third-person approach beyond science and technology to include law and politics. He calls this "justice reasoning," in the sense used also in care ethics. Gilligan likens justice reasoning to the algorithmic application of moral principles to moral problems. One of her young research subjects speaks of "doing a math problem with humans" (Gilligan 1982, 28). Similarly, in a 1986 interview, Levinas says, "'justice' is for me something which is a calculation, which is knowledge, and which supposes politics; it is inseparable from the political. It is something which I differentiate from ethics which is primary" (Wright et al. 1988, 171).

Justice reasoning, indeed all reasoning that depends on categorization, involves for Levinas a fundamental betrayal of the alterity of the Other. This is a betrayal that Levinas recognizes as both inevitable and necessary, given that we each encounter more than one Other. There are more than two, more than I and you, in the universe. "If the third is also a face," Levinas notes, "one must know whom to speak to first." One is compelled to ask "Who is the first face?"

---

10. Where Buber (1970) famously speaks of "I and thou" using the familiar form of "you" (*Du* in German, *tu* in French), Levinas insists on the asymmetrical relation of the I and what in French is expressed as *vous*, the formal "you."

Thus one is "led to compare the faces, to compare the two people. Which is a terrible task. It is entirely different from speaking to the face. To compare them is to place them in the same genre" (Wright et al. 1988, 174). Reasoning through genres, or with categories, involves assimilating the Other, that is, reducing the Other to the categories of *my understanding*. Otherness, which resists this reduction, is obscured and cannot be encountered this way. What is produced instead is an impersonal epistemological relation between the in principle universally accessible *perspective* of the knowing subject and the objectively known object. This can be called an epistemological third-person relation in contrast with the second-person orientation of the dialogical ethical relation. Both of these relations are further to be differentiated from an ontological relation between two entities that is independent of there being any knowledge of it.

Pregnancy clearly involves an ontological relation between two entities,[11] and this relation exists regardless of whether the pregnant woman or anyone else is aware of it. Whether this is a significant relation from a third-person justice perspective depends on what *kind* of an entity the fetus is understood to be and what kind of obligations one has to such entities on the relevant scheme of justice reasoning. But for Levinas focus on ontology is ethically misleading. For Levinas, the ethical relation occurs not in virtue of the mediation of the categories of scientific or justice reasoning but immediately through meeting the Other. This meeting requires receptive consciousness on the part of the one who encounters the Other. And, of course, there must really be an Other who is encountered, not just a hypothetical Other whom one imagines or anticipates encountering. Thus, insofar as one can be pregnant without knowing it, or think that one is pregnant when one is not, pregnancy itself cannot be a paradigm of ethical relation. Further, if we accept Levinas's use of "the maternal" to designate the ethical, pregnancy is not necessary for maternity.

Pregnancy does have some important characteristics, however, from a Levinasian perspective. Precisely because one can be pregnant without knowing it, one has no choice but to *discover* that one is pregnant. One can only find that one is in this specific relation rather than choose to enter it. I don't, of course, mean that it is impossible to choose whether to try and become pregnant or to try and avoid it. Rather, I mean that after the occurrence of the necessary events there are gaps between the coming into being of the other entity (when the

---

11. This is true even if the embryo or fetus is not strictly speaking a separate being. We can still understand it as distinct in the way that I can speak of my relation with my hand as something distinct from "me."

body becomes pregnant), the discovery that it exists (when one discovers that one is pregnant), the encounter with it (when one first "meets" one's child), and a coming to terms with that encounter (when one places the relationship with this Other into a larger context of competing ethical demands). These gaps separate the entity's ontic generation from its epistemological conceptualization as other, from its ethical birth as Other, from its political reconception as one who bears specific rights. The gaps are not only temporal ones. They are effects of qualitative difference. The ethical gap is entailed by the fact that one cannot choose to encounter the specific otherness of the Other prior to *encountering* him or her, never mind prior to his or her actual *existence*. The feature of having no choice but to discover relation rather than choosing to enter it in the way one might enter a contractual relation makes the relational consciousness of pregnancy a radical example of the kind of passivity and involuntariness that typifies Levinas's "maternity." Yet the distinction between pregnancy and maternity remains crucial.

Whether and when pregnancy becomes maternity depends on what sort of knowledge occurs when a pregnancy becomes known. Is it the kind of knowledge I have described as reasoning with categories and genres, or is it dialogical knowledge, the experience of meeting or encountering an Other in an ethical sense? These questions cannot be answered by ontological inquiry, by establishing what kind of a being a fetus is. This remains true even if we try to appeal to the category of "beings with a face" (Levinasian persons, so to speak). If we could it would mean that each of us already stands in maternal relation to the whole world (or at least to every person) simply by virtue of the fact that those beings exist.

Why might a Levinasian deny such global maternity? Not simply because we may lack intentions regarding those we have not met. Ethical status, for Levinas, does not depend on intentions. Moreover, he is keenly aware of the importance of those whom we unwittingly affect. "Thou shalt not kill," Levinas explains, "does not mean simply that you are not to go around firing a gun all the time." He continues, "It refers, rather, to the fact that in the course of your life, in different ways, you kill someone. For example, when we sit down at the table in the morning and drink coffee, we kill an Ethiopian who doesn't have any coffee" (Wright et al., 1988, 173)

If Levinas would allow talk of an *ethical ontology* (i.e., to express that we are the *kind* of beings who could encounter each other) we might say that we stand in a kind of proto-ethical relation to them. Each of us, we could say, is pregnant with the whole world, vulnerable to being held hostage by each person we might encounter. But even if Levinas allows this, pregnancy remains distinct from maternity.

3.2. Can Ultrasound Produce Maternity?

In light of the distinction between pregnancy and maternity we can reexamine the role ultrasound might play in generating a shift between these conditions. To review the distinction: pregnancy first constitutes a specific ontological relation between a woman and a zygote, embryo, or fetus. This relation may or may not be politically or legally significant, depending on which form of justice reasoning one applies. A woman who knows she is pregnant stands additionally in an epistemological relationship to the zygote, embryo, or fetus—a relationship, moreover, in which all third persons may stand insofar as they can also know that this woman is pregnant. This knowledge may also generate certain political or legal obligations on the part of the pregnant woman or others in the know, again depending on the kind of justice reasoning applied. Finally, anyone who encounters a zygote, embryo, fetus, or unborn child stands in (Levinasian) maternal relation to it.

The question that then presses itself on us is whether a zygote, embryo, or fetus can be encountered at all. That is, does it have a "face" in Levinasian terms? Further, can it only be encountered by a woman who is pregnant with it? Can it be encountered by anyone else? Does seeing a prenatal ultrasound image constitute an ethical encounter or simply evidence that a certain kind of being is there? In other words, is ultrasound imaging only capable of generating an epistemological relation? Depending on how we answer these questions we can consider the ethical meaning and political acceptability of various strategic uses of ultrasound technology during a woman's pregnancy.

First, it is important to note that the face need not be a literal face, according to Levinas. One may encounter a face, he says, even if all one can see is the slope of someone's shoulders or a gesture of his hand. Clearly hands, shoulders, and the backs and fronts of heads (not to mention the highly significant genitalia) appear in ultrasound images, yet certain comments made by Levinas warrant skepticism about the equation of seeing a prenatal ultrasound image and encountering the face of the Other. These comments occur in an interview in which Levinas is pressed to explain how we can tell whether we are confronted by a face or not. Specifically, why does he think we are not confronted by a face when confronted by an animal, a dog, for example? It is not because he countenances cruelty to animals, but that he insists on differentiating between face-to-face encounters and encounters which move us because they *recall* face-to-face encounters.[12] "We do not wish to make an animal suffer needlessly and so on. But the prototype of this is human ethics. Vegetarianism, for example, arises from the transference to animals of the idea of suffering. The animal suffers. It is because we, as human, know what suffering is that we can have this obligation" (Wright et al. 1988, 172).

According to Levinas, the obligations involved here arise from thinking about animals as beings of a certain category or "genre," for example, as beings that suffer. Thus our general obligation to beings that can suffer comes from the idea of suffering, rather than as a command from a particular one who is suffering. Thus we can rationally determine appropriate behavior in relation to an animal in light of what follows from our idea of the nature of suffering, and so we refrain from hurting it and act to protect it from harm. According to Levinas we sometimes also transfer the idea of the animal to our relations with humans. To illustrate, he compares our delight in animal company with our delight in the company of children. "I cannot say at what moment you have the right to be called 'face.' . . . But there is something in our attraction to an animal. . . . In the dog, what we like is perhaps the child like character. . . . Children are often loved for their animality. The child is not suspicious of anything. . . . It's delightful" (Wright et al. 1988, 171). Levinas's resistance to mistaking the *idea* of ethical encounter for actual encounter arises not merely from the possibility of ontological misidentification (regarding whether a dog or a fetus is the kind of being who ever could be encountered) but also from misidentification of "encounter." In comparing my ideas of encounters I recall, with the encounter I imagine or anticipate having with an animal, I see compelling similarities and conclude that I can have an encounter with an animal and interpret my experience accordingly.

The fundamental problem here derives from fixation on appearances and phenomena. But for Levinas the point of the face metaphor is not the visual appearance of the face. The face above all is not an *appearance* for Levinas. About this he is explicit: "The face does not give itself to be seen. It is not a vision. The face is not that which is seen" (Wright et al. 1988, 176). And for those who treat the ultrasound image as *evidence* of the fetal face the following statement is also important: "There is no evidence with regards to the face" (176). In the same conversation Levinas also cautions, "I am not at all sure that

---

12. For a critical discussion of Levinas's view of animals see Atterton (2004).

the face is a phenomenon. A phenomenon is what appears. Appearance is not the mode of being of the face. The face is, from the start, the demand" (171).

Levinas's critique of aesthetics has a similar basis. He calls taking art as meaningful in and of itself idolatry (Levinas 1989). A work of art, he says, freezes a moment or a finite perspective. Since ethical Otherness is characterized by *infinite* alterity, an appearance that in any way is taken to represent the Other seduces us away from encountering Otherness in its specific and infinite alterity. The problem is not with the creative dimension of art but with the finitude of appearances, with phenomenal images that threaten to replace rather than mediate relation with an Other. Thus, there is a risk that seeing an *image* of a fetus is mistaken for the ethical significance of a face-to-face encounter.

One encounters the face of an Other insofar as one is addressed (though not necessarily verbally) by him or her. In light of this approach, Levinas's resistance to acknowledging the face of the animal can be read as not necessarily an emphatic denial of the ethical significance of animals, but rather as an emphatic insistence on the difference between being moved by the idea of suffering (feeling as if one were addressed by a hypothetical third person or idea) versus actually being addressed by an Other who suffers. Thus, in the context of pregnancy we can say that ultrasound images certainly help to inform the ideas we have of the vulnerability, pleasures, suffering, and interests of a fetus. This much can be acknowledged without admitting to being addressed by the fetus. The importance of this distinction is that ideas, while rationally compelling, do not hold us hostage in the way that ethical address does, according to Levinas. Thus, *if* a zygote, embryo, or fetus does not address us, it remains, in principle, possible to decide against its interests (in part or in whole) without fundamentally threatening our ethical integrity from a Levinasian perspective.

Ultrasound imaging provides evidence about a pregnancy that enables one to think about what the pregnancy sustains, what the other being is *like:* a child for example, or an animal for whom one cares, or perhaps even like a parasite supported by a host body. Depending on how one understands what this being is like, and what sorts of rights might properly be understood to be possessed by beings like that, one can decide how best to act. To resolve disagreements on this level one must take up the morally deliberative third-person perspective. Disagreement on this level is disagreement that can be negotiated with reasoned argument.

A pregnant woman's access to this perspective is threatened by those who would play the role of ethical surrogate for her. A woman's ethical horizons are threatened by those who take it as given that pregnancy is maternity and thus that a pregnant woman is an ethical hostage whose condition can and should be revealed to her with the aid of ultrasound or who ought to be morally disqualified because she seems deaf to the ethical call of the unborn. The assumption of maternity to which the ethical surrogate appeals is a premature ideological projection of motherhood onto the women whose lives are situated at sites of pregnant embodiment.

4. FINALLY . . .

But what if pregnancy were maternity and a pregnant woman were addressed by the fetus she carries? Does it follow that she must put the fetus's interests before all others? No. Levinas recognizes that if she is also addressed by any others she may have no alternative but to choose between them.[13] She must resolve the conflict between competing ethical calls by comparing them, and in so doing, undertake the terrible, but as Levinas recognized, also necessary move into the realm of the political, that is justice reasoning (cf. Derrida 1995). Can this be reconciled with ethics? Feminist research and reflection on how women have struggled to come to terms with a decision not to meet the Other's demands as well as their explorations of how this struggle is enacted through dialogical, narrative accounting suggest that it is possible (Gilligan 1982; Tuttle Hansen 1997). Notably, this research includes the possibility of telling a maternally responsive story about relations that have been ruptured by relinquishing access to a child through adoption, abortion, and even infanticide.

I offer no easy solutions here to the question of how a woman should deliberatively resolve such conflict-ridden situations, or complete the task of adequate ethical accounting that is demanded by the address of the Other. My point is simply that the necessity of undertaking difficult deliberation, and accounting for one's decisions, cannot be trumped by an effort to hold a pregnant woman ethically hostage to an *image* of a fetus. The efforts of ethical surrogates to force a transition from pregnancy to maternity by brandishing the image of a face and vetriloquizing its voice are neither ethically responsible nor politically just. Speaking for the fetus in the voice of a child may well move a woman to behave like its mother, but this is not an ethically motivated response. A political

---

13. There remains some dispute among Levinasians as to whether one's self has an ethical call on one that can compete with the call any others may make on one. I leave this issue unresolved here. It is sufficient for present purposes that a pregnant woman be faced with the demands of more than one other besides herself, as is almost always the case in actual human lives.

discourse that resorts to such tactics should be unsettled by the faces of women who like any Other demand recognition.[14] Their voices must not be smothered. We must not allow our attention to be misdirected away from them toward an image of motherhood superimposed upon images of pregnancy.

Ethics do not demand, only the Other does. Looking at pregnancy through a Levinasian lens makes it clear that if a fetus is an Other who demands ethical response, and if that response conflicts with the call of a pregnant woman or any other Others, that conflict can only legitimately be addressed in the realm of the political, that is, through justice reasoning. It cannot be resolved by prematurely imposing motherhood on a woman by appeal to what ethics demands.

REFERENCES

Atterton, Peter. 2004. Face to Face with the Other Animal? In *Levinas and Buber: Dialogue and Difference,* ed. Peter Atterton, Matthew Calarco, and Maurice Friedman, 262–81. Pittsburgh: Duquesne University Press.

Atterton, Peter, Matthew Calarco, and Maurice Friedman, eds. 2004. *Levinas and Buber: Dialogue and Difference.* Pittsburgh: Duquesne University Press.

BBC News. 2004a. Scans Uncover Secrets of the Womb. June 28. http://news.bbc.co.uk/2/hi/ health/3846525.stm (accessed August 24, 2006).

———. 2004b. Viewpoints Abortion. July 29. http://bbc.co.uk/1/hi/health/3894245.stm (accessed August 24, 2006).

Bevis, Kathryn. 2007. "Better than Metaphors"? Dwelling and the Maternal Body in Emmanuel Levinas. *Literature and Theology* 21(3): 317–29.

Bordo, Susan. 1987. *The Flight to Objectivity: Essays on Cartesianism and Culture.* Albany: State University of New York Press.

Brody, Donna. 2001. Levinas's Maternal Method from Time and the Other Through Otherwise than Being. In *Feminist Interpretations of Emmanuel Levinas,* ed. Tina Chanter, 53–77. University Park: Pennsylvania State University Press.

Brownmiller, Susan. 1975. *Against Our Will: Men, Women, and Rape.* London: Secker and Warburg.

Buber, Martin. 1970. *I and Thou.* Trans. Walter Kaufmann. New York: Scribner's Sons.

Campbell, Stuart. 2004. *Watch Me Grow.* London: Carroll and Brown.

Card, Claudia. 1990. Caring and Evil. *Hypatia: A Journal of Feminist Philosophy* 5:101–8.

Derrida, Jacques. 1995. *The Gift of Death.* Trans. David Wills. Chicago: University of Chicago Press.

Diprose, Rosalyn. 2002. *Corporeal Generosity: On Giving with Nietzsche, Merleau-Ponty, and Levinas.* New York: State University of New York Press.

---

14. For further insight on the role of the maternal, that is ethics, in "unsettling" politics, see Murray (2003, chap. 6).

Foxnews.com. 2004. New Ultrasound Rekindles Abortion Debate. July 22. http://www.foxnews.com/story/0,2933,12651 (accessed August 26, 2005).

Gilligan, Carol. 1982. *In a Different Voice: Psychological Theory and Women's Development.* Cambridge: Harvard University Press.

Grandy, David. 2001. The Otherness of Light: Einstein and Levinas. *Postmodern Culture: An Electronic Journal of Interdisciplinary Criticism* 12(1). http://muse.jhu.edu/login?uri=/journals/pmc/v012/12.1grandy.html (accessed November 18, 2008).

Grosz, Elizabeth. 1994. *Volatile Bodies: Toward a Corporeal Feminism.* Bloomington: Indiana University Press.

Guenther, Lisa. 2006. *The Gift of the Other: Levinas and the Politics of Reproduction.* Albany: State University of New York Press.

Haraway, Donna. 1988. Situated Knowledges: The Science Question in Feminism and the Privilege of Partial Perspective. *Feminist Studies* 14:575–99.

Harding, Sandra. 1991. *Whose Science? Whose Knowledge? Thinking from Women's Lives.* Ithaca: Cornell University Press.

Houston, Barbara. 1990. Caring and Exploitation. *Hypatia: A Journal of Feminist Philosophy* 5:115–19.

Illinois Federation for the Right to Life Daily News. 2005. National Geographic Channel Explores the Hidden World "In the Womb." February 22. http://lifesite.net/ldn/2005/mar/05030301.html (accessed August 24, 2006).

Jay, Martin. 1993. *Downcast Eyes: The Denigration of Vision in Twentieth-Century French Thought.* Berkeley and Los Angeles: University of California Press.

Katz, Claire Elise. 2003. *Levinas, Judaism, and the Feminine: The Silent Footsteps of Rebecca.* Bloomington: Indiana University Press.

Knocked Up. 2007. Dir. Judd Apatow. Prod. Seth Rogen, Evan Goldberg and Shauna Robertson [motion picture]. Universal Pictures.

Kukla, Rebecca. 2005. *Mass Hysteria: Medicine, Culture, and Mothers' Bodies.* Lanham, Md.: Rowman and Littlefield.

Levin, David Michael. 1997. Keeping Foucault and Derrida in Sight: Panopticism and the Politics of Subversion. In *Sites of Vision: The Discursive Construction of Sight in the History of Philosophy,* ed. David Michael Levin, 397–465. Cambridge: MIT Press.

Levinas, Emmanuel. 1969. *Totality and Infinity.* Trans. A. Lingis. Pittsburgh: Duquesne University Press.

———. 1981. *Otherwise Than Being or Beyond Essence.* Trans. A. Lingis. The Hague: Martinus Nijhoff.

———. 1989. Reality and Its Shadow. In *The Levinas Reader,* ed. Sean Hand, 129–43. Oxford: Basil Blackwell.

———. 1993. *Outside the Subject.* Trans. Michael Smith. Stanford: Stanford University Press.

———. 1996. *Proper Names.* Trans. Michael Smith. Stanford: Stanford University Press.

Martin, Sheilah, and Murray Coleman. 1995. Judicial Intervention in Pregnancy. *McGill Law Journal* 40:947–91.

Mitchell, Lisa. 2001. *Baby's First Picture: Ultrasound and the Politics of Fetal Subjects.* Toronto: University of Toronto Press.

Morton, Christine. n.d.a. Ultrasound Babies and Their Imaginary Counterparts: Women's Experience of Fetal Visualization and Movements. http://christinemorton.com/CHM/CHM_Ultrasound%20Babies.htm (accessed August 20, 2005). Draft cited with author's permission.

———. n.d.b. Sociology of Reproduction Course Notes. Lecture 7, Case Study: Ultrasound. http://christinemorton.com/CHM/S000_week07.htm (accessed August 24, 2005).
Mullin, Amy. 2005. *Reconceiving Pregnancy and Childcare: Ethics, Experience, and Reproductive Labor.* Cambridge: Cambridge University Press.
Murray, Jeffrey. 2003. *Face to Face in Dialogue: Emmanuel Levinas and the Communication of Ethics.* Lanham, Md.: University Press of America.
Nelson, Erin, and Gerald Robertson. 2001. Liability for Wrongful Birth and Wrongful Life. *ISUMA: The Canadian Journal of Policy Research* 2(3): 103–5.
Newman, Marc. 2007. A Diamond in the Raunch: Pro-life Positions Emerge in *Knocked Up* and *Waitress.* LifeSiteNews.com. http://www.lifesite.net/ldn/2007/jul/07070402.html (accessed August 19, 2007).
Noddings, Nel. 1984. *Caring: A Feminist Approach to Ethics and Moral Education.* Berkeley and Los Angeles: University of California Press.
O'Keefe, Mark. 2003. Activists Tout Ultrasound Images to Discourage Abortion. *Values and Philanthropy.* Newhouse News Service. http://www.newhousenews.com/archive/okeef (accessed August 26, 2005).
Perpich, Diane. 2005. Figurative Language and the "Face" in Levinas's Philosophy. *Philosophy and Rhetoric* 38(2): 103–21.
Petchesky, Rosalind P. 1987. Foetal Images: The Power of Visual Culture in the Politics of Reproduction. In *Reproductive Technologies: Gender, Motherhood, and Medicine,* ed. Michelle Stanworth, 57–80. Minneapolis: University of Minnesota Press.
Rados, Carol. 2004. FDA Cautions Against Ultrasound "Keepsake" Images. *FDA Consumer Magazine,* January–February. http://fda.gov/fdac/features/2004/104_images.html (accessed August 25, 2006).
Rettig, Mary. 2005. "Option Ultrasound" Helps Many Women See Alternative to Abortion. *Agape Press,* May 3. http://headlines.agapepress.org/archive/5/32005c.asp (accessed August 26, 2005).
Rich, Adrienne. 1986. *Of Woman Born.* New York: Norton.
Sandelowski, Margarete. 1994. Separate but Less Unequal: Fetal Ultrasonography and the Transformation of Expectant Mother/Fatherhood. *Gender and Society* 8(2): 230–45.
Sherwin, Susan. 1991. Abortion Through a Feminist Lens. *Dialogue* 30:327–42.
Silent Scream. 1984. Dir. Bernard Nathanson. American Portrait Films. http://www.silentscream.org (accessed August 20, 2005).
Stabile, Carol A. 1992. Shooting the Mother: Fetal Photography and the Politics of Disappearance. *Camera Obscura* 28:179–206.
Taylor, Chloé. 2005. Levinasian Ethics and Feminist Ethics of Care. *Symposium: Canadian Journal of Continental Philosophy* 9(2): 217–40.
———. 2006. Hard Dry Eyes and Eyes That Weep: Vision and Ethics in Levinas and Derrida. *Postmodern Culture: An Electronic Journal of Interdisciplinary Criticism* 16(2). http://muse.jhu.edu/login?uri=/journals/pmc/v016/16.2taylor.html (accessed September 22, 2008).
Thomson, Judith Jarvis. 1971. A Defense of Abortion. *Philosophy and Public Affairs* 1(1): 47–66.
Tronto, Joan. 1993. *Moral Boundaries.* New York: Routledge.
Tuttle Hansen, Elaine. 1997. *Mother Without Child: Contemporary Fiction and the Crisis of Motherhood.* Berkeley and Los Angeles: University of California Press.

Wolfe-Devine, Celia. 1997. Abortion and the "Feminine Voice." In *The Problem of Abortion,* ed. Susan Dwyer and Joel Feinberg, 160–74. 3rd ed. Belmont, Calif.: Wadsworth.

Wright, Tamra, Peter Hughes, and Alison Ainley. 1988. The Paradox of Morality: An Interview with Emmanuel Levinas. Trans. Andrew Benjamin and Tamra Wright. In *The Provocation of Levinas: Rethinking the Other,* ed. Robert Bernasconi and David Wood, 168–80. London: Routledge.

TEN

INSIDE THE FRAME OF THE PAST:
MEMORY, DIVERSITY, AND SOLIDARITY

Sue Campbell

> The Northwest Resistance was remembered in many traditional European ways with medals, monuments, and naming opportunities. First Peoples remember the conflict with their own customs.
> —Canadian War Museum, Hall of Remembrance, "The Northwest Resistance Remembered"

1. INTRODUCTION

A critical resource that cultural and political diversity brings to a community is that of different and often oppositional perspectives on that community's past. These perspectives offer the potential epistemic enrichment of a more accurate grasp of collective histories, and their acknowledgment offers the potential political enrichment of conceptions of community that reflect rather than suppress heterogeneity of membership and relation. Yet dominant representations of the past, even ones that we might think of as discredited, can remain surprisingly compelling for dominant groups, and their persistence raises issues of how oppositional perspectives can be constituted effectively

---

I owe thanks to Richmond Campbell, Lea Caragata, David Checkland, Nancy Daukas, Rockney Jacobsen, Christine Koggel, Duncan Macintosh, Letitia Meynell, Jan Sutherland, and Alison Wylie for conversations that helped me develop the paper's themes. Michelle St. John (The Turtle Gals Performance Ensemble) kindly corrected my memory of some of lines from *The Scrubbing Project*. John Sutton drew my attention to the relevance of work by Christoph Hoerl and Teresa McCormack, and Christoph Hoerl was kind enough to immediately e-mail me their study. Letitia Meynell, Susan Sherwin, Seetal Sunga, and Jan Sutherland provided valuable and detailed feedback to an earlier version.

enough to have an impact on how a community experiences its past.[1] I contend that to support oppositional perspectives, we need to grasp how we share in the work of making others' pasts meaningful without this activity assuming prior common experience, perspective, or sensibility.

This paper explores performance theory as one resource for understanding how we participate in others' experiences of the past. Recollection is often publicly expressed and shared among those who do not share a past. Thus, when people remember, they often direct the imaginings of appreciators who may not share a past with them but who become participants in recollective activities.[2] I argue that as audience to memory performances, we make important contributions to how the past can be remembered. Our imaginative engagement can both facilitate or thwart the intentions of particular acts of memory, and fortify or undermine the resources that others need to reexperience their pasts in ways that meet their present needs and interests, including those of challenging dominant views of the past.

Sections 2 and 3 assert the social nature of recollection and introduce the importance of performance theory to its analysis. Using performance theory is one way to meet the demand of contemporary memory theorists that we conceive memory more dynamically and more relationally. Performance theorist Diana Taylor writes that performance "places us within its frame, implicating us in its ethics and politics" (Taylor 2003, 33). I am particularly interested in the capacity of performance theory to highlight the importance of communicative uptake to the constitution of memory meaning and to how we form relationships over the past. In sections 4 and 5, I focus on Taylor's contention that the meaning of memory performance is in situ and dependant on its audience.

Section 4 examines the dynamics of reanimating the past for one another in conversation. Even in circumstances where the past is not shared, such reanimation can create an environment of relationships, objects, and practices—"a potentially habitable world"—that invites imaginative participation (Middleton and Brown 2005, 122). As audience, we engage emotionally and kinesthetically in others' memories, a process of self-imagining that puts us inside the frame of alternative views of the past, affirming or contesting their

---

1. Susan Babbitt (2005) has raised the challenge of how we can be said to truly understand others' pasts if our knowledge of these pasts makes little difference to our identities or the directions in which we act. This paper attempts to model a kind of experiential understanding of others' pasts that meets her challenge.

2. I take the notion of following others' directions for imagining from Walton (1990).

values. But while Section 4 addresses the importance of audience appreciation to the meaning and success of memory performance, the conversational example I use focuses on memory engagement where participants arguably share a social imaginary, easing their way into the memory.

Section 5 considers a Canadian First Nations theater performance before a diverse audience in order to widen the scope of my analysis. As a non-Indigenous Canadian who attended, I consider the possibility that my participation in others' reanimations of the past can fortify the resources of a social imaginary other than my own; and I move beyond straightforward recollection to consider the creative reanimation of a past through which one such imaginary is offered. I show that audience engagement can help enable a shift from the dominant social imaginary as conflicting frameworks for memory interact in the imaginations, emotions, and bodies of audience members. Thus, I suggest that the performative and relational approach to memory that this paper explores illuminates important possibilities for thinking about projects of sharing memory in diverse communities.

2. RECOLLECTION AND RELATIONALITY

Propelled by studies of memory from a variety of theoretical orientations, researchers in the sciences and across the humanities now stress the dynamic, embodied, reconstructive, and social nature of human recollection.[3] We remember selectively and in response to the demands of the present and future; we remember with others and in response to their perceptions of the past. Though memory theorists have by no means abrogated the project of grasping how the mind retains information, they have increasingly turned attention to the contextual factors of memory's occasionings—to the where, why, how, and with whom we remember—as necessary to explain our sophisticated memory capacities and as contributing to the meaning of recollective events.

The turn to present context in the study of the recollected past acknowledges a complexity to memory that has a number of ramifications. The one I wish to highlight is the importance of sharing memory to thinking about the nature of recollection. Even the most rigorous of memory scientists use the metaphor of time travel to convey the complex temporal experience of a

---

3. For useful overviews of current interdisciplinary trends in memory research, see Sutton (2004) and Wertsch (2002).

creature who learns to live in a present, self-consciously, with and through its past (Schacter 1996, chap. 1; Tulving 2002, 3). This type of self-consciousness involves sophisticated cognitive abilities that are initially shaped in contexts of family or group reminiscence. Christoph Hoerl and Teresa McCormack argue, for example, that episodic memory requires attending to the past in ways "that grasp the causal significance of the temporal order in which events happen" (Hoerl and McCormack 2005, 279),[4] particularly the understanding that later events "can change the effect of earlier ones" (270). Their research suggests that it is through the activity of joint reminiscing that children develop the causal-temporal reasoning necessary for episodic memory, as their caretakers direct their attention to the significance of the sequencing of past events: that though first the child hurt his finger, because then his father put a bandage on and kissed it (changing the significance of the child having hurt himself), after that there was no reason to cry. An aspect of the research of particular interest to its authors is that to learn this type of reasoning is to be at the same time engaged in a kind of social interaction that fosters mutuality, as it is the development of a shared outlook on the past, a shared perspective on the significance of events, that facilitates the child's ability to grasp the import of temporal sequencing (Hoerl and McCormack 2005, 282).

To reframe their point to my purpose, the importance of memory to relationships is interwoven with the development of our memory capacities and memory experiences. Studies of joint reminiscence, such as Hoerl and McCormack's, focus on what seems to be clearly shared past experience, such as a family event or outing, where reminiscence takes place among those who were all present at the event, and can or do remember it under a particular description. Such examples may lead us to believe that having experienced the same past in roughly the same way is the prior condition of joint reminiscence. However, the authors offer a more dynamic picture. It is through the child's coming to experience and sequence the past as encouraged to do so by another that the occasion becomes one of joint reminiscence through the participants' development of a shared perspective (Hoerl and McCormack 2005, 282).

I contend that if we think about it at all, we will readily affirm that in adulthood sharing memory continues to be one of our most significant kinds of interpersonal engagement—one that shapes and reshapes our experience of the past, and thus who we become through the forming and negotiating of

---

4. The philosophical import of Hoerl and McCormack for theorizing social memory is discussed in Sutton (2006).

relationships with others. We do not know how different or shared our pasts will seem, even as to how we describe events, until we attempt to share memory. An expectation of joint reminiscence can become the sharing of different pasts. You and I may sit beside each other at a meeting and conclude recollectively that we were at quite different events. The significance of the remembered event may, in fact, shift again for each of us as we recognize the contrasting distinctiveness of our experiences, and our failure to find a common perspective may forestall our inclination to talk about how we remember the event. There is an inverse dynamic as well. Events are part of larger events and collective identifications are often contextual. In sharing distinct autobiographies, we may find common perspectives and identifications that cause us to harmonize the scope of events toward moments of joint reminiscence. We may jointly reminisce about a strike, though we were on different picket lines, or the war, though we fought in different theatres.

In other words, what my past is, the descriptions under which I remember and reexperience its events, is partly the unstable consequence of continuously sharing memory with others. I have elsewhere used the term "relational remembering" to capture the thought that we are often deeply involved in each others' experiencing of the past (Campbell 2003). How the events are experienced may depend on prior identifications—a child is perhaps disposed to remember a past as encouraged to do so by a parent—and sharing the past can shape or disrupt our identifications. I understand psychologists David Middleton and Steven Brown to be making something like these points when they call memory "the site at which the singularity and collectivity of experience intersect" (Middleton and Brown 2005, 15), and the self "a movement that is continuously refracted back through the stabilities it creates" (viii). Like me, Middleton and Brown are interested in how we move into engagement with others' pasts. They say that to understand the complexities of this activity "we need to get a handle on the complex and often ambiguous forms of experience that are central to how remembering is performed" (14).

In what follows, I draw out the significance of the language of performance for recollection. Performance theory has recently turned its attention to memory, and in the next two sections I look at everyday cases of recollection, including a developed example from Middleton and Brown, to show how the tools of performance theory can enhance an analysis of relational remembering. But performance theorists have also been specifically concerned with theorizing the possibilities of oppositional agency (Roach 1996; Taylor 2003). In the final section, I shall suggest that performance theory is one way of examining how we might share a past with others whose experiences may be oppositional to our own, as well as the kinds of mutuality and identification that may be possible in that encounter.[5]

3. PERFORMING RECOLLECTION

Performance theorists study what we might think of as traditional staged performance—for example, theater and dance—and train the methodological tools used for doing so as a lens on the significance of other types of social behavior (Taylor 2003, 3). They have revealed how our reiteration of forms of embodied behavior, such as the postures and activities of femininity, incorporate or induct us into dominant practices, norms, and identities, for example, those associated with being women in our culture (Butler 1990; Case 1990). Because performance theory turns its attention to what its theorists refer to as "restored" behaviors (Roach 1995), behaviors that we learn, adapt, and transmit from our cultural repertoires of how to sit, eat, gesture, and so on, it has been an important tool for theorists interested in the type of social memory that might be thought of as tradition. For example, in the widely referenced *How Societies Remember,* Paul Connerton studies how commemorative performance works to conserve and transfer values intergenerationally. He argues that disciplining bodies to perform ritual movements, such as kneeling in submission or laying a wreath in respectful remembrance, which if performed correctly enact the value, is essential to such transfer (Connerton 1989). Subsequent performance-minded theorists have flagged as foundational Connerton's claim that accounts of social memory require an analysis of embodied "acts of transfer" (Hirsch and Smith 2002; Middleton and Brown 2005; Taylor 2003). I contend that we can give performance theory wider scope in an analysis of memory than its role in explaining the embodied conservation and transfer of tradition. What we lack are theoretical vocabularies for conceiving of recollection as a primarily

---

5. I use the language of relational rather than social memory in this paper. I prefer with Middleton and Brown "to deliberately blur the boundaries between the individual and the collective, between what is held in common and what is most intensely personal" (2005, vii). Even when accounts of collective memory are formulated so as to accommodate diverse interpretations and valuings of a collective history, they tend to index the idea of shared memory to the idea of preexistent subgroup affiliations. Thus, they often position us as locked in group contest over the meaning of the past. A performative account of relational memory may be a more optimistic aid to projects of sharing memory in diverse communities.

relational activity, and the analysis of memory as performance can compel this focus.

Theorist Diana Taylor describes performance as the live embodied communication of information in the here and now, a description I adopt for this paper (Taylor 2003, chap. 1). Performative activities, for Taylor, thus include theater, dance, and ritual, but also political protest, acts of testimony, the teaching of skills, and conversation. Taylor's performance theory has a natural affinity with memory studies. She writes that through performance, "forms from the past" can be animated and "experienced as present" (24). She suggests that to understand how this is so, we must look beyond the idea of a cultural past conserved archivally to think of our embodied repertoires of skills, movements, and shared modes of expression; our social scripts and ways of embodied relating; and the material spaces in which our interactions take place. Taylor says we might begin to get at the performative qualities of our interactions by interpreting them through the theatrical lens of a scenario: attending to the material environment and the information encoded within it; to aspects of communication through movement; and to "the social construction of bodies in particular contexts," all of which may be necessary to a grasp of what is being communicated by the performance (28). Finally, Taylor contends that the meaning of performance is in situ and dependent on its audience: "As participants, spectators, or witnesses, we need to be there, part of the act of transfer" (32). She writes more provocatively that "the scenario places us within its frame, implicating us in its ethics and politics" (33).

Taylor's account of performance first seems to me apt for reframing quite ordinary occasions of recollection. The sharing of memory through practices of recollection is a performative activity. It is live embodied communication to an audience in the here and now. As our capacities for episodic memory require that we learn special skills of attending to the past (Hoerl and McCormick 2005), sharing memory with others requires that we learn to direct their attention to episodes in the past as we have experienced them. We reanimate the past for others, shaping salience through choice of detail, mode of expression, gesture, emotional tone, and the sharing of objects and place, and they participate in and help to shape our recollective scenarios.

I recently went hiking with a colleague in the Nova Scotian woods. Attending to the material environment and his embodied presence and movement within it were important to sharing his past—the granite boulders where we rested and the vistas that I followed the turn of his body to locate became the setting of his valued recollections. He had walked and run over the uneven ground so often that he moved without conscious attention to where he stepped. I was aware of walking with someone who *had been there* many times, and my attention to his embodied ease and familiarity with the trail helped me to experience it as part of his past. My own presence shaped his experience of the past into which I was drawn, as many of the people who became present to him as we walked, those who had accompanied him on past hikes, were people that I knew as well. It was easy to move into joint reminiscence about them. My being there, part of the act of transfer, contributed to how, who, and perhaps why he remembered, as he tried to make me comfortable in an unfamiliar environment by drawing me, at the same time, into a comfortable world of mutual friends.

To think of memory as the stored psychic record of episodes now beyond the effect of time, place, and context on their meaning takes us far away from the kind of daily recollection among intimates I have just described through the lens of a performance scenario. But I also want to explore whether performance theory allows us to enter the more challenging domain of thinking how we shape relationships through coming together to share the memory of more unfamiliar pasts. To adapt language from Maria Lugones, we can be more or less "at ease" in each others' world of recollection. Lugones specifies different ways of being at ease in a real, imagined, or, I shall add, recollected world: 1) we may share a cultural history that gives us a stock of shared references; 2) we may understand the norms of that world and thus how to "move confidently" in the environment; 3) we may be "normatively happy" in the world; we may "love the norms" of that world; 4) we may have important relationships in that world (Lugones 1989, 283–84).

My entrance into my colleague's past was eased by our overlapping autobiographies, our mutual sense of Nova Scotia as a home where one might expect to encounter friends in common, our shared ways of thinking and speaking, our joint values, our fondness for each other, and my fondness for those he remembered. Being at ease in all of the ways that Lugones specifies, I was "maximally at ease" in my colleague's memories (Lugones 1989, 283–84). In the remainder of this paper, I focus more closely on how performance works to draw people inside the frame of an unshared past, the ways it can implicate appreciators in the values being expressed, and the potential of sharing the past for forming rather simply affirming relationships. I shall ask whether our capacity to be at ease in one another's pasts sets limits on the nature of these engagements over memory.

4. MEMORY AND MEMBERSHIP

In a recent fascinating study of conversational remembering, Middleton and Brown premise their analysis of memory on a view of our temporal experience as a process in which the past and present are not sharply separated from each other, as they were not sharply separated in my hike in the Nova Scotian woods. They are intrigued then by how we mark out the past from the present by performing or "actualizing" the past for others through sharing memory (Middleton and Brown 2005, 74–79). They contend that in order to negotiate present environments, we etch out the past from its embedded and often inchoate life in experience, describing it in different and creative ways to provisionally secure its character and influence in the present. We often remember through relating scenarios, a type of conversational performance in which we direct the imaginings of appreciators who may not share that past with us but who become active participants in our recollecting. In analyzing participation, the theorists seek to show that processes of sharing memory are also used to give people a personal investment in others' versions of the past (Middleton and Brown 2005, 6, 86), and to create bonds of membership "that are made relevant" by the occasion of recollection (86).

Middleton and Brown draw much of their data from reminiscence groups, groups of elderly people brought together to share memories of their different pasts. In one such group, the joy of drinking has been the topic, and Sue, a former churchgoer and present teetotaler, enters the conversation to relate an event involving her younger self. Expecting a visit from the parson, she confronts her father about the bottle of stout he has warming on the fire grate or hob. Her father refuses to remove it and instead tells the parson, who says, "well, I've never heard such a thing in me life. I like one occasionally meself" (Middleton and Brown 2005, 121). In describing her actions as the object of her father and the parson's incredulity, Sue pulls up and describes a past that marks out her present identity as someone who may not like the taste of drink but who can be counted on to be a willing appreciator of others' drinking stories (95).

Sue describes her past by offering a vivid generalized image of her home life, perhaps drawn from many similar occasions, a very common kind of autobiographical memory (Middleton and Brown 2005, 125). She weaves others' experiences and voices into her account, positioning herself as having a place in a group "on whose behalf [she] presume[s] to speak" (122). Maurice Halbwachs argued that our tendencies to summate recollections from different times and project them onto the past as vivid images of group life create a shared repertoire of prototypical images that group members use to communicate about their pasts (Halbwachs 1992, 60). They can locate or "localize" their past experiences around these images. Our use of objects and places to organize our accounts of the past—the objects of Sue's environment play a crucial role in articulating the relationships—is so integral to this process of developing resources that the material environment often seems to hold memory for group members—a process Middleton and Brown describe as "territorialization" (Middleton and Brown 2005, 42, 121).

Yet even in circumstances where the past is not shared, the authors contend that use of a prototypical scene can create an environment of relationships, objects, and practices that invites imaginative participation. Sue's remembering creates "a potentially habitable world," and her directions for visualizing the scene facilitate a form of temporal engagement in the scenario (Middleton and Brown 2005, 122). Her interlocutors can attend to the details of the imagined material environment—in this case the patriarchal home—and to the social construction of bodies in a specific context—the two male authority figures and the young Sue—to anticipate the possibilities of the action. Through this anticipation, the other members of the reminiscence group can and do contribute to the scenario's development, anticipating and supplying details as the narrative unfolds. For example, when Sue describes the stout bubbling on the fire grate, Ted says "warming" (120).

Ted's contribution to the memory is not an act of joint reminiscence, as the occasion remains focused on an episode of Sue's past, but I contend it is a closely related process. Sue and Ted are involved in the joint project of reexperiencing Sue's past from her present perspective. Middleton and Brown write that "the detailed description of Sue's home" serves "as a means of incorporating the listener into a localized set of personal relationships, to vicariously experience what it might be like to move through that physical environment" (124). They stress that this experience is embodied and affective, "a matter of feeling that one could physically engage" as Ted imagines taking a sip of the warming stout, or as his eyes move back and forth, visualizing the interactions described (124). In other words, in imagining the scene, Ted is engaged in an act of self-imagining through his embodied uptake,[6] and Sue's memory scenario has been performed to invite exactly this type of participation. She has brought Ted inside the frame of her past to reexperience it with her.

---

6. See Walton (1990), chapters 1 and 6, for a detailed account of how our engagement with representations involves us in self-imagining.

One way of reading Taylor's claim that when a performance brings us inside the frame that it implicates "us in its ethics and politics" is that such self-imagining participation affirms the values of the scenarios in which we participate. Though I shall argue below that this may be only one of our responses to our engagement with scenarios, it will be useful to examine the dynamics of value affirmation through sharing memory; Middleton and Brown's remarks about forming bonds through memory seem to depend on this kind of affirmation.

The authors note that memory performances often establish a particular moral order embedded in the details of the scene and the activities. They thus find it quite remarkable that the interlocutors, who may never have experienced such an environment, and who "may take issue with the moral order," do not question or resist the moral order, but in fact participate so as to give the values weight in the present (Middleton and Brown 2005, 123). Their discussion of how this weighting comes about opens important possibilities for how our response may contribute to shaping the significance of the past for those who share memory with us.[7]

Middleton and Brown first point out that the moral order embedded in scenarios, in this case the Christian and patriarchal world of Sue's home, is often the taken-for-granted setting of the memory. It becomes the ground of the shared project of the memory's elaboration. Second, the values are expressed through the description of activities (hard-working fathers drinking beer by the fire); they are not articulated as available for explicit contestation (Middleton and Brown 2005, 126–27). Third, the description of the activities often has a sense of ritual to it. Our embodied participations in a scenario—Ted's incipient bodily movements as he lifts the glass of stout to pronounce it warming—"carry with them a set of moral sensibilities" (126). The authors here use Connerton (1989) to argue that some degree of value affirmation occurs through our imaginative participation in these activities.

Finally, because such scenarios are generalized and prototypical, the past becomes not historicized, but oddly somewhat naturalized. In recalling "the way things were" or "when I was young," in ways that do not seem to map onto a specific date in historical time, rememberers are "able to partially conflate their own recollections with an ahistorical past in general," placing their audience in the position of having to take issue, not just with the meaning of a particular

---

7. Middleton and Brown (2005) use several examples to fund this discussion. I am applying insights drawn from other examples back to Sue's scenario.

episode, but with the "entire weight of the past" in order to challenge the values "lacquered around" the objects and activities in the scenario (Middleton and Brown 2005, 131). Interlocutors may challenge, but the processes of reminiscence, the summation and projection of the past, mitigate this possibility. Giving values present weight by embedding them in the activities of a past invoked as somewhat timeless is, I would suggest, a critical function of actualizing the past that requires much more political attention.[8]

Audience engagement with Sue's memory establishes her relationship in the group. One of the most important foci of Middleton and Brown's analysis is how we negotiate our identities and form relationships through the ways in which we participate in and shape the significance of one another's pasts. It is of course the nature of the present occasion that prompts Sue to communicate a particular memory. But the participation of her audience in shaping the significance of her past goes far beyond the role of their presence in eliciting a certain recollection. It is only if the appreciators affirm a certain significance to the scene, which they do by laughing at the younger Sue's discomfort, that the performance succeeds in its intent of gaining Sue the present identity of one in no position to take the "moral high ground," that the affirmation of this identity becomes the meaning of her past as reexperienced and shared on that occasion (Middleton and Brown 2005, 123). It is through this identity that she bonds with the other members of the reminiscence group in their stories of happy drinking. Her audience is brought under the influence of her past in ways that affect how they go on to relate with each other. Ted is sharing a reexperiencing of Sue's past from her perspective and affirming its values in ways that give Sue membership in a new community of memory.

Middleton and Brown's analysis, read explicitly through performance theory, does give us a rich array of tools for thinking about heterogeneous communities of memory. But their example does not really identify such a community,[9] and seeing why this is so is significant in thinking of the kinds of relationships that sharing memory makes possible. Middleton and Brown suggest that we invest in each others' pasts through affirming the values of remembered ways of life via

---

8. For example, when three firefighters raised the U.S. flag amidst the destruction of the World Trade Center on September 11, 2001, the action also, for many Americans, actualized the past through the summated image of many occasions of flag-raising, the most powerful reference being Iwo Jima in 1942. The action projected an image of courage, defiance, hope, and resolve, with these values given weight in the present through a past invoked as somewhat timeless. For a description of the flag raising that captures this aspect of it, see The Bravest Fund, http://www.bravestfund.com (accessed May 24, 2006).

9. I do not mean to imply that they intend to identify such a community.

embodied engagement in the activities that express these values; and that this investment helps create membership made appropriate by the occasion. The performance of Sue's memory is an example of the above dynamic. But the very intent of drawing someone into the past may be to encourage the contesting rather than affirmation of values; if this alternative is a significant one, affirming value cannot be a straightforward effect of the performative processes of memory. In fact, in modeling value affirmation as an *effect* of memory processes, the authors tend to ignore the ways in which Sue's appreciators may already be multiply at ease in her the world of her recollection.

I shall say that those who share normative understandings and a body of cultural references, comprising two of Lugones's grounds for "ease" in a world, share a cultural imaginary. Sue's interlocutors may well share her imaginary. There is no confusion about the nature of the place and objects that anchor the relations of Sue's scenario—they all seem to know what hobs are—and Ted knows that the norms of the environment make the stout his for the tasting. We might also suspect that Sue's interlocutors are normatively happy in her world. They do laugh at her embarrassment rather than objecting to the patriarchal norms that have determined it. Her securing this laughter helps form her relationships with the reminiscence group while giving weight to the appropriateness of her embarrassment.

It is crucial to think about how people are at ease in recollection in order to assess the role of common experience and understanding in the affirmation of relations. Although Sue's interaction does create new bonds of membership by drawing others into an unshared past, the structure of the interaction is quite similar to my engagement with my colleague's memory. My colleague made me feel at ease in an unfamiliar environment by actualizing a past within it that made the environment the familiar and shared one of friends in common. Sue negotiates an environment in which she is perhaps uneasy by performing a past into which she draws others. She enters the world of happy drinking through engaging others in a past in which the values of drinking are affirmed, again creating a familiar and now shared environment. Thus, in both cases, the significance of performing the past on a particular occasion is to create an environment in which the participants have experience and perspective in common—in the first case to affirm relationship, in the second case to create it. Resting the analysis here might seem to limit the possibility of forming relationships via sharing the past to occasions on which we can be at ease in each other's recollection.[10]

---

10. Letitia Meynell made many useful comments on the Sue example, and Jan Sutherland has helped me see the parallel import of the Sue and colleague cases.

5. PERFORMING OPPOSITIONAL MEMORY

If we are not and perhaps cannot be at ease in others' worlds of recollection, what kinds of possibilities for engaging with the past and forming relationships might we nevertheless encounter? This is a pressing political question, and I want to use the theoretical tools so far developed to make some very preliminary suggestions about possibilities for engagement. Though I have challenged Middleton and Brown's reading of Sue's performance, I will use my participation at a recent theater forum, a forum at which I was ill at ease in a number of ways, to argue that the processes they describe can, if understood properly, also give insight into the sharing of oppositional memory. In entering worlds of memory in which we are not at ease, we can nevertheless engage with values, give weight to fragile cultural imaginaries, support identities, and undertake new relationships that I will characterize as relationships of solidarity.

Margaret Atwood, Canada's most famous novelist, wrote in 1972 that "the central symbol for Canada" as expressed through its literary traditions "is undoubtedly survival" (Atwood 1972, 32): the survival of explorers, colonists, and settlers in the harsh Canadian geography; the cultural survival of French Canadians in English Canada; and the survival of English Canada in a U.S.-dominated continent. In writing *Survival: A Thematic Guide to Canadian Literature,* Atwood located what was, at that time, a dominant cultural imaginary. Indigenous peoples have never been positioned as the subject of that imaginary, but they have been subjected through it: portrayed as a part of the harsh environment, or as engaged in a self-subordinating willingness to support the acts of appropriation necessary to white settler survival, or as those who have not survived but have irrevocably lost their culture and identity.[11] Many of us came as children to learn what *Canada* is by drawing the routes of explorers and fur traders, unaware of the ways in which these maps overlaid Indigenous paths and projects. We physically participated in the values of the imaginary of survival, and those of us who are of European heritage were probably quite at ease there. Although the dominant imaginary has no doubt shifted somewhat over the last thirty years, it remains compelling for some of us schooled in it.

---

11. In Atwood's words: "The Indians are, finally, a yardstick of suffering against which the whites can measure their own and find it lacking" (1972, 99).

In December 2005 a group of theater artists, cultural critics, and academics came together in Halifax, Nova Scotia, for the theater forum "Canadian Theatre Identity Crisis: Challenging Eurocentricity through Aboriginal Myth and Ritual" (OneLight Theatre 2005). The topic was provoked in part by the plans of a group called Theatre 400 to stage a commemorative reenactment of the *Theatre of Neptune in New France* on the four hundredth anniversary of its original performance at the site of the former Port Royal colony in Nova Scotia. Thought to be the first European play produced in the so-called "New World" the *Theatre of Neptune* was devised by a Port Royal lawyer and historian, Marc Lescarbot, to distract the colonists from the anticipated hardships of their third winter (Lescarbot 1982).[12] In the course of play's action, four "Indian" men speak in turn to affirm the sovereignty of the French in New France, pledge the devoted service of their skills, and symbolically offer up their land through furs and their women through love trinkets. Written and performed to aid white settler survival, the play positioned the "Indians" as willing contributors to the appropriations that would support this survival; and it was originally performed to an audience in which in which Mi'k Maq and their Grand Chief Membertou were present as spectators.[13] There was no indication that the reenactment was meant to animate or bring into "our" sense of the past what it may have been like for the Mi'k maq to be made spectator/participants to this complex appropriation. Perhaps remarkably, only the theme of settler survival seemed salient to the planners of the reenactment. One of them said: "Good theatre, real theatre has a purpose. This play was aimed at guaranteeing the survival of this group of people for the rest of the winter" (CBC Arts 2004).

The plans for the reenactment did not receive project funding from Canada Council, and the performance did not take place. The lack of institutional support for the reenactment as well as the protest at its prospect may indicate that some non-Indigenous Canadians are no longer normatively happy in the dominant imaginary of survival. Lugones notes that our being ill at ease in a world may help encourage us to travel to others. But our being ill at ease in this one way is compatible with the persistence of the dominant imaginary. The

---

12. My information about the play and the plans for its reenactment are drawn from a presentation and text by Donovan King (2005). King invited the public to participate in the "open-ended participatory 'meta-performance'" of *Sinking Neptune* (26). The reflections of this paper are my contribution to this meta-performance.

13. "Lescarbot had claimed the new world in a new way by enlisting the spectating bodies and appropriated voices of its inhabitants in his imaginary theatre." Alan Filewood (2002, xiv–xv), quoted in King (2005, 8).

questions remain: how do those subjected by this dominant imaginary muster the resources needed to reexperience their pasts and reshape their identities outside of it, and how do those of us who are not normatively happy as the subjects of this imaginary act in solidarity to precipitate this shift? Lugones argues that other people will be one of the primary resources for those in the process of becoming "non-subjected subjects" if we can help make sense of each other outside of the "rhetorical spaces" that affirm some people's identities through subjecting or degrading the identities of others (Lugones 2002, 56).[14] Different performances of the past can provide new rhetorical spaces but challenge us to learn to contribute to each other's meanings without the assumption that shared experience, perspective, or sensibility will ease this contribution.

At the same theater forum, the Turtle Gals Performance Ensemble performed the very powerful *Scrubbing Project,* an exploration of the attempted genocide of Indigenous peoples of the Americas and the internalized racism that is part of its legacy. I acknowledge that the complex meld of memory and imagination characteristic of many aesthetic representations of the past may complicate an epistemology of memory. I put aside this issue here, however, in order to focus on analyzing audience engagement.

The Turtle Gals take their name from Turtle Island, the Anishinabe name for North America, part of it now "territorialized" through countless acts of dominant imagination and memory as the Canada of Atwood's *Survival.* The intent of the performance is to remember Turtle Island: "We will build memory/A war memorial/A wailing wall that will stretch across this Grandmother Turtle" (Turtle Gals 2002). In trying to build the memory of Turtle Island, a wailing wall whose presence will challenge or replace a dominant cultural imaginary, the performers have the task of developing the resources through which memories of Turtle Island can be shared. *The Scrubbing Project* uses the technique of "storyweaving to entwine stories and fragments of stories with words, music, song, film, dance and movement" (Turtle Gals 2005). In particular, it uses vaudeville as "a madcap metaphor

---

14. Lugones takes the phrase "rhetorical spaces" from Code (1995). Code defines "rhetorical spaces" as "fictive but not fanciful or fixed locations, whose (tacit, rarely spoken) territorial imperatives structure and limit the kinds of utterances that can be voiced within them with a reasonable expectation of uptake and 'choral support': an expectation of being heard, understood, taken seriously" (ix–x). Lugones suggests that there are "infrapolitical rhetorical spaces" (2002, 63) where the intentions of non-subjected subjects do have credibility. I take Shulamith Lev-Aladgem (2006) to have recently argued that community theater can be such a space. I thank Cate Hundleby for this reference.

for the way we navigate our identities. It allows us to explore deep, sorrowful stories with zany comedy and character transformations that happen in the blink of an eye. Much like the way we live" (Turtle Gals 2005). Thus, in building memory through performance, the performers are also navigating their identities. At the end of *The Scrubbing Project* the performers pass up into the audience large paper scrolls with the names of their ancestors–which the audience simply holds. The end of the performance signaled the possibility that the participation of a diverse audience in *The Scrubbing Project* could contribute to the building of memory and the affirmation of identities that the performers intend.

I have used Middleton and Brown's discussion of Sue to provide some concrete reflection on how we might think of an audience as inside the frame of a memory scenario, contributing to the situated meaning of representing the past on a particular occasion. We can see these processes they describe: the creation of prototypical images that make the environment imaginable, our affective and embodied participation in value, and the affirmations of identities and creation of bonds though sharing memory also at work in our engagement with *The Scrubbing Project*. I reflect from my own audience position.

The activity of scrubbing in the title refers to a recurring image that emerged in the early conversations of the writer/performers: "Either we or someone we knew had at some point tried to scrub off or bleach out their colour" (Turtle Gals 2005). The title image of *The Scrubbing Project* functions as a prototypical image that has facilitated the communication of memory for the performers; they have localized and shared experience through this imagery. Its description in the program projects "the scrubbing project" onto the past as a vivid image of subjugation, and its dramatic development in the performance anchors our imaginative entrance into the scenario. Our participation in the performance may give weight to this image as one that complexly emblematizes both significant effects of colonization and the spirit and creativity to resist and overcome these effects. How the audience understands this imagery develops in our encounter with the performance.

The Turtle Gals direct salience by talking and singing about the past to one another and to the audience using vivid generalized images drawn from many occasions. Like Sue, they weave others' experiences and voices into the account, creating an entitlement to speak about the past. They position themselves as having a place in many groups. They do not, however, speak on behalf of these groups so much as they themselves try to imaginatively engage the groups' experiences while at the same time engaging the embodied participation of the audience:

> All: he said, he said, he said, he said, he said
> Esperanza: "I always knew when there'd been a massacre
>   by the shoes..."
>   I see the scattering of forlorn shoes
>   abandoned in the plaza
>   orphaned
>   left to lie on their sides upside down....
>   A man's oxford here, sneaker there
>   but mostly women's shoes
>   *tacones*
>   pink, turquoise, white and black high heels
>   debris....
> Ophelia: Did they jump straight out of those shoes?
> Esperanza: I wonder
> Branda: Did they bend to untie them?
> Esperanza: Did they struggle to squirm a foot out
>   over the back of the shoe with a desperate heel?
> Ophelia: did they step on glass as they ran?
> ALL: as they fell
>
> (*Turtle Gals* 2004)

In this sequence, as in Sue's scenario, a moral order is given weight in the present. It is the ground of an enacted and invited imagining. It is expressed through activities, and through the summated presentation of different occasions of massacre. It is actualized for us with a kind of timelessness. The performers encourage the audience's embodied engagement with this racist and genocidal political order made present and vivid through the objects and activities of the performance. We do not affirm these values, but the performance invites a discomfiting physical participation that compels us to feel their force. While Middleton and Brown suggest that we often take on others' pasts with a kind of personal commitment via enacting and thus affirming the values imaginatively engaged, their analysis does not reach this objective, nor ought it. Our mere bodily willingness to engage in activities does not affirm values in the ways that Connerton's account makes plausible. Our kinesthetic anticipations may sometimes affirm values. They may also cause us dis-ease and compel a confrontation with the values given weight through their presence in recollection. This confrontation may have been part of the intent of engaging the participation of a diverse audience.

The Scrubbing Project was a staged performance that will be restaged. But Taylor stresses that however repeatable the images, plots, and paradigms that form our repertoires, scenarios have situational meaning; they are "intelligible in the framework of the immediate environment and issues surrounding them" (Taylor 2003, 3). Part of the significance of performing *The Scrubbing Project* on the occasion I have described was one of helping to expose the myth of Eurocentricity in Canadian theater through performance founded in a different cultural repertoire. But I believe that there are other ways that the performance has situated meaning. Though I cannot presume to speak for the Turtle Gals' intentions, their description of *The Scrubbing Project* suggests this actualizing of the past is part of a project of becoming non-subjected subjects. Lugones has written that those who must travel between worlds, and who are subjected to degraded identities in some of these worlds, often develop the sense of having plural selves. They must develop different skills than those who simply remain in the worlds where they are maximally at ease. She affirms world-traveling as "skilful, creative, rich, and enriching" (Lugones 1989, 275). The Turtle Gals deliberately shape the past to emphasize the intelligibility and creativity to character transformations "undertaken in the blink of an eye. Much like the way we live." They do so by exploring "deep and sorrowful stories with zany comedy" (Turtle Gals 2002). The range of audience uptake—our imaginative involvement with imagery, our laughter at the comedy, and our uneasy embodied confrontation with racism as its perpetrators or victims—may be relevant to how the artists are able to affirm the intelligibility and creativity of their own and others' identities.

Finally, the performance was partly about the development of transient bonds made relevant by the occasion of remembering as we were brought physically and briefly into community with the names of the dead. I recognize that the nature of these bonds will differ radically depending on audience membership. I want to conclude by saying something about the nature of these bonds for those in the audience of European heritage.

Contemporary political theorists have argued that if we are interested in relations of political solidarity with others, we must move away from the search for shared experience and shared perspective, and instead seek out common interests.¹⁵ Lugones's work suggests that people's desire to become non-subjected subjects can be one such common interest, and the ability to appropriate one's own past in memory is essential to any such project of becoming. I hope to have made it plausible that to be brought inside the frame of another's past to aid in shaping its present significance does not require that we somehow share the same kind of experience of that past or perspectives that encourage our ease within it. Our engagement with the values performed through the activities of that scenario may nevertheless help give meaning to another's past, whether this is the situational affirmation of identities; the reinforcement of schemas, prototypes, and modes of expression that may give weight to a different cultural imaginary; or the acknowledgment of our own presence in that past. In other words, we can form relations of solidarity made relevant by the occasion of recollection.

I do not want to either exaggerate or trivialize the possibility or importance of these relationships. There are a number of reasons not to exaggerate the prospects of solidarity. To act in solidarity with others over remembering the past requires our accountability to them for the ways in which we are implicated in the ethics and politics of those projects. Insofar as the performance is a unique event, we need to see how we are contributing to the aims of actualizing the past on a particular occasion. Insofar as the performance develops the transposable resources of social memory, we need to reflect on the resources to which we contribute. Our reflexive understanding of ourselves as appreciators in others' worlds of memory may help us notice the added weight of our response in shaping prototypes and advancing acts of territorialization that support or undermine dominant or fragile imaginaries. To become aware of these possibilities, we must become critics to our own self-imaginings. I have chosen the setting of a theater forum that was meant to encourage this kind of reflection and accountability. Other settings may fail to encourage appropriate uptake. Moreover, we cannot expect that others will want to share their recollections with us or give us the opportunity to form relations. Making sense of one another outside of the institutional and "rhetorical spaces" that give only some people's intentions full credibility is, according to Lugones, a fragile project (Lugones 2002, 56). It is fragile in part because without the assumptions of shared experience,

---

15. See especially the work of Chandra Talpade Mohanty (2003). I take Lugones's work to be endorsing this same view of solidarity and, in "Impure Communities" (2002), to be giving it a quite radical application to how we interpret one another's meanings.

values, or perspective, one must attempt to shape the significance of one's experience in relational circumstances that are "without trust or assured reciprocity" (61). The Turtle Gals mark the fragility of this project in passing scrolls with the names of their ancestors into the hands of an audience they do not know and have no reason to trust.

Nevertheless, part of what seems most insightful to me in Middleton and Brown's (2005) analysis is their contention that sharing memory can give us an investment in each others' past and create bonds of membership made relevant by the occasion of recollection. Our moving inside the frame of others' pasts and thus investing their pasts with some influence on who we take ourselves to have been and on who we become is one of the central ways in which we affirm our identities as in-relation-to-others. The relationships formed in sharing memory may often be brief and occasion specific. But because of the importance of recollection to affirming identities and developing different cultural imaginaries, they do not seem to me trivial.

REFERENCES

Atwood, Margaret. 1972. *Survival: A Thematic Guide to Canadian Literature*. Toronto: Anasi Press.
Babbitt, Susan. 2005. Collective Memory or Knowledge: Covering Reality with Flowers. Paper presented at annual meeting of the Canadian Society for Women in Philosophy, Dalhousie University, Halifax.
Butler, Judith. 1990. *Gender Trouble: Feminism and the Subversion of Identity*. New York: Routledge.
Campbell, Sue. 2003. *Relational Remembering: Rethinking the Memory Wars*. Lanham, Md.: Rowman and Littlefield.
Case, Sue-Ellen. 1990. *Performing Feminisms: Feminist Critical Theory and Theatre*. Baltimore: Johns Hopkins University Press.
CBC Arts. 2004. Canada's First Play to Be Revived. December 8.
Code, Lorraine. 1995. *Rhetorical Spaces: Essays on Gendered Locations*. New York: Routledge.
Connerton, Paul. 1989. *How Societies Remember*. Cambridge: Cambridge University Press.
Filewood, Alan. 2002. *Performing Canada: The Nation Enacted in the Imagined Theatre*. Textual Studies in Canada 15. Kamloops, B.C.: University College of the Cariboo.
Halbwachs, Maurice. 1992. *On Collective Memory*. Ed. and trans. Lewis A. Coser. Chicago: University of Chicago Press.
Hirsch, Marianne, and Valerie Smith. 2002. Feminism and Cultural Memory: An Introduction. *Signs: Journal of Women in Culture and Society* 28:1–22.

Hoerl, Christoph, and Teresa McCormack. 2005. Joint Reminiscing as Joint Attention to the Past. In *Joint Attention, Communication, and Other Minds*, ed. N. Eilan, C. Hoerl, T. McCormack, and J. Roessler, 260–86. Oxford: Oxford University Press.

King, Donovan. 2005. A Dramaturgical Toolbox for *Sinking Neptune*. Montreal: Optative Theatrical Laboratories–Radical Dramaturgy Unit. http://optative.net/neptune/sinkingneptune.pdf (accessed September 23, 2008).

Lescarbot, Marc. 1982. *The Theatre of Neptune in New France*. Trans. Eugene Benson and Renate Benson. In *Colonial Quebec: French-Canadian Drama, 1606–1966*, ed. Anton Wagner and Richard Plant, 38–43. Vol. 4 of *Canada's Lost Plays*. Toronto: Canadian Theatre Review Publications.

Lev-Aladgem, Shulamith. 2006. Remembering Forbidden Memories: Community Theatre and the Politics of Memory. *Social Identities* 12(3): 269–83.

Lugones, Maria. 1989. Playfulness, "World"-Traveling, and Loving Perception. In *Women, Knowledge, and Reality: Explorations in Feminist Philosophy*, ed. Ann Garry and Marilyn Pearsall, 275–90. Boston: Unwin Hyman.

———. 2002. Impure Communities. In *Diversity and Community: An Interdisciplinary Reader*, ed. Philip Alperson, 58–64. Oxford: Basil Blackwell.

Middleton, David, and Steven D. Brown. 2005. *The Social Psychology of Experience: Studies in Remembering and Forgetting*. London: Sage Publications.

Mohanty, Chandra Talpade. 2003. *Feminism Without Borders: Decolonizing Theory, Practising Solidarity*. Durham: Duke University Press.

OneLight Theatre. 2005. Canadian Theatre Identity Crisis: Challenging Eurocentricity Through Aboriginal Myth and Ritual. Halifax.

Roach, Joseph. 1995. Culture and Performance in the Circum-Atlantic World. In *Performativity and Performance*, ed. Andrew Parker and Eve Kosofsky Sedgwick, 44–63. New York: Routledge.

———. 1996. *Cities of the Dead: Circum-Atlantic Performance*. New York: Columbia University Press.

Schacter, Daniel. 1996. *Searching for Memory: The Mind, the Brain, and the Past*. New York: HarperCollins.

Sutton, John. 2004. Representation, Reduction, and Interdisciplinarity in the Sciences of Memory. In *Representation in Mind*, vol. 1, *New Approaches to Mental Representation*, ed. Hugh Clapin, P. Staines, and P. Slezak, 187–216. Boston: Elsevier.

———. 2006. Investigating the Philosophy and Psychology of Memory: Two Case Studies. In *Cartographies of the Mind: The Interface Between Philosophy and Psychology*, ed. Massimo Marraffa, Mario DeCaro, and Francesco Ferretti, 81–92. Dordrecht: Springer.

Taylor, Diana. 2003. *The Archive and the Repertoire: Performing Cultural Memory in the Americas*. Durham: Duke University Press.

Tulving, Endel. 2002. Episodic Memory: From Mind to Brain. *Annual Review of Psychology* 53:1–25.

The Turtle Gals Performance Ensemble. 2002. *The Scrubbing Project*. Play.

———. 2004. The Scrubbing Project (excerpt). In *Beyond The Pale: Dramatic Writing From First Nations Writers and Writers of Colour*, ed. Yvette Nolan, 125–28. Toronto: Playwrights Canada Press.

———. 2005. *The Scrubbing Project*. Theater program presented at Dalhousie University, December 10, 2005.

Walton, Kendall. 1990. *Mimesis as Make-believe: On the Foundations of the Representational Arts*. Cambridge: Harvard University Press.

Wertsch, James. 2002. *Voices of Collective Remembering*. Cambridge: Cambridge University Press.

ELEVEN

COLLECTIVE MEMORY OR KNOWLEDGE OF THE PAST: "COVERING REALITY WITH FLOWERS"

Susan E. Babbitt

1. INTRODUCTION

In *I Saw Ramallah,* Mourid Barghouti comments that the Palestinian people still wait with "open eyes," but that the Palestinian media continue to "cover reality with flowers" (Barghouti 2003, 120). Being a philosopher, and not a political scientist, I do not comment on the accuracy of the claim about the Palestinians but rather on the significance of Barghouti's remarks for self- and social understanding. I am concerned, in particular, about the role of historical memory in questions about agency, especially in questions about collective agency. It is often commented, and it has been said in particular about the situation between Palestinians and Israelis, that "part of imagining a new future . . . is the ability to deal maturely and honestly with the past" (Kimmerling and Migdal 2003, xix). Yet dealing "maturely and honestly with the past," whether it is the past of a society or an individual, is not just a matter of telling the history differently or incorporating into the national story events that have been left out. It is not even a matter of describing events from a different perspective, taking into account, for instance, the interests of the opponent or of marginalized groups.

I am immensely grateful to Haideh Moghissi and Saeed Rahnema for making possible my participation in the *Gender, Displacement, Memory and Agency* Conference in Ramallah, Palestine, March 5–7, 2005, where this paper was first presented in a plenary session chaired by Hanan Ashrawi. I am also grateful to the Ministry of Women's Affairs in the West Bank for sponsoring that conference and to the SSHRC MCRI program for travel support. I am indebted to Sue Campbell, Letitia Meynell, and Sue Sherwin for the opportunity to present this paper at Dalhousie University in Halifax in October 2005, and for their patience, diligence and insight in preparing this volume.

Indeed, it may be a mistake to give primacy to historical memory in questions about collective or individual agency. Certainly it is true that we can understand nothing about the world without relying on background beliefs and assumptions. And certainly it is true that when we act and make life plans, we rely on stories we tell ourselves about the past.

Moreover, national identities are a matter of stories: we assume a national identity based on the way the national history has been told and understood, and it is often necessary to challenge established conceptions of history in order to promote social justice. As Toni Morrison points out, if racism is not recognized as part of the history of the United States, black Americans will never be full citizens (Morrison 1992). For unless it is acknowledged that the history has been racist, there is no need to question such racism. Yet it is also true, as Barghouti (2003) emphasizes, that stories about the past and our concern to retell them rob us of freedom and prevent rather than promote an ability to take responsibility for the present. In this context he distinguishes between those who "cover reality with flowers" in their concern about securing history and those who proceed, albeit more uncertainly, with "open eyes."

In this paper I try to identify and explain the philosophical importance of Barghouti's insight that looking toward the past can rob us of freedom because it robs us of understanding. My freedom and capacity to choose and act is promoted by more adequate understanding. In part, I take Barghouti to be making in a more political context a point that is well known in the philosophy of science: evidence only becomes meaningful when it plays a role in the pursuit of specific goals. In other words, scientists give importance to empirical evidence relative to specific interests. It is the interests that explain the importance of the evidence, not the other way around (e.g., Kitcher 1984, 45–54). The point about historical evidence, therefore, is not one about whether or not it's important to look at histories and how they are told. Rather, it is that in order to retell the histories in the right way—that is, in the way most likely to provide more adequate understanding—it is necessary to possess the right sorts of interests and directions of action. This insight about losing freedom when looking to the past is the motivation, I take it, for Barghouti's memoir, set in such a complex political context. I will argue that the memoir suggests a reversal of the traditional explanatory relationship between memories (or histories) and agency. We should not look toward the retelling of histories, or the recovery of memories, to explain the possibility of greater freedom for one group or another. Instead, we should pursue real commitments toward peace and justice, and toward more humane ways of being and interacting, in order to discover what to do with histories.

I suggest that what matters to collective memory—understood (roughly) as those background beliefs and stories that inform deliberation, individually or collectively, about action—is not primarily knowledge of the past, but rather specific and appropriate expectations for the future. In using "expectation," I indicate not just goals and ideals, but a way of being and moving forward in the world, with material needs and interests. For it is relative to such a direction of thought or action, based on what we might call "practical identity," that background information becomes specifically meaningful. The point is this: my background beliefs and stories (i.e., memories) do not determine how I understand myself and what impulses I choose to act upon; rather, it is how I identify myself and choose to act that determines what beliefs and stories are meaningful to me.

Therefore, as regards agency and embodiment, it is more important to address the question of responsibility for the present and what this might mean within specific circumstances and conditions, than that of content of memory, individual or collective. Agency is best promoted when we respond sensitively to a specific context, adopting an orientation—that is, a direction for both thought and action—adequate to the discovery of what is required to really live better in specific respects. We might think of this as taking responsibility for the present. I turn now to the sort of understanding that allows us to take responsibility and to choose and act more freely,[1] that is, to exercise agency.

2. KNOWLEDGE AND UNDERSTANDING

We give importance to events in the past when those events play an explanatory role in what we need to understand in order to proceed. It used to be thought that scientists understand the world by collecting facts, through careful observation. But it turns out that scientific understanding does not necessarily increase as our set of knowledge claims grows. Instead scientists tell stories that are meaningful to the extent that they explain what needs to be understood, that is, to the extent that they answer relevant questions. Charles Darwin's account of natural selection, for instance, raised questions that needed to be answered, and

---

1. I do not take up the meaning of freedom in this paper. However, by "freedom" I do not mean the capacity to do whatever we want, within limits, which is an understanding of freedom that is not defended by philosophers but rather assumed popularly by politicians. Defensible philosophical views about freedom all have something to do with realizing goals and plans, and living better.

his theory was successful to the extent that it provided resources to explain such phenomena, or at least to point in the direction of their explanation (Kitcher 1984, 45–54). What was important were the questions Darwin raised—about evolution—not the facts by themselves. The facts about evolution would have meant nothing if there were not a phenomenon that needed explaining, which is what Darwin had shown (Boyd 1985).

Knowledge by itself does not save us from ignorance. We have to be in a position to be able to give importance to knowledge, to be able to judge what such knowledge explains or might explain. What Darwin did was raise a set of questions. And to raise questions it is necessary to tell a story—an alternative story. A question becomes possible when we see that things could be otherwise, that is, that the world could be otherwise. And we see this because there is a story, which is theoretical. But the story itself only becomes possible, I suggest, because of a position—that is, because of a state of being in the world, in some sense, and not primarily because of knowledge. Darwin's theory provided resources for telling a different sort of story about the world, but such theoretical resources would not be meaningful unless there were something to explain.

The distinction between knowledge and understanding is not about the reliability of beliefs, but rather about the perspective according to which we judge the importance of knowledge and apply it. It is about the ability to see what the questions are, that is, to see what needs explaining. For instance, I can know all about the independence struggles in Cuba and still be ignorant about those struggles if I do not recognize the relevance of those struggles for explaining specific aspects of the situation in Cuba currently. And I may fail to see the relevance because I am not involved enough in the current situation, physically and emotionally, to care. If I am not involved enough in a situation to feel to some extent personally connected, I will not care enough to raise the questions toward which evidence matters. For instance, if I cannot appreciate the feeling of humiliation that resulted for Cubans from the U.S. intervention in 1898 at the end of a remarkable thirty-year war of independence that the Cubans were poised to win (Ferrer 1999), I might not wonder about the full explanation for that intervention. If I do not care enough to wonder how such an intervention occurred, and what it eventually brought about, I possess information but miss important dimensions of the picture. And I will not know that I am missing part of the picture, for I have not understood the questions. Thus, I am ignorant. In other words, if I do not identify the relevant explanatory role of knowledge I possess, there's a sense in which I also fail to fully understand such knowledge, even though I possess it.

The roles of understanding and explanation, as distinct from knowledge, are in fact important in most practical aspects of day-to-day life. Science fiction writer Samuel Delaney pointed out that whether or not he could make sense of facts about his own life—facts he remembered and knew to be true—depended upon whether such information played any role in supporting and promoting his idea of what he wanted to become, as a person (Delaney 1993, 443). So, for instance, if he did something that was inconsistent with his image of himself, his memory of that event would, as he put it, be "cut out" of the stock of stories that grounded his actions and expectations for himself. Delaney suggested, therefore, that the meaning that we give to memories of events in our lives, and, in fact, whether or not accounts of such events even become part of our stock of memories, depends on the self-image we assume and pursue. Events become meaningful, and are able to be articulated and acted upon, if such events are relevant to and consistent with what I want to become and what I think I need to do to become such a person. Otherwise, I can know that certain events happened, but if the knowledge of such events plays no explanatory role in my current pursuits, the beliefs are "cut off" from other beliefs and are forgotten. In an anecdote, Delaney remembers that he knew about certain events precisely at the point at which his self-understanding and life directions changed in such a way as to make the forgotten beliefs explanatorily relevant.

In a much reprinted article, "Cuba Libre," written in the 1960s, Leroi Jones (1966) describes how he came to doubt the dominant ideology of his country, the United States. He had gone to Cuba determined not to be "taken in" by the communists. But he interacts with Cubans in Cuba and describes his experience of their happiness. Jones's personal, emotional experience in Cuba contradicted certain expectations derived from his own social context, such as that these people should be dismissed. His expectations, perhaps implicit, were that these people might be somewhat crazy. As a result of the contradiction between his expectations and what he felt when he shared the Cubans' happiness, he becomes aware of those expectations and is able to question them. When he returns to the United States, Jones describes becoming aware of the "thin crust of lie that we cannot even detect in our own thinking," and from that awareness he went on to become a radical and effective critic of his own society (Jones 1966, 61).

My first point, then, is that knowledge by itself is not interesting, at least not in questions about agency, whether individual or collective. We can fail to fully grasp truths we know to be true because the way that we act and identify ourselves within a community makes such truths largely irrelevant to us. Knowledge becomes motivating and relevant to agency when it plays an explanatory role relative to needs for understanding. Thus, as regards agency, it is more urgent to ask how we acquire explanatory needs—that is, questions— that make meaningful and necessary the retrieval and appropriate application of background histories and memories.

3. TAKING RESPONSIBILITY FOR THE PRESENT

My second point is that explanatory need—that is, questions that motivate the telling of an alternative story, such as that pursued by Leroi Jones in the example above—arises out of a certain kind of directed, caring interest in present circumstances, even at the expense of consistency with established commitments and beliefs. Jones could have dismissed the contradictions between his deep-seated beliefs and his actual experiences in Cuba, and remained with his more comfortable assumptions. But he cared enough about the people with whom he engaged in Cuba, and what their reality might suggest for him, to pursue more adequate explanatory resources. And so he came to realize that some of his established beliefs were false and that he had good reason to question other such beliefs.

When Fidel Castro spoke to the General Assembly of the United Nations in 1960, in a speech entitled "The Case of Cuba Is the Case of Every Developing Country" (Castro 1992, 76), he invited the audience to imagine "that a person from outer space were to come to this assembly, someone who had read neither the Communist Manifesto of Karl Marx nor UPI or AP dispatches or any other monopoly-controlled publication. If such a visitor were to ask how the world was divided up and then saw on a map that the wealth was divided among the monopolies of four or five countries, he would say, 'The world has been badly divided up, the world has been exploited'" (Castro 1992, 76).

Castro's point here is not that the world is divided up badly. Indeed, the truth of the claim "the world is badly divided up" is hard to dispute. Yet although almost anyone can recognize the truth of the claim, "the world is badly divided up," relatively few think the claim needs explanation. That is, few are surprised by the truth of the claim and wonder how it came about. If such a truth is not explained, or in need of explanation, it is because it is assumed that that is how the world is supposed to be. Both Fidel Castro, and the Iranian nationalist Mohammed Mossadegh before him in 1952, tried to get the General Assembly of the United Nations to see that what was taken for granted—U.S. and British imperialism—was wrong. The facts about what was happening to the resources of the Third World were well known at the UN. The message of the anecdote is that it would take a visitor from outer space—someone from another world—to give to such facts moral importance, and to see that they need explanation. This is not to suggest, as some philosophers will think, that it takes someone from nowhere to see the importance of the fact that the world is divided as it is. Someone from outer space is not from nowhere but from somewhere else, not from this planet. Such a figure is not without interests, just without the interests of people living on *this* planet. The ideology that prevents giving importance to such facts is globally influential, and was even then, despite the existence of a second super power. The purpose of the example is that the true claim that the world is divided so that four-fifths of humanity suffer in order that one-fifth lives well is so striking that *anyone* not conditioned by a corrupt globally powerful ideology, generated by the wealth of that one-fifth, would see that such division is wrong.

Explanatory purpose is not just an issue about awareness or sensitivity. We can be aware of the facts about the world and sensitive to their importance, but still not think they matter to us in the relevant ways. Instead, the issue here is about a certain sort of awareness and sensitivity, namely, that generated by responsibility, or a sense of relevant caring about the situation and its implications. For if there is not the interest, there is no reason to pursue the explanation, that is, the alternative story.

Bertolt Brecht once commented that when someone falls down, other people faint, but if violence is falling like rain from the sky, people turn away when others suffer.[2] His point is that it is usually quite natural for people to react to the suffering of others, but if violence is everywhere, we cannot react because the suffering of others becomes unsurprising. If something is unsurprising, it doesn't even get explained, let alone generate action. But in order for there to be that surprise, we have to think the world could be different, and, importantly, we would have to consider that possibility important, that is, worth pursuing.

The point is this: we do not question, and often should not question, that which is the way it is supposed to be. If there is nothing strange about a situation, it makes no sense, usually, to ask why that situation is as it is. So we only ask questions about ourselves and the beliefs presupposed in thinking about ourselves if we think that perhaps we are not the way we should be. But we would only entertain such doubts if we understood our human possibilities

2. This anecdote was cited by Acosta (2003, 6).

well enough to see that we not only could, but really ought to, live differently in relevant respects. That is, we only ask questions—worth pursuing—if we think that we really could and ought to be otherwise.

To return to Barghouti: Barghouti says that he *saw* Ramallah, that is, he saw his past, when he saw himself as that which all his life he had criticized and distanced himself from, namely, a despot. A despot is someone who is immune to criticism (Barghouti 2003, 125). So intellectuals can be as despotic as politicians. Barghouti's point is that only when he understood something about himself, namely his despotism, did he develop the need to understand his own implication in the situation, and therefore raise the questions that helped him to recognize responsibility. His past, that is, the stories of others, cannot become relevantly meaningful, that is, meaningful to him personally, unless there is something that needs to be understood about himself as a person, but this would never be possible if, as in the case of the intellectual despot, he is fine as he is.

We like to "cover reality with flowers" because we like to make reality *into* something familiar. We like to fit it into the story we already have, that story about ourselves we presupposed in order to act, and to understand others. We do this often for good reason, in the interests of stability. But to do so always is a failure to appreciate the radical contingency of our understanding of the world, that is, that acquiring adequate understanding of a situation is dependent on our engagement with the world (Babbitt 1999). In some cases, we don't understand, not because we don't possess the facts, but because of our sort of involvement with current circumstances and conditions, or better, our lack of an appropriate, more responsible sort of involvement.

4. EXPERIENTIAL UNDERSTANDING

Understanding a current reality and taking responsibility, particularly in ways that promote understanding relevant to agency, is an example of the greater importance of experiential, and not merely intellectual, understanding in questions of agency specifically, and human development generally. By "experiential understanding" I mean here the understanding that becomes possible only as a result of a certain way of being situated in the world, and of awareness of that state of being so situated.

Robin Dillon refers to experiential understanding having to do with the role of emotional involvement in full understanding (Dillon 1997). She points out that someone can know intellectually that a close friend has died but only fully grasp that truth when she stands by the coffin. For instance, I more fully grasp what has happened when I am physically present at the funeral because at that moment I feel some part of the transformation happening to me in my life as a consequence of the truth of my belief. Dillon says that there are some truths that can be understood intellectually, some that can be understood experientially (such as what it is like to see yellow), and some truths that if they are only understood intellectually are not understood fully. It is the last category that is interesting to Dillon. There are some bits of knowledge that we can possess and know we possess, but if we have not experienced them in some way, we do not fully understand.

Dillon argues that there are some truths that must be felt in order to be fully grasped. Belief in my own self-worth is one such truth. Dillon points out that someone can believe truly that she has worth but fail to act appropriately upon such a belief—with confidence—because the belief is held only intellectually. Instead, when the truth of a belief is *felt*, the truth of that belief is presupposed in action and, according to Dillon, we then possess expectations appropriate to the truth of that belief. Without such expectations, it is difficult to act consistently with such a truth.

If my knowledge of my worth is only intellectual, and I do not possess the relevant expectations, I will be surprised, as Dillon points out, at any evidence of the truth of the belief in my worth, and I will look for alternative explanations. For instance, when I am successful, I think it is just a matter of luck. I do not expect to succeed and so do not see myself as the source of that success and seek another explanation. And when I fail to understand myself as relevantly connected to my actions, that is, as being the explanatory cause of what I have brought about, and instead assume that my success is just a fluke, I fail in agency.

But the idea of experiential understanding possesses even broader and more important applicability. In Dillon's example, we fail to fully understand a true belief, which we hold, and are unable to act appropriately on that belief, when we do not feel in some way the consequences of the truth of that belief. It is also the case, though, that if we do not act in a certain way appropriate for the circumstances, pursuing relevant objectives materially and epistemically, we will not have experiential access to true beliefs that we do in fact possess, beliefs that matter to that situation. Without specific actions and pursuits, we will not have reason to ask the questions allowing even the identification of background stories and memories, let alone their explanatory significance. We will possess such stories and histories and remain ignorant.

Drawing again on the philosophy of science, there is a question, once the thoroughly value- and theory-dependent nature of science is acknowledged, about how we ever discover anything about the world. If all our investigations are dependent on expectations determined by past patterns of regularity, how do we ever discover that our conceptual schemes and the expectations they give rise to are wrong? The answer in the philosophy of science is, roughly, *the world*. We can discover that our conceptual schemes, or paradigms, are wrong, or perhaps wrong, because we engage with the world, and the world reacts back. Since we all in fact engage, albeit from different points, and for different reasons, with the same physical world, we can hope that our theories converge and that we can work toward this goal through ongoing theoretical and practical engagement (Boyd 1980, 1990).

It is possible that understanding issues related to human well-being, in general and in specific contexts, has this same characteristic: namely, that the discovery that deep-seated beliefs and expectations may be wrong depends on the theoretical and practical consequences of actual engagement with the object of understanding, that is, human well-being or perhaps just human reality. Karl Marx thought that we become estranged from ourselves, and fail to understand ourselves, when we identify with abstractions, such as religion. There are of course other abstractions we identify with, including personal ideals such as being "progressive" or "self-aware." Such self-conceptions play an alienating role, just as religious beliefs might, when dependence on such abstractions is substituted for the real, productive creative life in which we take our own world in hand, and instead of merely thinking about it, actually set about changing it and thereby changing ourselves (see, e.g., Marx 1977 and Merton 1967). According to Marx, religious idolatries, and presumably any other ideology adopted for existential security, prevent people from being themselves and even from being human. For we define ourselves in terms of such abstractions rather than through the realistic collaboration of the work of daily living.

Alienation prevents understanding. The concept of alienation explains how it is that we become detached from our reality: we understand ourselves and our reality in terms of abstract conceptions and we fail to engage directly with the world. When we fail to engage directly, we also fail to be changed by the world, emotionally, intellectually, and physically. Marx recognized that if we avoid direct and concrete relationship with the material and social world, we deprive ourselves of the only possible resources for increased understanding of human well-being, which is collaborative action toward that very goal. Marxist humanists—such as Antonio Gramsci (1983) and Che Guevara (2003)—claimed that in order to change the world we have to be changed *by* the world. Above I suggested that position, directedness, and interests explain the raising of questions. And in the specific case of understanding human flourishing, we come to possess relevant sorts of direction and interests—in human well-being—as a result of change to ourselves and our present circumstances.

When Barghouti says that the Palestinian people still wait with "open eyes," but that the media deny this and continue to "cover reality with flowers" (2003, 120), I understand him to be referring to the epistemic benefits of this sort of concrete, contingent understanding and engagement. In his case, he is referring to a people: the Palestinian people. Rather than seeking ways to understand what is happening now mostly in terms of past myths and a sense of secure identity, in his view the Palestinian people look at what is before them and engage with that reality in a way that relevantly transforms who they are. "Open eyes," I take it, is the characteristic of interpretation that involves looking at and engaging with what is happening now, and determining from those results what should be, rather than relying solely on past expectations. It is easy, though, if one doesn't accept the inevitability of a certain amount of insecurity, to end up "covering reality with flowers," that is, looking primarily for unity and meaningfulness according to past expectations.

Experiential understanding, then, can be understood as the circumstantial and bodily position according to which truths become relevant and meaningful specifically as a result of such positionality. But there's a certain instability and discomfort in what Barghouti describes as proceeding with "open eyes." "Covering reality with flowers" is much more reassuring. But then we may end up understanding the evidence of experience as just more evidence for what we already expected.

5. AGENCY AND HUMILITY

Thomas Merton says that the great paradox of human existence is that the more we make of ourselves, the less we exist (Inchausti 2005, 1; Merton 1961, 267). Merton was not just referring to the ethical dimensions of building ourselves up, but rather, more urgently, to the epistemic barriers posed by self-indulgence, or even self-awareness or "mindfulness," when it is not directed toward relevant change. Merton points out that it is sometimes thought that the antidote to alienation is awareness of the present. However, the "elephantiasis of self-awareness," as he calls it, is a misunderstanding of the existentialists' significant insight about alienation (Merton 1968, 31). If "awareness of the present" is above all a means of self-description, another aspect of self identification and a way to make myself important, I am still relevantly alienated from my immediate experience. For if I do actually engage my immediate reality—personal and social—I cannot also be involved in building myself up, at least not in the first instance. For the result of such engagement is precisely the loss of existential security, through the effective raising of new questions.

Existentialists often refer to two sorts of community (e.g., Merton 1961). One is a false community in which members identify with a sense of collectivity not of their own making or even choice. The other is a more genuine sense of community in which members accept their own fragile lot, choosing to exist contingently, that is, with awareness of their ultimate existential insecurity, and in recognition of the ultimately solitary nature of such choice. The paradox is that it looks as if real communication and community depend more interestingly on solitude than on togetherness. For existential awareness results from solitude, at least occasionally, and is what makes it possible to understand what is shared between all human beings. One explanation for this might be that solitude is a position in the world that is in fact more effectively disruptive of arbitrarily derived expectations for togetherness, the false sort that existentialists worried about.

Merton, a Catholic, and Guevara, a Marxist, recognized that only if we are actually engaged in genuinely humane interactions, such that we ourselves become more humane in relevant respects, do we begin to interpret events more progressively, and so become more free, that is, more aware of arbitrarily imposed compulsions, such as the attraction of the false sorts of community that existentialists worried about. If we are falsely secure in our sense of moral importance, there is no reason to interpret experience other than as evidence for that same sense of importance and rightness, and we are then likely to be bound by inherited, often unexamined, values and less likely to be able to act spontaneously according to present circumstances and conditions.

Therefore, humility has an epistemic role because we can only discover new ways to pursue human well-being if we actually pursue human well-being, that is, if we do in fact engage the real possibility of more just and humane circumstances and conditions. And to the extent that such a pursuit in any unjust society requires questioning established conceptions, it is not possible if we are, as Barghouti says, intellectual despots, that is, fine as we are. For intellectual despots have no real need to pursue human well-being, at least not in any interesting sense involving discovery of misconceptions, which is the only sense in which increased understanding is possible.

This reflection brings us to the importance, and difficulty, of one sort of experiential understanding, the one that is, in my view, more urgent. Intellectually, the pursuit of human well-being involves no threat. As we pursue understanding of human flourishing—our own or that of a group—in theory, we continue to interpret reality in terms of background beliefs and stories, finding existential comfort in abstract ideas of togetherness, including individual togetherness or self-awareness. But when we actually engage with our individual and social reality, there *is* a threat because we may discover that deep-seated beliefs are unfounded. Or we may just discover the deep-seated beliefs, as Leroi Jones did. The experience of the insecurity of such situations, if properly acknowledged, motivates the pursuit of more adequate understanding, more adequate explanations and stories, as in Jones's case, which resulted in greater understanding of his social situation in the United States at that time. He would never have discovered such motivation if he had been stuck on himself, unable to relinquish his self-conception. Experiential understanding is also, in part, that sort of humility. Jones, for instance, would not have had a need for or interest in pursuing more adequate explanatory resources for his situation in the United States if his sense of self importance, derived from identification with his background beliefs and memories of that same situation, had been suitably dominant.

Barghouti's point about the impact of experiencing himself as an intellectual despot is a point about the epistemic barrier of self-importance. I will not discover arbitrarily derived, unself-conscious expectations regarding human development if I remain confident that I am all right as I am. For if I am all right as I am, I have no need to act in ways likely to provide evidence against such expectations. Barghouti's existential insight, namely that he is not in fact open to new directions but is in fact as despotic as those he has criticized, constituted a position from which he could raise questions about his expectations that could not have been raised previously.

Karl Marx said that the difference between human beings and other animals is that while all animals strive to realize their natures (e.g., dogs are happy when they do what dogs typically do), only human animals care about what it means to be doing that. There is an epistemological reason why this is so: what we give importance to and what impulses become reasons for action depends on what stories we tell ourselves about such impulses. Our reasons also depend on the concepts such stories rely on. We cannot expect to discover new, more adequate ways of investigating the question of human well-being if we rely only on the sense of communal togetherness resulting from the reigning conceptions of well-being, those depending for their content on inhumane ideologies. And such conceptions are what generally constitute the warm togetherness we rely on to escape loneliness. As Jean Vanier said, in Massey Lectures entitled *Becoming Human,* "When we refuse to accept that loneliness and insecurity are part of life, when we refuse to accept that they are the price of change, we close the door on many possibilities for ourselves; our lives become lessened, we are less then fully human" (Vanier 1988, 12–13).

One problem with the primacy of historical memory in questions about agency, especially collective agency, is that we look to the retelling of history to provide security. That security is about identity, including human identity, and the pursuit of such security is at odds with understanding relevant to agency.

Of course we do not have to seek security. We can also retell history and rearrange memories in order to make relevant sorts of insecurity understandable and acceptable. As Toni Morrison (1992) so eloquently argued, the history of the United States can be told in such a way that American racism is evident, so that even our deep-seated moral concepts are in question, having derived meaning from such racism. The retelling of history in this case promotes relevant insecurity, generating appropriate questions.

To reiterate: the point here is not one about whether or not it's important to retell histories. It is that there is a question about how to acquire the understanding that allows us to retell the histories in the right way, that is, in the way most conducive to peace and justice. This desire for a more adequate telling was the motivation, I take it, for Barghouti's memoir. Interest in and commitment to becoming more human, in thought and action, must explain the retelling of history, and not the reverse. We should not rely on storytelling to discover or define that commitment. We should pursue such a commitment in order to discover what to do with histories.

6. CONCLUSION

To conclude, it turns out that freedom must make one a stranger to the past, as Barghouti suggests. As long as I am attached to the past, and the sense of importance that my account of the past supports, I have no reason to raise the questions that might make meaningful histories that contradict that sense of identity and make possible more adequate understanding of human possibilities, individually or for a group. But perhaps effective agency is not primarily about historical memory at all, at least not in the first instance. Rather, it is about how to raise the appropriate questions about individual, group, or national identity, including about what we mean by freedom and democracy. Such questions can make the stories of those others stories about *us*, that is, about the human condition, because such stories can then become relevant to understanding such fundamental concepts as freedom and democracy.

It is not the possession of stories that explains understanding and freedom, but rather, the expectation that such stories matter to who we can be and, importantly, the desire to be more than we are. Desire for something better, indeed desire to be something better as persons, is more likely to produce better self-understanding. Effective agency is best explained by sensitivity to and awareness of a present reality, and not primarily stories of the past, marginalized or not. We are better off then to ask about how to live in and engage with a current reality than how to tell the history that explains it. For only if we succeed in engaging with others in a direction leading to greater human flourishing can the questions that arise in such a pursuit explain how to properly understand what we may already know to be true and to effectively act upon it.

REFERENCES

Acosta, Elíades. 2003. Intelectuales y artistas contra el fascismo. *Juventud Rebelde* (Havana), tabloide especial, no. 4 (April), 6.
Babbitt, Susan. 1999. Moral Risk and Dark Waters. In *Racism and Philosophy*, ed. S. Babbitt and S. Campbell, 235–54. Ithaca: Cornell University Press.
Barghouti, Mourid. 2003. *I Saw Ramallah*. Trans. Ahdaf Soueif. New York: Anchor Books.
Boyd, Richard N. 1980. Scientific Realism and Naturalistic Epistemology. *Proceedings of the Biennial Meeting of the Philosophy of Science Association* 2:613–62.
———. 1985. Observations, Explanatory Power, and Simplicity: Toward a Non-Humean Account. In *Observation, Experiment, and Hypothesis in Modern Physical Science*, ed. Peter Achinstein and Owen Hannaway, 47–94. Cambridge: MIT Press.
———. 1990. Realism, Conventionality, and "Realism About." In *Meaning and Method: Essays in Honour of H. Putnam*, ed. G. Boolos, 171–95. Cambridge: Cambridge University Press.
Castro, Fidel. 1992. The Case of Cuba Is the Case of Every Underdeveloped Country. Address to the U.N. General Assembly, September 26, 1960. Reprinted in *To Speak the Truth: Why Washington's "Cold War" Against Cuba Doesn't End*, ed. Fidel Castro and Che Guevara. New York: Pathfinder.

Delaney, Samuel D. 1993. *The Motion of Light in Water: Sex and Science Fiction Writing in the East Village, 1960–1965.* New York: Richard Kasak Books.
Dillon, Robin. 1997. Respect: Moral, Political, Emotional. *Ethics* 107:226–49.
Ferrer, Ada E. 1999. *Insurgent Cuba: Race, Nation, and Revolution, 1868–1898.* Chapel Hill: University of North Carolina Press.
Gramsci, Antonio. 1983. The Intellectuals. In *Selections from the Prison Notebooks of Antonio Gramsci,* ed. Q. Hoare and G. Nowell Smith, 3–14. New York: International Publishers.
Guevara, Ernesto Che. 2003. Socialism and Man in Cuba. In *Che Guevara Reader: Writings on Politics and Revolution,* 212–28. New York: International Publishers.
Inchausti, Robert, ed. 2005. *The Pocket Thomas Merton.* Boston: New Seeds.
Jones, Leroi. 1966. Cuba Libre. In *Home: Social Essays,* 11–62. New York: William Morrow.
Kimmerling, Baruch, and Joel S. Migdal. 2003. *The Palestinian People: A History.* Cambridge: Harvard University Press.
Kitcher, Phillip. 1984. *Abusing Science: The Case Against Creationism.* Cambridge: MIT Press.
Marx, Karl. 1977. Economic and Philosophic Manuscripts of 1844. In *Selected Writings,* ed. David McLellan. Oxford: Oxford University Press.
Merton, Thomas. 1961. *New Seeds of Contemplation.* New York: New Directions.
———. 1967. *Mystics and Zen Masters.* New York: Farrar, Strauss and Giroux.
———. 1968. *Zen and the Birds of Appetite.* New York: New Directions Books.
Morrison, Toni. 1992. *Playing in the Dark: Whiteness and the Literary Imagination.* New York: Vintage Books.
Vanier, Jean. 1998. *Becoming Human.* Toronto: House of Anansi Press.

TWELVE

AGENCY AND EMPOWERMENT:
EMBODIED REALITIES IN A GLOBALIZED WORLD

Christine M. Koggel

1. INTRODUCTION

Many development theorists and policy makers now reject well-being approaches that treat people in developing countries as passive recipients of aid in favor of agency approaches that treat people as active participants who can and ought to shape and control their own lives. In *Development as Freedom,* Amartya Sen argues that people "need not be seen primarily as passive recipients of the benefits of cunning development programs" (Sen 1999a, 11) and that they should be treated as agents who "can effectively shape their own destiny and help each other" (Sen 1999a, 11). For Sen, agency does not mean merely opening up a broader range of options from which people can choose. Rather, agency is about having effective power to remove barriers, to use the abilities one has to make use of opportunities, and to be free to participate in, deliberate about, and have a say about economic, social, and political institutions.

The sense of agency as having the power to effect positive changes in one's own life and the lives of those around one is captured in the more recent turn in development theory and policy to the concept of empowerment. Work on this concept is reflected in the recent World Bank titles *Empowerment and Poverty Reduction: A Sourcebook* (Narayan 2004) and *Measuring Empowerment: Cross-Disciplinary Perspectives* (Narayan 2005). In the latter, Deepa Narayan provides the following definition: "empowerment refers broadly to the expansion of freedom of choice and action to shape one's life. It implies control over resources and decisions" (2005, 4). Empowerment underscores the idea that individual agents are always already situated in social contexts that all too often determine how much control they actually have over their own lives. One connection between the concepts would have us say that enhancing agency involves empowering people individually and collectively to take purposeful and effective action in contexts in which their power to do so is affected by institutional, economic, social, and political factors. One distinction would have us say that unlike agency, empowerment is a *process* of change—from conditions of disempowerment to ones of empowerment. Crucially, this process involves treating people as agents of change on the road to giving them greater control over and a say about resources and decisions that affect their life prospects.

Conceiving empowerment as a process suggests that agency approaches need to be contextual, relational, and responsive to changing conditions and circumstances. Where people are located, what opportunities and resources are available, what roles and functions are performed and by whom, and whether local conditions are affected by national and global factors and actors are issues relevant to an analysis of empowerment. I shall argue that features of feminist relational theory position it to provide the kind of contextual and detailed descriptions and analyses needed for understanding what empowerment involves. But I also argue that two aspects missing in both feminist relational theory and the current literature on empowerment need to be added to the analysis. First, facts of embodied realities and bodily needs matter to accounts of agency and empowerment. Taking agency seriously involves taking embodiment seriously, and this is because empowerment is enabled through bodies—bodies that are fed, sheltered, safe, healthy, and engaged in meaningful participation and communal activities. Because a key aspect of feminist relational theory is its call for responding in morally appropriate ways to the needs of others, this theory can only be enriched when embodiment and bodily needs are incorporated and developed. Second, because embodied realities and bodily needs are increasingly affected and shaped by features of globalization, attention needs to be paid to relationships of power at local, national, and global levels that have the effect of disempowering bodies. The central argument of this paper is that factors of embodied realities and bodily needs as shaped and reshaped by factors of globalization matter to accounts of agency and empowerment. I begin by using relational insights to develop the argument. I then defend the argument by discussing two case studies: features of embodied realities as captured through an examination of homelessness in the United States and the impact of globalization on bodies as captured in a study of Mexican women affected by a family planning policy implemented in the early 1990s.

2. EXPANDING A FEMINIST RELATIONAL CRITIQUE OF AGENCY

As developed by a number of feminists (e.g., Nedelsky 1989 and 1993; Minow 1990; Code 1991 and 2000; Koggel 1998 and 2003b; Sherwin 1998; Brennan 1999; Mackenzie and Stoljar 2000; and Campbell 2002 and 2003), relational theory uses as its starting point the fact that human beings exist in relationships and do not come into the world as the independent, autonomous, and self-sufficient agents assumed by many traditional liberal theorists.[1] Feminists have argued that paying attention to the relationships people are in draws special attention to the workings of power and to the ways in which factors such as race, gender, disability, and so on often reduce or prevent agency. In my own work, I argue that moving beyond the dyadic relationships examined in early feminist relational accounts of an ethic of care to the broad network of relationships in which people are situated allows us to identify several features distinctive to an expanded feminist relational approach. Such an approach 1) is contextual in that it allows us to attend to the details of the lives of those affected by various kinds of unequal and oppressive relationships, relationships that are in turn shaped by particular social practices and political contexts; 2) uncovers the governing norms and practices that sustain various inequalities for those who are powerless and disadvantaged; and 3) reveals the importance of the perspectives of those adversely affected by relationships of power as sources for learning about various kinds of inequalities and the structures that sustain them.[2] This approach, thereby, draws on perspectives as vantage points for revealing and analyzing the social structures that sustain oppressive relationships and shape the material lives of those in them.

Liberal theory's cherished notions of autonomy and agency are not relinquished in a relational approach; instead they are reinterpreted as capacities that are shaped in and through the network of complex and ever-changing relationships in which each of us is situated (Koggel 1998). Expanding the reach of relationships from the personal to those at public, national, and global levels allows us to capture the complexity of agency: lives, relationships, and conditions are affected by local, national, and global policies in ways that

---

1. For a fuller discussion of individualism in liberal theory, consult chapter 2 of my *Perspectives on Equality: Constructing a Relational Theory* (1998).

2. Features 2 and 3 can be viewed as distinguishing a feminist relational approach from other contextual approaches like virtue ethics and utilitarianism. Margaret Walker (1989) argues that what she refers to as an ethic of care (and I a feminist relational ethic) is a unified approach that challenges and is distinct from traditional accounts of morality evident in a justice approach.

determine possibilities for empowering agents. By this account, agency emerges through engagement with particular others in a network of relationships shaped by social practices and political contexts, a network that can enhance but also hinder an agent's capacity to make choices and determine the course of his or her life. So far, relational theory captures well the idea that empowerment is a process whereby agents are enabled to use abilities and resources to effect change in ways that remove or alleviate conditions of oppression.

To this call by relational theorists for an analysis of the complex network of relationships in which each of us is situated, I now want to highlight two additional features. First, assessing agency and empowerment requires accounts of embodied realities and bodily needs. In *Body Images: Embodiment as Intercorporeality*, Gail Weiss surveys literature by ethic of care theorists to argue that while many acknowledge the importance of bodies in their accounts of caring for others, they either tend to focus on unambiguous mother-child relationships to the exclusion of an account of the broader network of relationships that also require ethical responses to bodily imperatives, or they fail to foreground the "role that the body itself plays in our moral interactions" (Weiss 1999, 136–46). Weiss argues that feminists often "subvert their own goals by failing to do justice to the particularities of the lived body, particularities which are an indispensable feature of our moral practices and which have yet to become an equally indispensable feature of our moral theorizing" (1999, 143).

Weiss uses Simone de Beauvoir's discussion of the network of personal relationships that changed in the course of responding to her mother dying of cancer (Weiss 1999, 146–63). I want to apply Weiss's idea of bodily imperatives to the realm of public relationships by examining homelessness in the United States, an issue that would seem to foreground embodied realities and bodily needs. While Weiss's discussion of Beauvoir shows a process by which those involved gained insight into appropriate ethical responses to a particular dying body, the discussion of homelessness presents a case of a failure to respond to the bodily needs of those who are fellow citizens and strangers.

Second, the contemporary context of globalization requires an analysis of embodied realities and bodily imperatives attentive to a reality in which virtually all relationships are being shaped and reshaped by local, national, and global factors and in ways that often disempower people and hinder possibilities for agency. A brief discussion of the World Bank's multivolume work *Voices of the Poor* (Narayan 2000; 2001; 2002) will allow me to capture why relational theory is relevant to assessing empowerment and also why it demands that we think about embodied realities in the contemporary context of globalization.

In the foreword to the first volume, the president of the World Bank describes the work as "an unprecedented effort to gather the views, experiences, and aspirations of more than 60,000 poor men and women from 60 countries" (Narayan 2000, ix). In the introduction to the first chapter, the authors explain that the project was undertaken "to set a precedent for the participation of poor men and women in global policy debates" (Narayan 2000, 4). There is much to applaud in this World Bank project that makes the *voices* of the poor central to its analysis of poverty and to policies for alleviating it. What is missing in this use of perspectives, however, becomes evident soon into reading the volumes.

The authors describe the study as providing "rich descriptions of poor people's realities, drawing on their experiences of poverty and the quality of their interactions with a range of institutions, from the state to the household" (Narayan 2000, 3). They define the range of institutions as fitting two broad divisions of state and civil: "State institutions include national, regional, and local governments; the judiciary; and the police. Civil institutions include NGOs, trade unions, community-based organizations, social associations, kinship networks, and so forth" (Narayan 2000, 9). They pay attention to context when they argue that state institutions intersect with and shape civil institutions in specific ways in particular locations. They rightly avoid giving an account of people's lives in isolation from the local and state institutions that shape them. However, what is glaringly absent is any discussion of global institutions and their intersections with and shaping of state and civil institutions in particular locations, including the World Bank itself that produced the study. Absent is recognition of the relationship between the World Bank doing the study and those being studied, a relationship of power that would seem to be relevant to the results of the study itself in terms of what is said, heard, and reported when the World Bank listens to the voices of the poor. This explains why the study merely *seems* to attend to the perspectives of the poor. It lacks the kind of analysis provided by a relational account of global structures that shape relationships of power, and it ignores the disempowering effects of these relationships on those affected by them.

As described thus far, feminist relational theory has us pay attention to relationships of power and to the ways in which factors such as race, gender, disability, and so on affect and sometimes reduce or prevent agency. But taking this insight seriously also demands that we pay attention to embodied realities in the particularity of people who are unable to satisfy bodily needs or who perform functions and roles based on the bodies they have. The World Bank's multivolume work on poverty draws attention to the importance of voice, but this raises the question of whether hearing and reporting what is heard absent an account of the lived and concrete realities of bodies and bodily needs is sufficient for uncovering norms and taking perspective seriously. In taking into account the relevance of perspectives, but merely in terms of listening, interpreting, and recording different voices, are we missing features of embodied realities and bodily imperatives that are relevant to an account of agency and empowerment? Are we missing an analysis of how perspectives as they exist in relationships of power shape people's lives and reduce possibilities for agency? Do we run the risk of reinforcing the very power structures that contribute to processes of disempowerment? A discussion of the issue of homelessness in the following section and of women in Mexico in the final section highlights problems in an account of perspectives that takes listening to, interpreting, and recording voices to be sufficient. In the process, questions are raised about whose perspectives count and which bodies matter in an understanding of agency and in the formulation of policies for empowering agents.

3. AGENCY AND BODILY IMPERATIVES: DISEMPOWERING THE HOMELESS

In "Homelessness and the Issue of Freedom," Jeremy Waldron highlights contradictions in the United States, where commitment to the primacy of negative freedom (or freedom from interference) is espoused at the same time as laws are being passed that restrict what the homeless can do and where. By restricting what can be done on common property such as streets, parks, and subways, these increasingly popular laws, he argues, limit where activities such as eating, sleeping, washing, and going to the bathroom can be performed by those without homes. Because these bodily functions are necessary for life itself, the homeless, Waldron provocatively states, are "allowed to *be* in our society only to the extent that our society is communist" (Waldron 1991, 433, his emphasis). In other words, they are allowed to be only when they are allowed to use public or common property to perform the necessary bodily functions of urinating and defecating and to satisfy the basic bodily needs of eating, sleeping, and washing.

Significantly, laws that bar sleeping on subways or on park benches, for example, not only restrict what can be done on common property, they also have the effect of physically removing homeless people from places where they can be seen or encountered. Waldron argues that the laws are intended to have this effect because "people do not want to be confronted with the sight of the homeless... and they are willing to deprive these people of their last opportunity to sleep in order to protect themselves from this discomfort" (Waldron 1991, 437). It can be said, then, that these increasingly popular policies to deal with the "problem of homelessness" free those who have property and are more powerful from being confronted with the bodily imperatives that would require them to respond at all, let alone to respond in morally appropriate ways. Being free to ignore the fact that people have needs that demand a response is to be free to believe that the responsibility for homelessness rests with others, either the state or the homeless themselves. Moreover and more generally, not encountering the homeless in common and public areas means that many people can come to believe that the problem of homelessness has been solved—there are fewer or no homeless people to be seen, so it must be that they now have homes. And if we do not need to see or interact with them, we need not know anything about them; not even that their numbers continue to rise or that they live in conditions unimaginable to those who take for granted that they can perform basic human functions and satisfy basic needs in the privacy of their own homes.[3] They have become invisible; so much so that it takes the creation of a film to make it known that they exist and in large numbers.

Dark Days (2001) documents a community of homeless people living in a train tunnel beneath Manhattan, a virtual city underneath a city. The film has us learn that for some who are interviewed, this has been their home for as long as twenty-five years. Through the interviews we are invited to see "them" as like "us" in having relationships, dreams, goals, and hopes for the future. The story line of *Dark Days* is centered on Amtrak's effort in the late 1990s to remove these homeless people from the train tunnel. By the end of the film those who have lived in this underground community become the beneficiaries of policies that provide them with housing—a happy ending to the depiction of them as leading horrific lives without sunlight and surrounded by rats. This policy of providing homes fits the approach of treating people as passive recipients of aid. Waldron's provocative paper suggests that there may be something missing or problematic both in the *Dark Days* description of these lives lived underground and in the "happy" ending that has them evicted from the tunnels and moved into homes.

Waldron attempts to make the details of homelessness vivid and visible by describing in concrete ways their lack of bodily freedom to wash, urinate,

---

3. A *New York Times* article estimated that in 2006 there were 88,000 homeless in Los Angeles, making it the city with the highest population of homeless. Moreover, L.A. was ranked eighteenth out of twenty cities for being the "meanest" in treating its homeless (Archibold 2006b).

sleep, and eat. At the same time, Waldron explicitly rejects any suggestion that the lack of freedom resulting from increasingly restrictive laws implies that the homeless lack agency: "people remain agents, with ideas and initiatives of their own, even when they are poor. Indeed, since they are on their own, in a situation of danger, without any place of safety, they must often be more resourceful . . . than the comfortable autonomous agent that we imagine in a family with a house and a job in an office or university" (Waldron 1991, 434). Waldron suggests that homeless people have agency because they need to act and be aware of the implications of those actions in ways not confronted by most: they need to know the laws and policies that affect them, they need to be resourceful in finding places where they can do what others do privately and without thought, and they need to make decisions that allow them to stay alive. Avoiding homeless shelters that turn out to be dangerous, or creating communities underground are decisions born from experiences of coping with conditions dictated by laws and policies designed to "solve the problem of homelessness."

But the agency Waldron finds is not the same as that outlined in Sen's account, where agency is connected with having the power to shape a life one has "reason to value" (Sen 1999a, 14). Even if we follow Waldron's important insight that homeless people need to be conceived of as agents, it is also important to acknowledge that they have no control over resources or over the conditions, laws, and policies that determine the choices they can make. Because the capacity for controlling one's environment gives the concept of empowerment its force, describing these embodied realities and bodily needs is important for capturing features of disempowerment that otherwise go unnoticed.

Waldron recognizes that structures, laws, and ideology work to prevent homeless people from having the freedoms endorsed in a country that prides itself on being "the land of the free," but his main concern in this essay is to criticize the conception of freedom as that which any and all individuals have to shape their own lives by taking advantage of the opportunities hailed as available to all. Commitment to this picture of freedom and of agency as "calling up the power from within" is evident in prevalent beliefs such as that homeless people, and poor people more generally, can change their lives and pull themselves out of the rut they are in by just getting a job—like anyone else. There are no laws that bar them from getting a job or buying a house, so the choices they make and the lives they lead are taken to be the result of their lack of effort, discipline, or willingness to change. As Waldron argues, however, it is just not clear how those who are homeless can apply for jobs without an address or phone number, or how they can go to a job interview with no place to shower or change and with all their worldly possessions in a shopping cart. Here, the language of equality of opportunity is empty because, as Waldron puts it, "one cannot pee in an opportunity" (Waldron 1991, 440). The concrete details of bodily functions and needs matter to the analysis of freedom and equal opportunity, but they are invisible to those in homes who need not think of them or be in places where they are forced to respond to them.

While *Dark Days* begins by listening to and documenting life stories, the film does not focus our attention on the relations of power that construct the norms resulting in homelessness. The film ends with clips of people who end up in homes and are grateful for getting them. In other words, the film endorses the idea that private property is the solution to homelessness with no thought on how relations of power have constructed the institutions of property that disempower the homeless in the first place. By contrast, because the purpose of Waldron's essay is to challenge liberals on the issue of whether the homeless have even negative freedom, his own remarks on policy are directed at the need to ameliorate those restrictions on common property that hamper the homeless from meeting their basic bodily needs. While Waldron may be right to suggest that acceptance of the primacy of negative freedom in the United States calls for, at the very least, increasing the number of public washrooms so that people are free to go to the bathroom and wash, this policy hardly seems sufficient for enhancing agency in the sense of being able to live a life one has reason to value by having a say in the policies that shape it.

I suggest that we can get better answers to questions of policy if we reject the liberal framework within which the debate is conducted and the policy options are structured: either removing laws that limit freedom for some (negative rights) or providing resources that enhance freedom for all (positive rights). New possibilities for theory and for policy emerge when we shift the focus from individuals as such to individuals in relationships needing to respond in morally appropriate ways to embodied realities and bodily needs. Doing so also allows me to pay more explicit attention than does Waldron to two features central to the relational approach: the relevance of revealing norms that are in place and the significance of a developed relational account of perspectives to theory and policy.

On Waldron's account, those counted as poor display their agency in the skills and resourcefulness they need to respond to conditions beyond their control and the knowledge they have of those conditions and the structures that perpetuate them. Although Waldron does not himself highlight this point, his account explains why it is more apparent to the homeless than to those with homes just how meaningless is the language of rights to free speech, to vote, to run for office, or to assemble when freedoms to wash, urinate, sleep, and cook are restricted. But listening, learning, and reporting these perspectives will not do all the work, and this is so for reasons that point to how norms are invisible, assumed, and accepted by those who derive benefits from the system and from the structures that are already in place.

A central feature of relational theory is that a focus on relationships highlights the role of perspectives in uncovering norms that reflect dominant beliefs and expectations about what it means to live and act in circumstances very different from those with which people in power are familiar. Norms shape "outsider" perspectives to structures of power differently from "insider" perspectives on that power. A feature of the expanded relational approach I have sketched is its responsiveness to the particularities of kinds of relationships and, therefore, to various bodily needs demanded in and through them. Learning about the details of homelessness from reading or from viewing films allows one to gain some imaginative access to the kind of embodied experience that the homeless face. But this imagining and then making policies may not have the effect of empowering those who are powerless in varied ways and at multiple levels. Taking perspectives seriously involves more, in that it needs to involve caring about the breakdown of relationships and the failure to respond to the bodily imperatives of others. The expanded understanding of the role of perspectives when coupled with the reality of bodily needs shifts the focus from thinking about what we can do for "them" to what we can and should do about relationships of power that many of us continue to accept, endorse, or leave unchallenged. In the case of homelessness in liberal societies, this shift opens up possibilities for questioning the relationships, or absence of them, that are set up between those with property and those without.

Confronting the material realities of homelessness allows us to become aware that the relationships we fail to confront, form, or respond to are relevant to the lack of power that some people have to effectively shape their lives as full members of a community. But there is some reason for pessimism when even those who are aware and care are prevented from responding to the bodily needs of the homeless. Laws and ordinances are now being adopted in places like Las Vegas to limit the distribution of charitable meals in parks by "restricting the time and place of such handouts, hoping to discourage homeless people from congregating and, in the view of officials, ruining efforts to beautify downtowns and neighborhoods" (Archibold 2006a). A relational approach insists that we are individually and collectively accountable for the ways in which we interact or fail to interact with or respond to those whose embodied realities yield bodily imperatives which demand a moral response.

The discussion of homelessness shows how specific conceptions of property and freedom shape beliefs, expectations, and policies in the United States with respect to homelessness. When we move to the global context, it can be said that beliefs and expectations about the virtues of globalization dominate and in ways that reach into the lives of people all over the world. One way to connect the discussion of homelessness in the United States with a discussion of the global context is to think about the ways in which the conceptions of property and freedom just discussed now dominate the world scene. More important for my purposes of connecting the two case studies are the lessons to be learned about the need to link conceptions of agency and empowerment to embodied realities and bodily imperatives. As mentioned in section 1, the World Bank highlights the importance of paying attention to the poor in its multivolume work *Voices of the Poor* (Narayan 2000; 2001; 2002). In its more recent work on empowerment, the World Bank reiterates its claim that poor people need to be the proper focus—this time to achieve the goal of measuring gains in levels and kinds of empowerment (Narayan 2005, ix, 4–5).

In the discussion of homelessness, doubt was cast on the idea that listening, interpreting, and reporting what people say is sufficient for capturing aspects of the embodied realities of those who are identified as poor. We need to pay attention to the role of power as it manifests itself in norms and perspectives that go unnoticed because they are prevalent or globally dominant. This was evident in the discussion of homelessness, where norms have the effect of removing the homeless from sight and from relations with those in or with power. In the global context, the voices of the poor can be silenced or reinterpreted when people commissioned by international bodies such as the World Bank have power over what is said and heard, and when these bodies assume dominant norms and expectations about what globalization has achieved and can achieve.[4] The lesson is that much more can be learned by and through perspectives when their situatedness in relationships of power is taken into account. The following section picks up on the second issue I identified as missing in the literature

---

4. In *We the Peoples*, the United Nations notes that "Countries that a mere generation ago were struggling with underdevelopment are now vibrant centres of *global economic activity* and domestic well-being" (United Nations 2000, 19, my emphasis). While the report admits that economic globalization has not made a significant impact on reducing levels of poverty or closing the gap between the rich and poor, it accepts that economic globalization, with its commitments to free markets and neoliberal policies, is here to stay and can be made to work.

on agency and empowerment: the contemporary context of globalization requires broadening the analysis of relationships from those at the level of the personal and local to those at the level of the public, national, and global, where relationships of power shape and reshape embodied realities and bodily needs in ways that enhance but also hinder processes of empowerment.

4. AGENCY AND EMPOWERMENT IN THE GLOBAL CONTEXT

An overarching feature of globalization is that we live in a context of *economic* globalization, one in which markets, multinational corporations, international financial institutions, and world trade organizations shape the issues and circumscribe their effects on people. I have argued elsewhere that it is problematic to make general claims about economic globalization as either all bad or all good (Koggel 2003a, 2003b, 2006). Larger and more open markets have provided jobs for people where little opportunity existed before, jobs that have in turn increased levels of income and national wealth, improved access to education and health care, and challenged gender norms and practices in many parts of the world. But economic globalization has also resulted in the exploitation of workers in Third World countries and the destruction of families, ways of life, and communities when corporations move to countries with even lower cost wage labor or when rich countries or international financial institutions place conditions on aid or debt payments. While economic globalization may have positive effects, these sorts of negative effects have magnified the imbalances of power between rich and poor countries and in ways that shape its effects on citizens of a country and the power they have to change oppressive conditions. To assess the effects of globalization, we need detailed accounts of location, beliefs, and practices and of economic, social, and political conditions and structures. The attention to context and relationships called for by feminist relational theorists can now be used to identify specific features of economic globalization that shape material realities in ways that have the effect of disempowering agents in specific contexts.[5]

---

5. My work on relational theory in the global context has benefited from Chandra Mohanty's postcolonial feminist account of how women's specific kind of work, whether of lace makers in a specific region of India or of electronics workers in factories in the Silicon Valley, is embedded in the local particularities of social practices and political contexts at the same time as global markets utilize and reshape local particularities. In other words, her analysis of the local is always cognizant of various forces of power at the global level that have an impact on women's workplace experiences and their lives more generally (Mohanty 1997).

In "Does Contraception Benefit Women? Structure, Agency, and Well-Being in Rural Mexico," Austreberta Beutelspacher, Emma Martelo, and Verónica García apply insights from Sen's account of agency to a discussion of the family planning program implemented by the Mexican government in the early 1990s. The slogan "fight poverty" reflected the government's belief that encouraging women to use contraceptives to limit the number of children they had would give them the freedom to pursue educational and work opportunities and thereby make them better off (Beutelspacher, Martelo, and García 2003, 218). Rural parts of Mexico such as Chiapas were specific targets of the program because these areas "had the highest poverty levels and fertility rates in Mexico as well as the lowest contraception rates" (218). The authors compile data through interviews and questionnaires from six rural communities in Chiapas and then assess whether the government's promise of enhancing women's agency and improving their lives was met. Based on what women had to say about the effects of the family planning program on them, the study then divided women into four categories: "willingly home based," "unwillingly home based," "willingly employed," and "unwillingly employed" (224).

The study is to be applauded for capturing the fact that context and details matter: the family planning program had different impacts on women in specific locations and circumstances and did not result in improving the lives or increasing the agency of some women. But the study stops short of providing an analysis of the broader network of relationships in which these women are embedded. For example, the study notes that some women from the "willingly home based" category were forced to undergo sterilization by health care professionals and husbands. These women were specifically targeted because their wanting to stay home and raise children did not fit with a program to fight poverty by encouraging women to work outside the home. But raising children and even having large families need not by itself be taken as signifying poverty or oppression. We need to know whether expectations about women's proper role in the home determine women's choices and whether women are negatively affected by this choice in order to know whether paid work enhances agency or improves well-being.

There is yet more to learn in the case of these women who are categorized or perceive themselves as willingly home based. Globally dominant beliefs (evident in this family planning policy) that poverty can be alleviated by increased access to jobs, education, and global markets means that women who care for children are perceived not only as non–market contributors but also as unable to feed, clothe, and care for their children. Moreover, if they live on subsistence farms, what they and their families do neither counts as work nor gets counted in measuring gains to educational and work opportunities. What is invisible or ignored, in other words, are the material realities of subsistence farming as a viable means of responding to bodily needs. To assess agency or empowerment in terms of opportunities in the market is to deny that choosing to engage in subsistence farming can result in responsible ways of responding to the material conditions and bodily needs of children, families, and communities.

To get an accurate assessment of whether people are empowered, we need to know the details of subsistence farming in particular places and in the context of globalization. What are the mortality rates and life expectancies in these rural areas? Is there access to clean water? Is the choice to subsist on farms undermined or removed by a forced dependence on the purchase of seeds, pesticides, and fertilizers sold by global corporations? Are markets for farm produce affected by global agricultural policies designed to protect farmers in rich countries? Are lives improved when one-time subsistence farmers are forced into urban areas? When globalization reduces possibilities for subsistence farming as a livelihood option, then it is true that access to education and work become means of empowerment. But this is so only because choices have been restricted or removed from people who once led lives they had reason to value.

Returning to other aspects of the study, whether women perceive education and jobs as opportunities depends on conditions such as whether families own and live off the land, whether there are jobs available in a particular location, whether one has already had education and how much, whether the jobs that are available are desirable, and whether one's identity and life plans are integrally connected with the important work of caring for children. In other words, whether women perceive themselves to be better off or in control of their lives by using contraception and having fewer children is dependent on myriad factors, some of which are shaped by local traditions, norms, and ways of life and some of which are beyond the control of women to reject or change because they are controlled by national policies or multinational corporations.

Sen's persuasive argument that coercive policies of population control are less effective than collaborative policies would make him critical of the coercive aspects of Mexico's family planning policy. Collaborative strategies view such resources as health care, education, and work opportunities as important conditions for empowering women to make choices reflective of lives they have reason to value: "Central to reducing birth rates, then, is a close connection between women's well-being and their power to make their own decisions and bring about the changes in the fertility pattern" (Sen 1999b, 479). But two points need to be made to expand the analysis beyond Sen. First, providing resources should not override decisions and ways of life that do not fit the free market ideology that having a job and earning a salary inevitably enhance agency and well-being. We saw in the case of homelessness that entrenched assumptions about connections between property and freedom are contradicted by the embodied realities and bodily needs of homeless people. We also saw that giving homeless people property may increase their freedom to perform bodily functions, but it does not empower them in the sense of expanding their opportunities or enabling them to participate and have a say. Second, an assessment of national policies of population control needs an understanding of how these policies are often shaped by features of economic globalization in ways that reduce women's power or even the power of the state to make choices or shape policy for its citizens.

The significance of the latter point is highlighted through a broadened discussion of the "willingly employed" and "unwillingly employed" in the Mexico study. The basic point is that the employment opportunities a woman has may have less to do with her willingness or unwillingness to work than with government policies and the shaping of them by global institutions. Whether there is work and what kind of work there is are controlled by such factors as Mexico's economy, labor laws and regulations, free trade agreements, access to labor markets by multinational corporations, and policies tied to debt payments to lending countries and to institutions such as the IMF and the World Bank. An assessment of whether paid work is chosen or whether choosing it empowers agents needs an analysis of local conditions and opportunities in the areas under study and of how these are in turn shaped by national and global factors. An assessment of whether women's lives are positively affected by government policies and in ways that enhance agency needs an analysis of whether women are empowered to have a say in national policies of all sorts, of family planning programs and health care more generally, of access to and conditions of paid work, of educational opportunities, and of participation in social and political structures.

While women described as willingly employed can be said to have benefited from the family planning program, this may depend less on their "choice" to work than on factors external to their lives, their communities, and even their country. Economic globalization often drives developing countries to create jobs by luring multinational corporations through policies such as removing minimum-wage policies for labor or creating tax incentives for the companies to open up shop. This is not to say that job creation does not have positive effects, but we need an assessment of the impact on empowerment of factors such as the availability of education and health care programs, the kind and conditions of paid work, access to information about jobs and transportation to them, social norms and institutions that shape perceptions and roles of members of certain groups, and the value women place on having and caring for children. As with the discussion of homelessness, this kind of assessment provides a critical perspective on issues of listening to and reporting what is heard. In the Mexico study, women's experiences and preferences need to be understood in terms of their material realities and this can be provided through an analysis of the broader network of local, national, and global relationships that shape those experiences and lives in complex and ever-changing ways.

5. CONCLUSION

Early in the paper, I described empowerment as a process of enabling people, individually and collectively, to take purposeful and effective action in contexts in which their power to do so is affected by institutional, social, and political factors. Empowerment needs to be conceived of as a process in which people are treated as agents of change and through which they are able to use their skills and abilities to have control over and a say about resources and decisions that affect their life prospects. But if the forces of economic globalization have such an overarching impact on lives in all corners of the world, then it is fair to say that people in many locations have little or no control over resources and decisions that affect their lives and that their embodied realities and bodily needs are being shaped from the outside by these economic forces. As argued in the case of women in Mexico, their very freedom to make significant life choices about having and raising children is being shaped by national policies and global forces in ways that determine what they do with their bodies and where. And whether they are able to respond to the bodily needs of others is increasingly dependent on changes to markets, economic conditions, currency rates, free trade agreements, policies tied to aid and debt payment, prices dictated by powerful pharmaceutical companies, neoliberal agendas, and so on.

Globally dominant expectations that economic globalization in the form of markets, multinational corporations, and global financial institutions can and will empower people and increase their well-being, no matter what conditions or embodied realities present themselves in particular locations, can be said to be disempowering if it means that embodied realities and bodily needs are themselves shaped and reshaped by these forces. Entrenched beliefs and expectations of what it means to be homeless or what economic globalization can achieve make it difficult for those in relationships of powerlessness to be heard and these embodied realities to be visible or understood.

An examination of the new literature on empowerment shows that little or no attention is given to the features of economic globalization that can disempower individuals, communities, and nations. In these cases what gets empowered are multinational corporations, international financial institutions, world trade organizations, neoliberal policies, and market economies. To be effective, empowerment projects need an analysis of embodied realities and bodily needs as affected by complex networks of relationships now being shaped and reshaped by economic globalization. The study of women's experiences and lives under Mexico's family planning policy shows that agency in the domain of reproductive choice is not only tied up with empowering women in other domains, but also with the impact of the global on local conditions and national policies. For many of these women, their embodied and material realities were determined by factors beyond their control.

In this paper, I have used insights from feminist relational theory to develop an account of agency and empowerment that pays attention to embodied realities and bodily needs in the context of how these are being shaped and reshaped in complex ways by the multidimensional and varied intersections of state, civil, and *global* institutions. Because economic globalization affects differently situated people in diverse ways, detailed accounts of conditions, practices, policies, embodied realities, and relationships are needed. A framework for conceptualizing and measuring empowerment that assumes or unquestioningly promotes economic globalization may not reveal the whole story about kinds of barriers, including those that may be created by economic globalization itself. We need to pay attention to how the multidimensional and varied intersections of state, civil, and global institutions shape and reshape embodied realities when globalization increases gaps between the rich and the poor, when it destroys ways of life that once sustained families and communities, when it pushes people into densely populated urban centers where basic material needs are not being met, when it exploits embodied realities of race, ethnicity, gender, and disability to increase profits, and when it exacerbates relations of power with and in countries that have colonial and imperial histories. To move from treating people as passive victims of development policies to treating them as agents empowered to have control over their lives demands awareness of the processes of economic globalization that shape embodied realities and create bodily needs in ways that undermine agency and empowerment.

REFERENCES

Archibold, Randal. 2006a. Las Vegas Makes It Illegal to Feed Homeless in Park. *New York Times*, July 28. http://www.nytimes.com/2006/07/28/us/28homeless.html (accessed August 1, 2006).

———. 2006b. Problem of Homelessness in Los Angeles and Environs Draws Renewed Calls for Attention. *New York Times*, January 15. http://nytimes.com/2006/01/15/national/15homeless.html (accessed August 1, 2006).

Beutelspacher, Austreberta Nazar, Emma Zapata Martelo, and Verónica Vázquez García. 2003. Does Contraception Benefit Women? Structure, Agency, and Well-Being in Rural Mexico. Special issue (on the ideas and work of Amartya Sen), *Feminist Economics* 9(2–3): 213–38.

Brennan, Samantha. 1999. Recent Work in Feminist Ethics. *Ethics* 109:858–93.

Campbell, Sue. 2002. Dependence in Client-Therapist Relationships: A Relational Reading of O'Connor and Mills. In *Personal Relationships of Dependence and Interdependence in Law*, ed. Law Commission of Canada, 3–39. Vancouver: University of British Columbia Press.

———. 2003. *Relational Remembering: Rethinking the Memory Wars*. Lanham, Md.: Rowman and Littlefield.

Code, Lorraine. 1991. *What Can She Know: Feminist Theory and the Construction of Knowledge*. Ithaca: Cornell University Press.

———. 2000. How to Think Globally: Stretching the Limits of Imagination. In *Decentering the Center: Philosophy for a Multicultural, Postcolonial, and Feminist World*, ed. Uma Narayan and Sandra Harding, 67–79. Bloomington: Indiana University Press.

Dark Days. 2001. Dir. and prod. Marc Sanger [DVD]. Palm Pictures, New York.

Koggel, Christine M. 1998. *Perspectives on Equality: Constructing a Relational Theory*. Lanham, Md.: Rowman and Littlefield.

———. 2003a. Globalization and Women's Paid Work: Expanding Freedom? Special issue on the ideas and work of Amartya Sen, *Feminist Economics* 9(2): 163–83.

———. 2003b. Equality Analysis in a Global Context: A Relational Approach. *Feminist Moral Philosophy*, ed. Samantha Brennan. *Canadian Journal of Philosophy*, suppl. 28:247–72.

———. 2006. Equality Analysis: Local and Global Relations of Power. In *Moral Issues in Global Perspective*, ed. Christine Koggel, vol. 2, *Human Diversity and Equality*, 376–88. 2nd ed. Peterborough, Ont.: Broadview Press.

Mackenzie, Catriona, and Natalie Stoljar, eds. 2000. *Relational Autonomy: Feminist Perspectives on Autonomy, Agency, and the Social Self*. New York: Oxford University Press.

Minow, Martha. 1990. *Making All the Difference: Inclusion, Exclusion, and American Law.* Ithaca: Cornell University Press.

Mohanty, Chandra. 1997. Women Workers and Capitalist Scripts: Ideologies of Domination, Common Interests, and the Politics of Solidarity. In *Feminist Genealogies, Colonial Legacies, Democratic Futures,* ed. M. J. Alexander and C. Mohanty, 3–29. New York: Routledge.

Narayan, Deepa. 2000. *Voices of the Poor: Can Anyone Hear Us?* Washington, D.C.: World Bank.

———. 2001. *Voices of the Poor: Crying Out for Change.* Washington, D.C.: World Bank.

———. 2002. *Voices of the Poor: From Many Lands.* Washington, D.C.: World Bank.

———. 2004. *Empowerment and Poverty Reduction: A Sourcebook.* Washington, D.C.: World Bank.

———. 2005. *Measuring Empowerment: Cross-Disciplinary Perspectives.* Washington, D.C.: World Bank.

Nedelsky, Jennifer. 1989. Reconceiving Autonomy: Sources, Thoughts, and Possibilities. *Yale Journal of Law and Feminism* 1:7–36.

———. 1993. Reconceiving Rights as Relationship. *Review of Constitutional Studies/Revue d'etudes constitutionnelles* 1(1): 1–26.

Sen, Amartya. 1999a. *Development as Freedom.* New York: Anchor Books.

———. 1999b. Population: Delusion and Reality. In *Moral Issues in Global Perspective,* ed. Christine M. Koggel, 469–85. Peterborough, Ont.: Broadview Press.

Sherwin, Susan. 1998. A Relational Approach to Autonomy in Health Care. In *The Politics of Women's Health: Exploring Agency and Autonomy,* ed. Feminist Health Care Ethics Research Network, coord. Susan Sherwin, 19–47. Philadelphia: Temple University Press.

United Nations. 2000. *We the Peoples: The Role of the United Nations in the 21st Century.* New York: Department of Public Information.

Waldron, Jeremy. 1991. Homelessness and the Issue of Freedom. Reprinted in *Moral Issues in Global Perspective,* ed. Christine M. Koggel, 430–43. Peterborough, Ont.: Broadview Press, 1999.

Walker, Margaret. 1989. What Does the Different Voice Say? Gilligan's Women and Moral Philosophy. *Journal of Value Inquiry* 23:123–43.

Weiss, Gail. 1999. *Body Images: Embodiment as Intercorporeality.* New York: Routledge.

CONTRIBUTORS

SUSAN E. BABBITT has been teaching philosophy at Queen's University in Kingston since 1990. Her current research is on the work of nineteenth-century Cuban philosopher José Martí.

SYLVIA BURROW is Associate Professor in the Department of Philosophy and Religious Studies at Cape Breton University in Sydney, Nova Scotia. Her research centers on moral psychology, with recent research exploring the emotions and attitudes central to moral understanding, moral perception, autonomy, and integrity. Her martial arts experience informs and inspires related research addressing the problem of violence against women.

SUE CAMPBELL is Professor of Philosophy and Gender and Women's Studies at Dalhousie University in Halifax. She works in the area of moral and political psychology and feminist theory. Her previous books are *Interpreting the Personal* (Cornell, 1997); *Racism and Philosophy* (with Susan Babbitt, Cornell, 1999); and *Relational Remembering: Rethinking the Memory Wars* (Rowman and Littlefield, 2003), which won the North American Society for Social Philosophy 2003 Book Award.

JACQUELINE M. DAVIES is Associate Professor of Philosophy at Queen's University in Kingston where she is also cross-appointed to Women's Studies and Jewish Studies. Her research focuses on intersections between the narrative dimensions of feminist care ethics and what contemporary Jewish Studies scholars call textual reasoning.

ANGELA FAILLER is Assistant Professor of Sociology and Women's & Gender Studies at the University of Winnipeg. Her general areas of teaching and research include feminist and queer theory, cultural studies, and psychoanalysis. Currently, she is interested in questions emerging from the politics of memory and loss, memorial/counter-memorial practices, and the field of remembrance studies.

CHRISTINE M. KOGGEL is Director of the Centre on Values and Ethics (COVE) at Carleton University in Ottawa. She is the author of *Perspectives on Equality: Constructing a Relational Theory* (Rowman and Littlefield, 1998) and editor of the expanded three-volume second edition of *Moral Issues in Global Perspective* (Broadview Press, 2006). Her current research in the area of development ethics is on the concept of empowerment.

REBECCA KUKLA is Professor of Philosophy, Professor of Obstetrics and Gynecology, and Affiliated Professor of Women's Studies at the University of South Florida in Sarasota. She is the author of *Mass Hysteria: Medicine, Culture, and Mothers' Bodies* (Rowman and Littlefield, 2005) and, with Mark Lance, *'Yo!' and 'Lo!': The Pragmatic Topography of the Space of Reasons* (Harvard University Press, 2008). She is the editor of *Aesthetics and Cognition in Kant's Critical Philosophy* (Cambridge University Press, 2006).

MONIQUE LANOIX is Assistant Professor of Philosophy in the Department of Philosophy and Religious Studies at Appalachian State University in Boone, North Carolina. Her research focuses on the rights of citizens to ancillary health care services. Another aspect of her work involves an examination of the philosophical dimensions of care-giving labor.

CATRIONA MACKENZIE is Associate Professor in Philosophy at Macquarie University, Sydney. She is co-editor of *Practical Identity and Narrative Agency* (Routledge, 2008) and *Relational Autonomy: Feminist Perspectives on Autonomy, Agency and the Social Self* (Oxford University Press, 2000). Her articles have appeared in a variety of edited collections and journals, including *Australasian Journal of Philosophy, Hypatia, Journal of Applied Philosophy,* and *Philosophical Explorations*. Mackenzie was awarded the Australian Museum 2007 Eureka Prize for Research in Ethics.

KYM MACLAREN is Assistant Professor of Philosophy at Ryerson University in Toronto. She is the author of articles on emotion, embodiment, intersubjectivity, and the philosophy of Merleau-Ponty and Hegel. She is currently writing a book on emotion and embodiment, which proposes a phenomenological response to current theories of emotion.

LETITIA MEYNELL is Assistant Professor of Philosophy and Gender and Women's Studies at Dalhousie University in Halifax. Her current research explores the epistemology of images in science and various intersections between feminist theory and contemporary trends in biology.

SUSAN SHERWIN is University Research Professor Emerita of Philosophy and Gender and Women's Studies at Dalhousie University in Halifax. She works particularly in the areas of feminist health ethics and relational theory. Earlier books include *No Longer Patient* (Temple University Press, 1992) and *The Politics of Women's Health* (co-ordinator, Temple University Press, 1998).

ALEXIS SHOTWELL is Assistant Professor of Philosophy and English at Laurentian University in Sudbury, Ontario. Her academic work addresses racial formation, unspeakable and unspoken knowledge, gender, and political transformation.

INDEX

abortion, 146–48, 159–61, 188, 190, 196
activities of daily living (ADLs), 164–66, 168
ageism, 178, 180
agency, 1–8, 10, 13, 25–26, 47–48, 53–55, 105, 122, 145, 161–62, 166, 179–80, 198, 235–36, 238–39, 247–48, 250–55, 257, 258, 266–67
    melancholic, 49, 53–55
    moral, 146, 149–54
aging, 164–65, 178–79, 180
aid programs, 250, 256
alienation, 44, 120–23, 171–74, 243–44
alterity, 16, 200, 205
Ansara, Gavriel Alejandro Levi, 68
Aristotle, 79, 91
Aronson, Jane, 171, 178, 180
audience, 212, 217, 222, 227
autonomy, 8, 12, 14, 40, 73, 126–31, 133, 135, 137–38, 140–41, 176, 179, 189
    and emotion, 25, 43, 109, 136
    consumer, 16, 166, 176–77
    embodied, 129–30, 135, 140
    relational, 7, 16, 72, 122n, 128, 141, 252 (*see also* self, relational)
    traditional liberal theories of, 4–5, 127–28, 252

Babbitt, Susan, 15, 17–18, 59, 212n
Bacchi, Carol Lee, 178–79
Baier, Annette, 151
Barghouti, Mourid, 17, 234–35, 241, 242, 245–47
Bartky, Sandra, 61
bathing 173–75
Beasly, Chris, 178–79
Beauvoir, Simone de, 37, 253
becoming subject. *See under* subject
belief
    background, 239–41, 246
    true, 242–43
Benjamin, Henry, 62n
Benson, Paul, 135
Beutelspacher, Austreberta, 262
Blum, Virginia, 92n, 94
body, 2–3, 7–11, 13, 77, 80–81, 82–88, 90–92, 95–97, 112–19, 129, 165, 171, 173–74, 177–79
    bodily continuity, 101–2, 112–14
    bodily integrity, 136
    bodily intentionality, 29–32, 33, 41, 119

bodily needs, 251, 253, 255–59, 260, 263
bodily perspective, 103, 114–19, 120, 122
body-as-home, 13, 59, 67–69, 71, 73
body image, 14, 116–17, 118–19
body-mind interaction, 2–3, 89–90, 144
body schema, 14, 115–16
    See also mind-body distinction
Bordo, Susan, 92
Brecht, Bertolt, 240
Brison, Susan, 101n, 122, 127, 130
Brooks, Geraldine, 103–5
Brown, Steven, 215–16, 219–24, 227–31
Brown, Wendy, 53–54
Buber, Martin, 198, 200
Butler, Judith, 10, 54

Calhoun, Cheshire, 38n
Campbell, Stuart, 188, 196
Campbell, Sue, 38n
Canadian Broadcasting Corporation (CBC), 94n
capitalism, 4, 172
care, 15–16, 35, 155–59, 166, 175, 181, 186
    acute, 169, 179
    ethics of (*see* care *under* ethics)
    giving, 155, 157, 160–61, 165–76, 180–81
    institutional practices of, 166–76
    labor, 16, 156–57, 165–72
    receiving, 155, 157, 161, 165–66, 170–71, 173–81
    See also health care
Castro, Fidel, 239
character, 14, 77–82, 86, 89–90, 94–97
characterization, 82, 93, 101–2, 108
Cheng, Anne Anlin, 13, 46, 48–55
Claire, Eli, 59, 64–68, 70–71
Coetzee, J. M., 175n
colonialism, 48, 225–30
Combe, George, 86
compulsion, 38, 42
Connerton, Paul, 216, 221, 228
continuity, bodily. *See* bodily continuity *under* body
continuity, psychological. *See* psychological continuity
corporations, multinational, 261, 263–65
cosmetic surgery, 92–94, 96–97, 120

Cuba, 237–39
Cushing, Pamela, 180

Dark Days, 256–58
Darwin, Charles, 236–37
Davis, Kathy, 94
Delaney, Samuel, 238
Descartes, René, 2, 27, 28n, 30
De Sousa, Ronald, 109n
Dillon, Robin, 241–42
disability, 118–19, 138
disempowerment, 189, 194, 254, 257, 266
Dolto-Marette, Françoise, 34–43

embodiment, 1, 3, 5, 9–11, 13, 60, 62–69, 112, 114, 117, 120–22, 128–30, 151, 153, 172, 174, 251, 253–55
    embodied realities, 18, 251, 253–55, 257–60, 265–67
    embodied self, 126–27, 129–31, 135–36, 140
    racial, 48–50, 55
    social, 217
emotions, 3, 9, 25–26, 28–29, 33–34, 41–43, 136
    emotional tension, 32–33
empowerment, 18, 175, 188–89, 250–51, 253, 257, 260, 263–67
Enlightenment, the, 4, 6, 80–81, 88, 90
epistemology, 2, 11. *See also* belief; knowledge *and* understanding
ethics, 2, 11, 14, 184, 186, 190, 198, 206–7
    of care, 155, 157, 166, 166, 186
    ethical encounter, 185, 188–90, 196, 202, 204
        ethical obligations, 201, 204
        relational, 198 (*see also* relational theory)
    See also morality
Eurocentrism, 2n, 225, 229
existential community, 245
existentialism, 28n, 36–37, 40n, 243–46
experience, lived, 28, 36–38, 41, 115–17
    of the past, 212–15, 217–20, 222, 226 (*see also* memory)
Extreme Makeover, 93, 95–97

face of the Other, 16, 189–90, 200, 203–5. *See also* Other, the
family planning, 262–64
Feinberg, Leslie, 65n, 67n, 71
Felman, Shoshana, 48
femininity, 15, 129, 135
fetus, 16–17, 145–48, 152–54, 159–62, 184, 187, 189–97, 201–7
    fetal rights, 192–94

Fiore, Robin, 170
First Peoples, 153n, 211, 224, 225–29
    flourishing, 59, 64, 73, 245–46, 248
Focus on the Family, 187–88
Foucault, Michel, 58
Fowler, O. S., and L. N. Fowler, 84, 85, 88–89
FoxNews, 190
freedom, 4–5, 18, 37, 47, 69, 72–73, 235–36, 245, 247–48, 257–58, 260, 265
Freud, Sigmund, 49–50
Frye, Marilyn, 129

Gallagher, Shaun, 115–16
Garcia, Verónica Vázquez, 262
gender, 73, 78–79
    dysphoria, 116, 120–22
    genderfusion, 68–69
    genderqueer, 13, 59, 62, 64, 66, 71
    sex-gender distinction, 6–7
Gilligan, Carol, 186, 200
globalization, 15, 251, 253–54, 260–67
Goldie, Peter, 107n
Gordon, Avery, 58, 60, 63, 71–73
Govier, Trudy, 134–35
Gramsci, Antonio, 243–44
Grosz, Elizabeth, 10
Guevara, Che, 243–44, 245

habits, 116–17
Halbwachs, Maurice, 219
Haraway, Donna, 10, 191–92
Harding, Sandra, 7
health care, 145–46, 156, 161, 164, 166, 168–69
Hegel, G. W. F., 37, 77–78, 80–82, 84–88, 91
Heidegger, Martin, 3, 28n, 29, 30n
Hilhorst, Medard, 93
Hoerl, Christoph, 214
Holstein, Martha, 181
homelessness, 253, 255–60
Hume, David, 3

identity, 121–22, 219, 222, 224–31
    formation, 11, 92, 195, 196 (*see also* becoming *under* subject)
    maternal, 189, 194
    narrative, 14, 105, 107–9
    national, 224, 235, 248
    personal, 14, 100–102, 105, 107–9, 112–13, 120–22
    practical, 105, 236
    racial, 46–47, 49–53, 55, 235, 248
    victim, 48, 53–54

images, visual, 191–93
imagination, 212
  self-imagination, 212, 219–20
  See also social imaginary
In the Womb, 188
integrity, bodily. *See* bodily integrity *under* body.
intersubjectivity. *See under* subject, the
irrationality, 25, 35–38, 43

James, Nicky, 170
Johnson, Mark, 107n
Jones, Karen, 134
Jones, Leroi, 238, 246
Jorgensen, Christine, 71
justice, 15–16, 247
  justice reasoning, 200, 206–7
  justice, social, 18, 155–57, 158, 181–82, 235

Kant, Immanuel, 27, 80
Katz, Claire Elise, 199
Kelley, Robin, 72
Kierkegaard, Søren, 36–37
Kingston, Maxine Hong, 51–54, 55
Kittay, Eva Feder, 166–67
Knocked Up, 188, 190
knowledge, 81, 188–89, 236–39
  bodily, 116–17
  in relation to the ethical and the political, 200–203
  self, 110
  sensuous, 13, 58–63, 65, 66, 70–72, 73
  situated, 191–92
  social, 60
Korsgaard, Christine, 105n, 107n, 111n
Krone, Ray. *See* Snaggletooth Killer, the

labor, 7, 156–57, 172
Lamas, Juan-Alejandro, 68
Lane, Christopher, 47
L'Arche homes, 180–81
Lavater, John Casper, 81n
Lescarbot, Marc, 224
Levinas, Emmanuel, 16, 184–87, 189, 191, 196–207
Lewis, Tanya, 180
liberalism, 4, 252, 258
liberation, 59, 61, 63, 68
localization, 219–23
Lorde, Audre, 67, 71
Lugones, Maria, 7, 17, 218, 223, 225–26, 229–31

March, 103–5, 108
Martelo, Emma Zapata, 262

Marx, Karl, 171–72, 243, 246
maternity, 184–87, 189–90, 194, 197, 199–200, 206–7
  maternal sacrifice, 184–85, 186–87, 192, 199
McCormack, Teresa, 214
McLeod, Carolyn, 134
McNay, Lois, 11
melancholy, 49–50, 54–55
  racial, 13, 49–51, 54–55
memory, 17, 212, 213–24
  collective, 17, 224–30, 234–36, 247
  oppositional, 211–12
  relational, 215, 216
  shared, 212–23, 230–31
Merleau-Ponty, Maurice, 3, 10–12, 27, 28n, 29–32, 34, 39, 40, 40n, 115–17
Merton, Holmes, 81, 83, 86n
Merton, Thomas, 244–45
Meyerowitz, Joanne, 71n
Mexico, 262–65
Meyers, Diana Tietjens, 14, 128–31
Middleton, David, 215–16, 219–24, 227–31
Mill, John Stuart, 11–12
mind-body distinction, 1–5, 8–11, 78, 80, 86, 88, 91–92, 114
Mohanty, Chandra Talpade, 1n, 261n
moralism, 25–26, 33, 42–43, 89
morality
  moral community, 151–53, 162
  moral values, 147–50, 151–54, 157–59, 161–62
  obligations, 15, 146
  relational, 154–59 (*see also* relational theory)
  See also ethics
Morrison, Toni, 69, 235, 247
Morton, Christine, 195–96
motherhood. *See* maternity
Mullin, Amy, 184–85, 186n, 187, 193, 198–99

Namaste, Viviane, 62
Narayan, Deepa, 250, 260
narrative theory, 106–9
Nathanson, Bernard, 192
naturalness, 90–91, 93–94, 96
needs, basic, 156, 161, 256. *See also* bodily needs *under* body
Newman, Marc T., 190–91
Neysmith, Sheila, 177
Nietzsche, Friedrich, 80
norms, 89–92, 189, 218, 223, 252, 258–59, 260
Now, Voyager, 113n

objectification, 171–72, 174–75
objectivity, 191, 194

O'Brien, Michelle, 69
O'Keefe, Mark, 189
oppression, 9, 13, 126, 130–31, 135–36, 252, 262
Other, the, 185, 189, 196–98, 200–202, 203, 205–7
otherness, 49, 197, 201, 202, 205.
    See also alterity

Palestinian people, 234, 244
Parfit, Derek, 104n, 107n
Parks, Jennifer, 169–70
past, the, 211–13, 215, 217–23, 224–25, 230–31, 234, 241, 247–48
Paul, the Apostle, 6
performance theory, 17, 212, 215–18, 221–23, 230
persistent vegetative state (PVS), 145–48, 152–53, 159–62
personhood, 16, 110–12, 114, 119, 146, 148–54, 161, 195–96
    social dimensions of personhood, 110, 114, 151
perspectives, 237, 240, 252, 255, 258–60
    bodily (see bodily perspectives *under* body)
    first person, 110
    third person, 103, 110–14, 119, 200–201, 205
    oppositional, 211–12, 224–31
phenomenology, 10–11, 12, 26–30, 111
phrenology, 77, 78, 81, 82–92, 94, 97
physiognomy, 77, 82, 84, 87
Plato, 2, 79
political issues, 11, 13, 14, 60, 67, 69, 71–73, 138–39, 146, 199
    political change, 59–61, 63, 66–73
    political relations (see relations, political *under* relational theory)
    political structures, 47
Poulain de la Barre, François, 6n
poverty, 254, 258, 260, 262
power, 10, 18, 51, 175, 251, 254–55, 258–59, 260, 261
    powerlessness, 48, 127, 173, 176–77, 179–80, 266
    relationship to powerlessness, 49
    See also empowerment
pregnancy, 16, 160, 172, 186–88, 192–203, 205–7
property, 255, 258, 260
Prosser, Jay, 62–63, 67n, 69
psychoanalysis, 13, 46–47, 49
psychological continuity, 101–2, 112–14
public policy, 15–16, 146–50, 158–59, 161–62, 166–67, 178–79, 258, 262

quickening, 193, 195

race, 78–79
    relations, American, 49–53

racialization and racism, 47–48, 50–55, 225–30, 235, 247
racial embodiment (*see* embodiment, racial)
racial identity (*see* identity, racial)
racial melancholy (*see* melancholy, racial)
radical reflection, 27
rationality, 25–26
reasoning, 200, 205
reidentification, 101–2, 113
relational theory, 18, 198, 251–55, 258–59, 261, 266
    relationality, 7, 185, 198–99
    relations, dialogical, 200–201
    relations, political, 199–203, 206–7
    relationship, maternal, 195–98
    relationship, personal, 15, 170–71, 173, 179
    relationship, sibling, 12
    relationship, social, 149–54, 217–18, 219–22, 228–30, 252, 264–65
religion, 2, 4, 15, 149, 152, 187–88, 243
resistance, 10, 69, 132, 135
responsibility, 155, 158, 160–61, 236, 241
Ricoeur, Paul, 107n, 111n
Romanow Report, 169n
Rostand, François, 40n
Rousseau, Jean-Jacques, 76–77, 91n
Ruti, Mari, 55

Sartre, Jean-Paul, 28n
Schechtman, Marya, 101–3, 105–15, 119, 122
Scheman, Naomi, 63
Schiavo, Theresa (Terri), 145
Schiebinger, Londa, 6, 8, 9
Schreber, Daniel Moritz, 89–90, 91
science, 9, 235, 236, 243.
    See also phrenology
science fiction, 100–101, 112
Scrubbing Project, The. See Turtle Gals
self, 7, 116–18, 127–28
    -becoming, 14, 120, 238, 247 (*see also* becoming, *under* subject)
    -confidence, 127, 132–34, 140
    -conception, narrative.
        (*see* -constitution, narrative, *under* self)
    -constitution, narrative, 14, 102–3, 105, 107–11, 113–14, 118–19, 122–23
    -defense, 14, 127, 131–33, 136–40
    embodied (*see* embodied self)
    -esteem, 134–36, 174
    -imagination (*see* imagination, self)
    -narrative, 14, 108–9, 110–12

relational, 7, 128
　(*see also* relational theory)
　-sacrifice, maternal (*see* maternal sacrifice *under* maternity)
　-trust, 134, 136, 140
　-worth, 242
Sen, Amartya, 250, 257, 263
sense data, 27
Sevenhuijsen, Selma, 166
Sheldon, William, 77
Sherman, Nancy, 78
Sherwin, Susan, 7
sibling jealousy, 34–38, 42–43
Silent Scream, The, 192
Snaggletooth Killer, the, 95–97
social imaginary, 213, 223, 224, 226, 230–31
social movement, 58–59, 63, 70–73
socialization, 47–48
Socrates, 79
somatophobia, 2–4
somatotype theory, 77
Spelman, Elizabeth V., 2
Stoics, 80, 88
Stone, Sandy, 63
Strawson, Galen, 106n
subject, the, 12, 36–41
　becoming, 32–33, 34–39, 43, 226, 229–30
　persisting, 105, 107, 111
　-object dichotomy, 27
subjectivity, 111, 117–18, 120–21
　intersubjectivity, 32–33, 34–39, 43, 61
　embodied, 14, 114
　epsychological, 114
Taylor, Chloe, 189
Taylor, Diana, 212, 217, 221, 229
temporal experience. *See* experience of the past
Theatre of Neptune in New France, 225
Thomson, Judith Jarvis, 199
Toombs, Kay, 118–19, 121
trans, 61–65, 68

transgender, 61–62, 63
transliberation, 59, 63
transsexuality, 61–62
transformation, 13, 35–41, 42, 59–60, 70, 72
trauma, 130
Tronto, Joan, 154–57, 166, 181, 186
Turtle Gals, 226–31
Twigg, Julia, 173n

ultrasound imaging, 16–17, 184–91, 192, 194–96, 203, 205
understanding, 235–39, 241–42, 247–48
　experiential, 238, 241–44, 246–47
　sensuous (*see* sensuous knowledge *under* knowledge)
Ungerson, Clare, 175
United Nations, General Assembly of, 239–40
Utopia, 73
Uttal, William, 81n

value affirmation, 221–22, 228–30
Vanier, Jean, 247
van Wyhe, John, 89n
Vice, Samantha, 106n
victimization, 53–54. *See also* victim identity
violence, 126–27, 130–31, 136, 139–41

Waerness, Kari, 167–68, 175
Waldron, Jeremy, 255–57
Walker, Margaret Urban, 154, 157–59
Wall, Glenda, 187
Watch Me Grow, 188
Weberman, David, 28n
Weiss, Gail, 10, 18, 253
well-being, human. *See* flourishing
Wendell, Susan, 10, 178n
Widgerow, A., 92
Wolf, Naomi, 129
Wollheim, Richard, 105n
World Bank, 250, 253–54, 260, 264

Young, Iris Marion, 8, 10, 118, 129, 172

Body ownership
~~Black~~ + ageist assumptions
(The aging body violates the self-sufficiency discourse (p 178, this volume)

The politics of body management
Passive – active bodies (C8 this book)

The body and sub-citizenhood (p 179 this book)
        " → sub-personhood (Charles Mills black ~~book~~)

Those who need care are deemed deviant bodies since society is constructed for the young male body

Managed bodies – p 180 this book

– Who owns a body? See Julie Ann Scott-Pollock in autoethnography, field notes, Facebook.

SEE P122: PUT THIS AT START OF C1, WPAE AS A KEY PREMISE: "OUR MORE OR LESS INTEGRATED BODILY RESPECTIVE FUNCTIONS AS A BACKGROUND CONDITIONS FOR THE ONGOING UNITY AND INTELLIGIBILITY OF OUR LIVES."